ONLY IN ALABAMA

To: Lenwood + Mike
Anthon + Family

Niece, Godchild and
fellow kinsmen

We are enjoying the
great wedding of Patrick
+ Emily + being here in
St Louis again. What a
great job you have done
with your four sons.
May God continue to
bless you all.

Uncle Julian + Aunt
Leslie - 8/10/2019

ONLY IN ALABAMA

More Colorful True Stories from a Lawyer's Life, 2016–2019

Julian L. McPhillips Jr.

Foreword by Bill Baxley

NewSouth Books

Montgomery

NewSouth Books

105 S. Court Street

Montgomery, AL 36104

Copyright © 2019 by Julian L. McPhillips, Jr.

All rights reserved under International and Pan-American Copyright Conventions.
Published in the United States by NewSouth Books, a division of NewSouth, Inc.,
Montgomery, Alabama.

Publisher's Cataloging-in-Publication Data

McPhillips, Julian L., Jr.
Only in Alabama : more colorful true stories from a lawyer's life, 2016–2019 / Julian
L. McPhillips Jr. ;
with a foreword by Bill Baxley.
p. cm.

ISBN 978-1-58838-405-8 (print, $26.95)

ISBN 978-1-58838-406-5 (ebook; $9.99)

1. McPhillips, Julian L., Jr. 2. Lawyers—Alabama—Biography. I. Title.

2019943629

Design by Randall Williams

Printed in the United States of America
by Versa Press

This book is dedicated first and foremost to God the Father, Son and Holy Spirit. The God Who created me, Who has Redeemed me, and Who Sustains Me.

In the earthly realm, this book is dedicated to my awesome wife, Leslie, the love of my life, and to my three grown children, Rachel, Grace, and David, and to their current brood of our five grandchildren, Laurel, Jude, Nanette, Sage and Emmanuelle.

It is also dedicated to the many clients I have represented over my forty years of law practice, and to my current partners and fellow attorneys Kenneth Shinbaum, Aaron Luck, Jim Bodin, Joe Guillot, Chase Estes, David Sawyer, Tanika Finney, and my office manager, Amy Strickland, whose assistance has been invaluable and necessary.

Finally, this book is also dedicated to the State of Alabama at its Bicentennial. The state has provided a foundation for my life and work.

Contents

Foreword

BILL BAXLEY

In January 1975 I began serving my second four-year term as attorney general of Alabama. Soon thereafter, an interesting letter arrived from a young man applying for a position as an assistant attorney general. The applicant was an attorney in the legal department of the American Express Company in New York City. Earlier he had served a stint with one of the better and larger New York law firms. He had received his undergraduate degree from Princeton, then his law degree from Columbia Law School. Nobody had to remind me of the admission standards of either of these respected institutions. It was also well known that this particular law firm only offered jobs to "top of the class" applicants.

Two other more subtle or intangible factors about this young man interested me even more. First, he was a member of the Princeton varsity wrestling team. Secondly, he was an Alabama native and wanted to come home. The wrestling background tweaked my curiosity simply because it was so unusual. The thought did occur to me that this might possibly be indicative of an aggressive, don't-back-down character trait.

The desire to come back to Alabama was more substantive. I knew that he would be taking a tremendous pay cut even factoring in Alabama's lower cost of living. I also knew that he would certainly be well aware of this. His letter indicated he was also aware of and agreed with some of the positions our office had taken and wanted to be a part of our efforts to effect changes in Alabama. He obviously was willing to make sacrifices, financially and otherwise, to help achieve what he thought was in the public good for our state.

In addition, I was well aware of the McPhillips family in our state even though I did not know any of them personally. They were well respected in both the Mobile and Cullman areas and the family members enjoyed a reputation for being extremely public-spirited.

Shortly after I received Julian's letter one of our talented assistant attorneys general, Bill Stephens, approached me. Bill, a Huntsville native and an Auburn grad, had finished Harvard Law School and had also gone to work for a large, prestigious New York firm. He had also taken a giant cut in pay to be a part of our team when he joined the office early in my first term. Bill told me that I had or would be getting an application from a guy named Julian McPhillips whom he had known in New York. He gave him a glowing recommendation and said "his heart was right." He also said that he thought several good law firms in Alabama were trying to recruit Julian.

I walked down to the office of Walter Turner, the chief assistant attorney general, handed him Julian's application letter, and told him I didn't need to do an interview—hire him before somebody else did. Being hired without an interview was most unusual for our office. Walter offered Julian a position, Julian accepted, and he and Leslie moved to Montgomery in April 1975. Thus began my nearly fifty-year association with Julian McPhillips.

The people of Alabama have benefited from his move for four decades and counting. Julian hit the ground running. He never shirked from tough assignments or difficult cases. I soon learned that Julian, more than most anybody I have known, personifies the description of someone as a "bulldog." That term is meant as a high compliment. Once he is convinced of the rightness of his position, he sinks his teeth in and simply will not let go. He doesn't let adversity or difficulties discourage or dissuade him. I suppose a less colorful descriptive adjective would be persistent. In any event, it is a good quality for a lawyer, and Julian possesses it in spades.

This does not imply that I agree with every position Julian takes or with every issue that he espouses. In fact, I don't agree with everything he says in this book. But people not agreeing with him has never prevented him from letting you know what he thinks concerning either individuals or issues. Julian has never expected everyone to agree with him on every issue. He wasn't like that as a young assistant attorney general, and he isn't like that today. The bottom line is that Julian does not take a position or a case because he thinks the position may be popular with the public at large or with any particular individual. Nor has he ever been shy or hesitant about stating his opinion or position publicly.

I am hesitant to inject too many of my own comments about the contents of the book that await the reader's discovery and enjoyment. Nevertheless, I will temper this reluctance in the following two instances.

Surprisingly, my favorite chapter does not concern a court case or a legal matter. It is Chapter 25 about Scott and Zelda Fitzgerald and Helen Keller. Without the generosity and vision of Julian and Leslie, the Fitzgerald Museum in Montgomery would simply not exist. Because of them it does exist, and thus tangible ties of Scott and Zelda's relationship with Alabama have been preserved as evidence of our state's connection with this talented but troubled young couple. In addition, Julian's background on and explanation of his deep feelings for Helen Keller give us a little peek into what makes him tick and what has motivated him to be the strong pillar of support for and defender of so many righteous causes.

In summary, this book is an enjoyable and easy read. For lawyers, it offers some fascinating shop talk from one of their colorful and noteworthy fellows. For non-lawyers, it offers some useful and candid insights into how the legal profession is practiced and how lawyers interact with each other, the courts, and their clients.

Julian's love for our state is evident in every chapter. I am very thankful that he came back to Alabama four decades ago and has spent his life and career trying to improve the quality of life for all our citizens.

William J. Baxley became the youngest state attorney general in U.S. history when he was elected in 1970 to the first of his two terms, during which he successfully prosecuted violent racists, industrial polluters, and corrupt politicians. He later served as lieutenant governor, and he still practices law in Birmingham.

Preface

Only in Alabama. How did I come up with that name as a title for this book? And what does it mean? What does it infer?

The name "Alabama" rings different bells for different people. Yes, we are a state, and the first in the alphabet of fifty states. However, is Alabama not more, as in a state of mind, or a culture, or a spirit?

When I first attended Princeton in 1964, given all the state's racial history and the then-recent notorious church bombing in Birmingham, my being from Alabama was sometimes challenging. During my four years at Princeton, followed by three more at Columbia Law School, I doubted I'd ever go back to live. An article about me in a college newspaper, intending to be humorous, said, "Julian McPhillips, who comes from Birmingham where people use bricks and bats rather than wrestling mats . . ."

Certainly record-breaking coaches, piling up national football championships then and now, projected a different image and gave Alabamians a boost of confidence, to cite just one example of aspects in which our state excels. We also have great music and artistic culture and beautiful lakes, valleys, rivers and forests. We have many wonderful people, although recently the publisher of a west Alabama newspaper again played into the bad stereotypes of the state in the national press.

Of course, bizarre and strange situations can happen anywhere, so some of the chapters of this book might well have occurred in other states. Yet the sum total of the stories I share here illustrates the case that Alabama is unique—delightfully so in many ways, woefully so in many others. Nonetheless, except for the interlude about traveling abroad, the accounts shared in this book did take place "only in Alabama."

Most of the chapters use the real names for real live people who were involved in events that truly happened. But in chapters one and eleven, some names have been changed to protect the guilty. Confidential settlement agreements sometimes prevent the disclosure of spectacular results, but that is usually a price worth paying.

Most of the chapters involve the true legal challenges of struggling people whom I have represented, oftentimes against the odds. Interesting exceptions are chapter eight on the "King of the DUI's," about distinguished senior attorney Tommy Kirk, and chapter thirteen, the "Ghee-Whiz Gang of Eight," about a dynamic family of eight Anniston attorneys. Both chapters add color to Alabama's legal landscape. There are two other exceptions. Chapter 25 talks about Scott and Zelda Fitzgerald in Montgomery's Old Cloverdale neighborhood in 1931–32 and marvels that during the same time period Helen Keller stayed often only two houses down the street (in the house where Leslie and I now live). And my last chapter shares insights from seventy-two years of living.

The clients I talk about are primarily from communities in central and south Alabama, including Selma, Tuskegee, Dothan, LaFayette, Auburn, Camden, Camp Hill, Troy, Enterprise, Pike Road, Wetumpka, Oxford, Montgomery, and Birmingham. However, one client was from Florence, in Lauderdale County, in the northwest corner of Alabama, adjacent to both Mississippi and Tennessee. Another hails from Chatom in Washington County, Alabama's oldest county, in southwest Alabama. Though this book covers recent cases, over the forty-four years since returning with Leslie to Alabama, I have represented clients from all sixty-seven of the state's counties. Counting two statewide political campaigns in 1978 and 2002, I have been in all of Alabama's counties and cities and most of its towns. The Alabama places that have most influenced my life include Mobile, my ancestral home; Birmingham, where I was born on November 13, 1946, Dad's twenty-sixth birthday; Cullman, where I grew up 1946–59; Montgomery, where I have lived the longest, and Huntsville, where my oldest and youngest children live.

WHEN THE CALENDAR TURNED over to 2019, Alabama began celebrating two hundred years of statehood. I am enthusiastically participating in our bicentennial, partially because my heritage in Alabama goes back to the Colonial era before we were even a territory, especially in 1700s' Mobile with Spanish, French, and Choctaw Indian ancestors.

One of Dad's direct forebears was Don Manuel Gonzalez, an early Spanish colonial governor of Florida. Dad's triple great-grandfather, Ignacio Sierra, was the 1790s' Spanish harbormaster for both Mobile and Pensacola. One paternal ancestral line goes back ten generations from me, through mostly female branches, to a French forebear, Jean-Baptiste Baudreau dit Grevilene (1671–1762), who married a Choctaw Indian princess, Ocqui Pany (1680–1735). She was the daughter of Chief Pierre Panyouasas in what is now southwest Alabama.

My McPhillips family name originated with an Irish immigrant great-great-grandfather, James McPhillips (1833–1910), who came to Mobile in the 1850s, and served as a baker and cook at Fort Morgan during the Civil War. After meeting and marrying Mobile Cathedral organist Rose Woodworth and raising four boys and four girls to adulthood, this Irish forebear became the first generation of the McPhillips family in the food business in Alabama from 1865–1975. It was through the second-generation son, James McPhillips, Jr. (1871–1927), my great-grandfather, who married my great-grandmother, Petronilla Greenwood, that the Spanish,

My paternal great-great-grandparents, James and Rose McPhillips.

French, and Indian heritage entered our family. (My appreciation goes to two sibling-in-laws, Johnny Williams, and Louise Jones McPhillips for their ancestral research.)

My father and uncle were the fourth generation in the food business occupational line, but my brother Frank and I instead entered the legal profession, him in Birmingham as a bond lawyer, me in Montgomery as a civil rights attorney and trial lawyer. Actually, my father, the Reverend Julian L. McPhillips Sr. had already changed the family's direction by going to seminary to become an Episcopal priest.

Dad's father, Julian B. McPhillips (1897–1978), played football while studying law at the University of Alabama in 1914–15. After he returned from fighting in WWI, "Poppy" founded the McPhillips Shrimp Company, based in Bayou La Batre in the 1920s–30s, and later King Pharr Canning Company in 1945 when his two sons Julian Jr. and Warren returned from World War II. King Pharr was a vegetable canning business based in Cullman, with plants in Selma and Uniontown, Alabama, and also in Georgia and Louisiana.

Dad's mother, Lillybelle McGowin McPhillips, brought into the family an energetic Scotch heritage. Lillybelle was part of the "Brewton McGowins," as opposed to her second cousins, the "Chapman McGowins" in rural Chapman, near Greenville. Although grandmother "Ibby," as we called her, was raised Baptist, she descended from an early 1800s' Methodist minister in south Alabama, the Reverend John S. Moore.

Interestingly, a leading member of the Chapman set of McGowins was Earl McGowin, chairman of the \ in Alabama—he recused himself in December 1967 from voting on me because of his kinship to my grandmother. Notwithstanding, he proceeded to ask me a number of questions about the civil rights movement and the anti-Vietnam War movement, which smoked out how liberal I was on both subjects, and thus presumably unacceptable to the committee.

I AM ALSO DEEPLY rooted in Alabama on my mother's side, descending from her great-grandfather, the Reverend David Davidson Sanderson, born in 1821 in Juniata County, Pennsylvania. A babe in his mother's arms, Sanderson and his parents stagecoached through dangerous Indian country in 1822 into Marion in Perry County in west Alabama. There David Sanderson grew up in the 1820s–'30s before leaving for Princeton in 1841. A member of Princeton's undergraduate class of 1845 and its graduating seminary class in 1848, Sanderson returned to Alabama, serving as a Presbyterian minister in Eutaw in Greene County, 1860–91. Remarkably, the congregation of his First Presbyterian Church before, during, and after the Civil War was half black and half white. Sanderson, along with his colleague and best friend, the Reverend Charles Alan Stillman, co-founded the Tuscaloosa College for Black Preachers in 1871. In 1895 its name was changed to Stillman College. In 1987, I purchased an original charcoal portrait of Dr. Sanderson from his grandson Robert Sanderson of Monroeville, my first cousin twice removed. The 1870s' portrait was by Sanderson's daughter-in-law Ellen Gilmer Bocock Sanderson, my great-grandmother.

Another set of Mom's forebears, the Bococks of Virginia, included her great-grandfather Henry Flood Bocock, clerk of the Appomattox County Courthouse, who witnessed Lee's surrender to Grant in 1865.

Two maternal great-great-grandfathers, Henry Flood Bocock, left, and Dr. David Davidson Sanderson.

One of his brothers, Thomas, was speaker of the Confederate House of Representatives. Another brother, Willie Joe, was Attorney General of Virginia. A fourth brother, Nicholas, was a Virginia Supreme Court justice. This was during the Civil War and before. How challenging life must have been. Maybe this is where my public service genes came from. When the Civil War was over, some Bocock family members migrated to Hale County in the Black Belt of Alabama. Great-great Uncle Willie Joe is buried in Greensboro. My famous New Orleans uncle, Dave Dixon, mother's brother, bore such a strong resemblance to Willie Joe—nose and all according to pictures—that it became a subject of great humor in the maternal side of my family.

Descending from both the Bococks and the Sandersons was my maternal grandmother, "Stu," as we called Stuart Sanderson Dixon. Her generosity and compassion were contagious and inherited by my mother. She gave all her grandchildren fifty cents for every "A" we made in school. She also paid for all our college educations.

Another of mother's ancestral lines, descending from John Poole of Massachusetts in the 1630s, goes back thirteen generations in America down to me. This came through the only grandparent I never knew, David Frank Dixon, 1892–1937, founder of the Great Southern Box Company, based in New Orleans, which later merged with Continental Can Company. His mother was a Poole from Mississippi. Both maternal grandparents went to Ole Miss, where in the 1910s they knew William Faulkner well.

Mom and Dad were both born in 1920. She, from a long line of Presbyterians, and Dad from devout Jesuit Catholics in Mobile—three of his first cousins once removed were Catholic priests—decided in 1950 to "split the difference" and become Episcopalians. Thus, at age four, I was involved in ground zero of the building of Grace Episcopal Church in Cullman. The enthusiasm of it spread to me and spilled over into two similar church beginnings, first in Pell City at St. Simon Peter, which Mom and Dad founded and where Dad ministered from 1975–85, and, overlapping in time, at Christ the Redeemer in Montgomery from 1980 to the present, which Leslie, and I and a few others co-founded, and where today we co-minister.

GROWING UP IN CULLMAN included playing sports at an early age in our backyard and driveway. This was the neighborhood playground for football, baseball, and basketball. Before leaving Cullman in 1959, I had played three years of organized "Pee Wee" football, was the pitcher for the Cullman County Little League All-Star baseball team, and was the only sixth grade player on the undefeated junior high basketball team. Only later at Sewanee, Princeton, and New York did I get into my favorite sport, wrestling. Summers included substantial time water-skiing and fishing on Guntersville Lake, and there were frequent trips to Mobile, Point Clear, and Gulf Shores.

My toddler years (the late '40s) also involved riding all over north Alabama in Dad's blue pickup truck that raised clouds of dust on dirt roads. Dad was negotiating with farmers to buy their vegetables for King Pharr Canning Company, only two blocks away from our Cullman home.

My parents, the Reverend Julian L. and Eleanor Dixon McPhillips, depicted in a portrait for their forty-fifth wedding anniversary, 1986.

Such deep roots in Alabama and America make it appropriate to dedicate this book to the 2019 Alabama Bicentennial. My stories, however, are modern-day sagas, painting a picture of Alabama's twenty-first-century legal culture, at least in central Alabama during the last three years of the 2010s.

MOST OF THE CLIENTS I have portrayed are honored to be recognized as a part of Alabama's history. I have been careful not to disclose confidences. If anyone on the opposite side feels shortchanged by these accounts, or unduly pictured, please remember that my comments are opinions based on memory and analysis, which I've never claimed to be perfect. If someone feels strongly otherwise, please write your own story in response, or send a letter to the editor, or write your own book. Indeed, I encourage you to do so.

Although I'm still active as a lawyer at seventy-two and plan to practice a little longer, being a wordsmith is part of my profession. Good writing and literature are much more than grammar and syntax. Writing lyrically or musically is an art. As you will see, literary icons Scott and Zelda Fitzgerald have influenced me in this regard. I do not pretend to have their skills, or their lifestyles, and my work is nonfiction, theirs entirely fiction. Yet their engaging literary styles have been absorbed via osmosis through my relationship over the years with the Fitzgerald Museum. And Helen Keller, longtime occupant of my home, continually inspires Leslie and me.

One widely admired Alabama historian, Mary Ann Neeley, passed away at eighty-five in August 2018. In her 2004 *Montgomery and the River Region Sketchbook*, she quoted me as saying about my law firm:

> We don't represent any big corporations or insurance companies; we don't represent any agencies or departments of state and we don't represent the city or county of Montgomery. We just represent the people who have problems with them all.

That approach to my profession has given me the freedom to pursue my heart's interest, namely representing the underdog against more powerful interests. It has also provided me with a mélange of experiences and stories worth preserving in this book.

Yes, good writing is an art, as much as painting, acting, dancing, etc. A painter I am not, nor a dancer. Of necessity, occasionally I am an actor in the courtroom, albeit one in need of more polish. In the literary arts I am at most a dabbler, writing in bits and pieces, as time and professional work allow. My legal career has nonetheless provided a rich reserve for real-life, pulsating stories worth preserving. Most of my clients consider it an honor to be a part of history. I also consider it a high honor, and a mission and calling, to share interesting episodes, preserving them for future generations, that is, for my grands, great-grands, and beyond. Hopefully.

I hope that readers will find my stories interesting and entertaining. Given the format, you can skip around. I also hope my example will encourage some to get in touch with their inner being to record their own stories and share them with others.

Acknowledgments

I have many to thank who helped make this book possible, as set forth in the appendices at the end. Directly or indirectly, they contributed to the foundation of life experiences molding and motivating this writer.

1

Beautiful Young Woman Entrapped

When twenty-two-year-old Ansley Jackson, an African American woman, came to my office on August 25, 2014, her sound character, sharp mind, and good looks were strikingly noticeable. So how did Ansley end up being criminally charged by the Alabama Alcoholic Beverage Control Board (ABC) with selling alcohol to a minor? Further, how did Ansley's picture get plastered on the cover of the magazine *BOOKED!* and spread all over town? This magazine is found in filling stations and convenience stores and flaunts the mug shots of those charged with crimes in Montgomery, Autauga, and Elmore counties. Beneath Ansley's captivating full-page photo were the poignant words:

> The most beautiful mug shot of 2014. We don't remember what she did.

To say that Ansley was embarrassed, humiliated, and deeply mortified is a classic understatement.

My legal representation of Ansley (her name and the restaurant's name have been changed in this account) was twofold, as reflected in our attorney-client agreement:

> (a) to pursue a claim against R. T. Restaurant, due to its negligent failure to train Ansley as a bartender, resulting in Ms. Jackson's being arrested in an ABC sting operation for serving a minor with a false ID, and in (b) representing Ansley in an entrapment defense arising out of criminal charges.

My first cannon shot came in a letter of April 25, 2014, to the CEO of
R. T. Restaurant, headquartered in Tennessee. I wrote:

> She (Ansley) was first employed there as a hostess from June until No-
> vember 2013. After taking a break for college exams, she came back to work
> in January, 2014 as a bartender.
>
> Ms. Jackson was given very little training as a bartender, other than
> how to make and mix drinks. She was given absolutely no training about
> how to check IDs, not from management, and not from other bartenders.
> Nonetheless, she (Ansley) did consistently attempt to check IDs of anyone
> who remotely appeared young enough to not be drinking.
>
> Ms. Jackson had no problems and did good work as a bartender until
> April 11, 2014, when the Alabama Beverage Control Board decided to do
> a sting operation, and sent several underage youth (two white males) into
> (the) R. T. Restaurant, with fake IDs reflecting they were old enough to be
> served drinks.
>
> Ms. Jackson checked their IDs, and after determining (that) they were
> old enough, she served them drinks (Bud Light bottles). Almost immediately
> thereafter, ABC representatives showed up, and placed Ms. Jackson under
> arrest. Ms. Jackson, of course, was horrified. She comes from a very good
> family, with two responsible parents, and is a graduate of one of the top
> secondary schools in Montgomery. She is also a college student at Alabama
> State University.
>
> The Montgomery Police . . . handcuffed Ms. Jackson and took her in
> a police car down to the City Jail, where she was further booked, with her
> photograph taken, and placed in a holding cell for at least two hours. This
> whole experience caused her (Ansley) much mental and emotional anguish,
> from which Ms. Jackson still suffers today. In addition she is having to cope
> with the criminal law process, and has to hire my law firm as her attorney.
>
> Adding insult to injury, Ms. Jackson discovered this past Saturday of
> Easter weekend that her mug shot down at the city jail is now on the cover
> of a magazine with the title *BOOKED!* Her (Ansley's) entire name is also
> mentioned on the front of the cover, and her name is repeated on the inside
> of the magazine, along with a statement of the criminal charges against her.

We strongly believe that R. T. Restaurant had a duty to properly train its bartenders on how to check identifications in order to determine which ones are false and which are valid. However, R. T. Restaurant negligently failed to provide Ms. Jackson with any such training and as a proximate result of that negligence, Ms. Jackson was arrested, charged criminally, and has had to go to the great expense of defending herself. She has also suffered enormous mental and emotional anguish.

This therefore is to give notice of Ms. Jackson's claim of negligence against R. T. Restaurant. This is also to request that you put your insurance company, if you have one, on notice of this claim. This is to further request that I hear back from you within 7 days of this date (Please note that I am faxing this letter today, as well as sending the original by regular mail), if you're interested in forestalling legal action. We recognize that a lawsuit will probably need to be filed, but we are giving you this one last opportunity to resolve it short of that."

Long story short, after extended negotiations, on June 18, 2014, Ansley's claim against the R. T. Restaurant settled for $20,000. Not pocket change, but Ansley and her father considered the amount significant.

That still left us with the criminal case to deal with. Despite my willingness to raise the entrapment defense in the Montgomery County District Court, the father and daughter together concluded that the safest course was for Ansley to accept a pretrial diversion route. To obtain this favorable outcome, one must first acknowledge wrongdoing (Ansley could not deny she sold liquor to an underage man). After that, one must complete numerous hours of community service and undergo other requirements. Upon successful completion, all charges are dismissed.

Time flew by during 2014 and 2015. Unfortunately, due to exams and other obligations, Ms. Jackson did not complete her assigned voluntary work in a timely manner. Hence, in early 2016 the District Attorney's office moved to set aside the pre-trial diversion agreement. That necessitated that Ansley and I return to court to try her case.

Ansley and her father accordingly returned to my office on January 18, 2016, to defend her against criminal charges. Trial was set for March 28,

2016, before Montgomery County District Court Judge Troy Massey. An ABC manager testified that, on the night of April 11, 2014, his agents were out scouting several Montgomery restaurants, hoping to snare a bartender serving alcoholic beverage to a minor.

The "ABC bait" used that night was a younger male agent whom we'll rename "Jacob McGinty." Although only eighteen years old when purchasing alcohol from Ms. Jackson, and only twenty at the time of the trial, Jacob had a distinct patch of gray hair, causing him to look much older. I was amazed. Talk about unseemly entrapment! Talk about baiting a field to shoot a deer!

On March 28, 2016, Judge Massey rendered justice by finding Ms. Jackson "Not Guilty."

Thus, a double victory was ultimately scored for Ms. Jackson. Although two years' worth of legalities was a nuisance and cost her money, Ansley was twice vindicated, having won both her civil and criminal cases. Still beautiful enough to be a model, Ms. Jackson is also very smart. I wouldn't be surprised to see her someday practicing law, or even donning judicial robes.

2

Pike Road Fire Chief Abused

Michael Green arrived on Planet Earth on February 15, 1964. He was no exception to the rule that to grow up one must encounter his or her share of bumps, bruises, and the potholes of life. Firefighting was in his blood. Mike put out many fires, especially the types that destroy people's houses. But he had more trouble with the type of fires that cost people their jobs, including his.

Mike began his firefighting career as a nineteen-year-old with the Montgomery Fire Department (MFD). Meanwhile, Mike was doing volunteer work with the fledgling Pike Road Volunteer Fire Protection Authority in the suburban community of Pike Road, due east of Montgomery.

Given his winsome personality and talents, Mike developed a loyal following among professional firemen, local and statewide. In 2002, he was elected president of the Montgomery County Association of Volunteer Fire Departments. In 2013, he was elected state president of the Alabama Association of Volunteer Fire Departments.

In March 2007, twenty-three years after he began as a rookie fireman, Mike retired as the MFD's assistant fire chief. In 2008, he became the first paid fire chief of the new Pike Road Fire Department.

The rough physical demands of firefighting eventually caused Mike to suffer disc problems in his neck. Artificial discs were implanted, causing him pain. He took ten days off in April 2012 for treatment and recovery. Mike's health concerns were shared with his board directors: Jack Jackson, Jane James, and Ty Glassford. His short-term need for prescribed medication included Oxycodone. Notwithstanding, Mike was careful not to let his medical condition interfere with the necessary duties and functions of his job.

An odd twist of legal history is that in 2012, another client of mine, Ms. Randa McCartha, a female Pike Road firefighter, opened up a Pandora's box that helped lead to Mike's downfall. Years before I met Mike, Randa came to see me about being sexually harassed by other Pike Road firefighters. Mike himself was not one of the accused. A few months later Randa's case settled on a confidential basis, but Randa was pleased. Notwithstanding, Mike, though temporarily away from his office with neck pain, insisted on attending a board meeting at Bridlebrook Station to help defend his men against the harassment charges. Mike wanted to protect the firefighters from false accusations that might upset their wives. Nonetheless, Mike was in such great pain at Bridlebrook that Chairwoman Jane James declared him "pumped up on Oxycodone and alcohol." Mike responded that he was fine, and not addicted to any substance.

Unfortunately for Mike, another pothole was just around the corner on January 4, 2014. While enjoying off-time on an extended New Year's weekend at his personal hunting lodge in Tallapoosa County, Mike went to a nearby country store to purchase food. But the store was closed. Returning, Mike paused at a stop sign. A Tallapoosa County deputy sheriff wheeled in behind him, stopped him, and declared him DUI. Mike protested that he was not, but the deputy arrested him anyway.

Soon thereafter, Mike advised the Pike Road directors of the DUI charge but asserted his innocence. Unfortunately, Jane James and Jack Jackson asked him to resign. Mike refused, and was backed by director Ty Glassford. At the meeting, Ms. James declared this was not the first time Mike had abused drugs or alcohol. She pointed back to the 2012 Bridlebrook incident. Undeterred, director Glassford persuaded colleagues James and Jackson to place Mike on restricted duty for two weeks. A termination decision was postponed for a later April meeting.

On April 29, 2014, the complaining directors and Mike Green collided at a public meeting. Proclaiming that Green's DUI was not his first offense, but his second, Ms. James publicly ripped Green for being "pumped up on Oxycodone and alcohol at the Bridlebrook station in 2012." Over Glassford's objections, directors Jackson and James voted 2–1 to terminate Green.

Mr. Green hustled down to our firm, accompanied by director Glassford.

After listening carefully, I decided Michael had a claim under the Americans with Disabilities Act. We concluded that Mr. Green was mistakenly perceived by the majority of directors as being disabled by "substance abuse," when he truly was not.

On May 15, 2014, we crafted a disability discrimination charge against the Pike Road Fire Department and filed it with the Equal Employment Opportunity Commission in Birmingham. On January 23, 2015, Green received his right-to-sue letter from the EEOC. Shortly thereafter, we filed suit for him in federal court.

A defense attorney from Ohio wrote me a scathing letter sanctimoniously denying liability, and she threatened sanctions against Mike if we pursued the case. We were not intimidated. The battle lines were drawn. Written statements from ten firefighters and a retired brigadier general living in Pike Road were good ammunition. All contradicted Jane James's denial that she ever said Mike Green was "pumped up on alcohol and Oxycodone."

Two able Birmingham attorneys, Michael Cooper and Dudley Motlow, swept down upon us from the distinguished law firm of Porterfield, Harper, Mills, Motlow and Ireland. They defended the Pike Road Authority and Ms. James, with Chase Estes ably assisting me.

This case rocked through several rounds of depositions, including a long-winded seven hours of attack questions against Michael Green. In response, in their depositions I turned Jane James and Jack Jackson every way but loose. Independent director Ty Glassford was also aggressively deposed by the defense lawyers, who also filed a lengthy motion for summary judgment. I give credit to associate Chase Estes for helping prepare a good brief in response.

The Honorable Harold Albritton, a seventy-eight-year-old federal judge, ruled on our case. He is generally conservative on employment cases, but in late July 2016 he denied summary judgment for our opponents. His opinion included language very helpful to us.

Both sides geared up for an August 22, 2016, trial date. Two weeks before trial, the Birmingham defense lawyers moved substantially in our direction. The case settled on confidential terms, but Michael Green was a happy camper.

3

Serendipity Has Its Place

S erendipity has its place, but more often anxiety in the extreme walks into my office, looking for relief.

Such was the case of thirty-three-year-old Tonya Snow of Birmingham, an African American female, who came to see me on May 5, 2016. The office questionnaire she filled out described her opposing party as Dillard's Department Store and her legal problem as the Montgomery Police Department. After I pieced through the babble about how badly she was treated, I finally got to the punch line. Tonya had been charged with third-degree theft of property (a class D felony) for shoplifting a $700-plus dress from Dillard's. Tonya was also charged with the felony of escape.

The police officer's report stated that on April 27, 2016, he:

> was notified by the camera operator that a subject was in the men's area putting clothes in her purse. At that time the subject attempted to hit me, but I grabbed her and took her to the ground. While on the ground she was able to get up again, so I took her to the ground a second time. While attempting to take her into custody, she received a minor laceration on the lip as a result of falling to the floor. I was then able to get one side of my handcuffs on her, but she stood up and ran out the door. I ran out the door after her and deployed my taser in an attempt to take her into custody . . . While in the parking lot I was able to take her into custody . . .

Tonya was obviously no girl scout. I didn't learn about her prior record until the day of trial, mainly because I didn't think she was going to pay the modest fee I had quoted her for representation. However, on November 29,

2016, the day of the trial, she finally paid two-thirds of the $1,500 fee. I quickly filed a motion for continuance, expecting to obtain it, having just been retained. Judge Johnny Hardwick just as quickly denied the motion, citing Ms. Snow's many previous delays.

Her court-appointed attorney, Chris East, gave me a copy of Ms. Snow's file in court that same day, including the State of Alabama's "Notice of Prior Convictions." I was astonished. Tonya's record, all from Jefferson County, included Theft of Property II in 2008, another Theft of Property I and II, and Receiving Stolen Property in 2009, and another Theft of Property conviction in 2010. Dismissed on prior plea deals were charges for Robbery III, three Receiving Stolen Property charges, and three more Theft of Property III charges. Tonya's first probation in 2008 was revoked in 2009. After serving time in prison, she was eventually released.

The State of Alabama had long given notice of its intention to "invoke all sentencing enhancements required or permitted by law." That included (a) the Habitual Offender Act; (b) enhancement for use of a firearm or deadly weapon; (c) a five-year enhancement for possession of a firearm; (d) a five-year enhancement for sale of drugs within three miles of a school or housing project; and (e) fines and suspension of her driver's license.

With my continuance motion denied, and my client looking at ten to fifteen years if convicted, it took some quick thinking, standing in front of Judge Hardwick, with Ms. Snow by my side. Ms. Snow had a teenage son for whom she was the only parent. I played that card, but Judge Hardwick's reply was Ms. Snow "should have thought of that before she committed the crime."

Before a packed courtroom crowd, including multiple attorneys, Judge Hardwick pushed us as only he can do to either plead or stand trial. The air was thick with tension and drama. However, the judge quickly told the young assistant district attorney he was throwing out the escape charge, because the security officer from whom Tonya "escaped" was "not really a law enforcement officer."

Tonya and I whispered anxiously back and forth about what to do, while standing before the judge. Shaking on the inside and outside, Ms. Snow was "scared to death." I told the judge that we both knew that a guilty plea meant substantial time. All of a sudden it occurred to me that the value of the dress might not be as much as the $700 alleged. If the value were $500 or less, Ms. Snow could only be charged with the misdemeanor charge, Theft of Property III, for which there was a one-year maximum, and no habitual felony enhancement. So I told Judge Hardwick we were "ready to try the case." I challenged the value of the dress, claiming its true value was less than $500. I didn't really know. I was simply being creative.

Judge Hardwick quickly asked the young assistant district attorney, Carrie Shaw, if she had her store witness ready to confirm the value of the dress. A look of anxiety crossed the prosecutor's face. She said, "Yes, your Honor." The judge said, "Produce them." The district attorney's staff first went to the witness room, and then out in the hallway, looking for the witness, who, lo and behold, was nowhere to be found. Apparently the prosecutor had expected a plea, and with so many cases on her plate, the detail of witness availability had slipped past her team.

Thus, the young Ms. Shaw reported back to the judge that her witness could not be found. Looking impatient and unhappy, Judge Hardwick candidly addressed Ms. Shaw, "You know what motion you should make." A chagrined Ms. Shaw replied, "Yes, sir. The State hereby moves to *nolle prosse* the case."

Judge Hardwick quickly granted the motion. All charges were dismissed. The rumble and sighs in the courtroom were just short of an outburst, to which the judge banged his gavel and called, "Order in the courtroom."

Tonya Snow and I quickly left the courthouse, while our luck was still good, and before someone changed his or her mind. That afternoon, I received an electronic copy of the judge's order dismissing the case.

My client was in tears and swore she would never shoplift again, or commit any other crime. Before she got out of my car, back in the driveway of my office building, Tonya and I had a spirited prayer together, thanking God for the miracle he had just given us.

So far, and to my knowledge, Ms. Snow has stayed completely away from crime. She is trying her best to be the mother she needs to be to her teenage son.

In the end, serendipity did find its place. Thank you, Lord.

4

Jailed for Getting
Behind in Her Bills

"Go ye to Dothan" is the famous Old Testament verse from which Alabama's fifth largest city appears to have drawn its name. Located in the southeastern corner of the state, it is the largest municipality in the "Wiregrass" region. Dothan's close proximity to both Florida and Georgia has provided avenues of escape for some of its more unsavory characters. On the other hand, the community has produced great patriots of high character like former Alabama Attorney General Bill Baxley, the almost-governor, and many other public-spirited citizens. Lately, however, other local problems have made the city appear toxic. One such example was the spider web Debra Raslevich fell into.

If you've never been behind in your bills, skip this chapter—you may not be sympathetic enough to commiserate with Ms. Raslevich, a sixty-one-year-old white female who was born in Fowler, Kansas. First married at age seventeen, and then again at thirty-one to her children's dad, Debra was for the most part a responsible adult. She raised a good daughter and a good son into adulthood before divorcing again and settling in another Wiregrass municipality, the smaller town of Ozark.

Debra's coming to see me grew out of her purchase of a washer and dryer from Aaron's Rent-A-Center in Dothan. Her contract called for her to lease these items. After paying the full amount she would own the machines. Debra's payments the first two years, from 2010 to 2012, stayed current.

In June 2012, Debra's father died unexpectedly, and her luck took a turn for the worse. She picked up her father's mortgage payments, to avoid foreclosure, and the loss of her house. That domino caused Debra to slip behind on her other bills. She tried to return the machines to Aaron's, but the store refused. At this point she was unable to make payments.

One day in August 2014, Ms. Raslevich went to the Ozark Police Department on another matter. The police would not let her leave. A "hold" had been placed on Debra for criminal charges in neighboring Houston County, where Dothan is the county seat.

Debra had no idea why criminal charges were against her. Finally, she discovered that Aaron's had placed a felony charge of "theft by leasing" against her in Dothan, after she got behind in her payments.

A $12,500 bond was too much for her to pay, given the bottomless pit she had fallen into, and she had no available help. Thus, Ms. Raslevich languished in jail for twenty-two days, sleeping on a cold concrete floor. Her picture was plastered on Facebook and other public media sites, proclaiming her a thief. Debra's spirits sank to an all-time low. When she finally got out of jail, she was a basket case and lacked money for even temporary lodging. She spent many nights sleeping in her car.

Ms. Raslevich finally meandered out to Utah where her thirty-year-old son lived. She called me from Utah on November 1, 2015.

In tears in her phone call, Debra described her pathetic misfortune to me. Follow-up emails confirmed her plight. Learning that all criminal charges against her had been dismissed, a year and a half after they were filed, I smelled a malicious prosecution case. The elements, first an unsuccessful criminal outcome, accompanied by malice and the absence of probable cause, all appeared to exist.

I turned the materials over to associate Chase Estes for him to review the law and facts. Chase consulted with law partner Kenneth Shinbaum and office manager Amy Strickland. Their unanimous recommendation was not to pursue the case. It had too many problems.

One problem was that the Code of Alabama 13A-8–142 authorized criminal charges against a consumer behind in payments, if written demand for return of leased property went unheeded. This was statutory law in the boonies of Alabama. Of course, Ms. Raslevich insisted she never received any such notice, and Aaron's could not produce a copy. Moreover, she had tried to return the merchandise, but Aaron's refused to accept it.

A second problem was that a grand jury indictment arguably established "probable cause," according to Alabama case law, with narrow exceptions. A third problem was that Dothan was and is a conservative venue, and Aaron's owners were local citizens, as opposed to a woman from Utah not paying her bills. Referred to in some publications as the "redneck capital" of Alabama, Dothan was often harsh on outsiders, and vice-versa. Admittedly, Debra's case tugged at my heartstrings. I saw light in the darkness. I also consider it highly unethical for anyone to use, or even threaten to use, criminal process for civil gain, as Aaron's did. For a lawyer to do so is a violation of Alabama Bar Association rules of ethics.

The final call was with me. Ms. Raslevich lacked resources to fund litigation expenses, but I took her case on a contingency fee basis, common in plaintiff's cases.

Not surprisingly, initial letters to Aaron's owner accomplished nothing. At least I discovered that Cincinnati Insurance Company provided coverage. Aaron's had a fine Dothan attorney in Kevin Walding. (Kevin later revealed that he had traveled in Israel with my parents in 1988, as part of a Methodist group. He recalled how nice my folks were and my dad's great sense of humor.) Yet correspondence with him accomplished nothing. Hence, I filed suit for Ms. Raslevich in the Houston County Circuit Court on May 24, 2016.

Soon discovery began, including depositions and requests for production of documents, which took months. About that time a young African American law clerk, Adam Andrews, came to work for me and breathed new energy into the case. Once we received Aaron's initial file production, we discovered some amazing things in its contract. First, on page six of the contract, Aaron's had given Ms. Raslevich a "preferred customer coupon." That meant that the contract actually gave the customer ownership of the leased property, even before final payments were made. Hence Aaron's totally lacked the right to file criminal charges.

Even more outrageous was that Aaron's contract with Ms. Raslevich contained an arbitration clause, requiring submission of all disputes to binding arbitration. Normally I despise arbitration as a rip-off on consumers, but here Aaron's ignored its own contract, jumping the gun to initiate criminal charges. The contract also said either party could go to Small Claims Court (with its $3,000 damages limit) but to no other court. Such an agreement would prevent seeking the unlimited damages in the Houston County Circuit Court, but Aaron's had opened the door to the circuit court when it filed its criminal charges against Ms. Raslevich.

On these three different grounds Aaron's had breached its own contract with Ms. Raslevich, I strongly believed. So I amended our complaint in August 2016, and deposed Aaron's owner and the manager who authorized the charges.

Meanwhile Ms. Raslevich moved back to Ozark. She began living in Section 8 federal housing and was still badly hurting financially. Given the court's schedule, and with a trial at least a year away, Mr. Walding and I agreed to mediation. We had a seasoned mediator in attorney Randy James of Montgomery. Long story short, the case settled for $20,000. The award was nothing to brag about, but Ms. Raslevich's share brought her substantial relief. Civil justice was rendered, but not the absurd type of criminal justice Aaron's Rent-A-Center wrongfully sought against Debra in the first place.

It was vindication in the Wiregrass of Alabama.

Don't get me wrong about Dothan. There are many good people in it, including the family of Damion Heersink, who dated my daughter Grace while they were both in high school in the 1990s. I also know a number of fine attorneys there. But fast-forwarding to 2018–19, I read about how local millionaire businessman Larry Blumberg was offering $50,000 per family to get Jewish families to move to Dothan. Yet the January 6, 2019, edition of the *Birmingham News*, reported that eleven families had accepted the offer, but one family had already experienced anti-Semitism and was wondering if they should stay.

5

Philadelphia Comes to Alabama

This is a compelling story about a young man from Philadelphia of great energy and enthusiasm known as Adam Andrews. He first came to see me as a client in May 2016, but stayed on as a law clerk for a year while preparing for the Alabama bar exam.

Originally growing up in the "Mainline" upper-middle-class suburb of Philadelphia, thirty-year-old Adam was an anomaly. A conservative Republican African American man, he was also the grand-nephew of Viola Desmond, "the Rosa Parks of Nova Scotia." (Her image is on a Canadian stamp and is soon to be on the Canadian $10 bill.) Adam was comfortable with Caucasians but sensitive to slights against his own race.

That is why Adam came to see me. He had just been terminated from a waiter's job at the Montgomery Country Club on grounds he deemed were racial. I had no conflict with handling his case. Even though Leslie and I have friends at the MCC, we had never joined, primarily due to its "whites only" membership policies, a remnant of Montgomery's apartheid past. We successfully settled Adam's case eight months later, in January 2017, just before I left on a southeast Asia-Australia trip.

Adam impressed me from the beginning as smart, personable, and one who didn't mind working hard. On the downside, Adam was sometimes argumentative, but I knew that quality could be chiseled into a talent. Since he was planning to take the bar exam, and I had space available upstairs, I gave Adam a third-floor office to study and prepare in. I added that we might even get him to help on a few cases, which would be good training for him and yield some compensation. It wasn't long before Adam became helpful on several cases.

Especially needed was Adam's assistance on my Vanessa Gill habeas corpus brief to the Eleventh Circuit Court of Appeals. This was a mountainous effort, requiring nights and weekends, and the piecing together of issues and facts from five previous courts in the preceding eight years. We strongly believed that Ms. Gill was wrongfully convicted of capital murder and wrongfully sentenced to life without parole (read more about this case in my book, *Civil Rights in My Bones*). Her family was paying us peanuts —$500 a month over ten months for a gigantic effort—because they couldn't afford more. With my turning seventy, the late nights were taking their toll, especially after a full day's work. Adam was exceedingly helpful, both legally and psychologically.

Adam had rendered great assistance on Lindsey Semmes's case, challenging her wrongful dismissal by the Pike County Department of Human Resources. Adam was also enormously helpful in my successful representations of former Alabama Department of Corrections officers Cornelius Simpson and Myron Chappell in their wrongful dismissals and criminal prosecutions [see Chapter 6]. Simpson was falsely accused of abusing an inmate and Chappell was criminally charged for misreporting where he found marijuana on an inmate. Both clients' cases required first a defense of criminal charges, and secondly, personnel board hearings to regain their jobs. Both cases were enormous legal projects. Adam helped at each stage, and he enjoyed the media coverage on both TV and in the *Montgomery Advertiser*. Adam's deep, infectious laugh echoed a celebration of all four victories, two in criminal court, two before State Personnel Board judges.

Adam also helped with two other plaintiff's cases, first the Debra Raslevich malicious prosecution lawsuit in Dothan, followed by the Avery family wrongful arrest in Chambers County. Adam energetically assisted me as well in pursuing white female Holly O'Dell's reverse race discrimination claims against the Elmore County Board of Education in late 2016. And he provided enthusiastic energy in our successful defense of a Montgomery fireman wrongfully terminated over false accusations of sexual harassment.

To my delight, Adam also joined Christ the Redeemer Episcopal Church, where I have served as senior minister since the church's re-opening in April 2013. Adam frequently visited with Leslie and me over Sunday night dinners after church services, and he came to our home for occasional meals, advice, and fellowship, needing a parental-like touch. During the 2016 presidential campaign, Adam and Leslie had lively exchanges. Leslie defended Hillary and questioned Trump, while Adam staunchly supported the eventual president.

In late October 2016, a new and demanding client came to the law firm, namely Ms. Dee Parks. Her pharmacy business had been wrongfully attacked from three different directions: (a) a bogus class action lawsuit charging a violation of HIPAA and medical malpractice laws; (b) the Alabama Board of Pharmacy's suspending and fining her pharmacies, and (c) Alabama Medicaid's not reimbursing her money, causing great financial damage. Adam helped me maintain contact with Ms. Parks on multiple issues. In court on Ms. Parks's cases, Judge J. R. Gaines took a liking to Adam, affectionately nicknaming him "Philadelphia." Adam didn't mind, adding that he had left the "City of Brotherly Love" due to its latter-day problems with drugs and crime.

Adam took the bar exam on February 20–21, 2017. In mid-April he got the unfortunate word that only 41 percent of the candidates passed, and he was not among them. To Adam's credit, he bounced back quickly from that deep discouragement. The DOC cases of Cornelius Simpson and Myron Chappell were still ongoing, and I needed assistance. Adam saw holes in the prosecution and helped me take advantage of them.

In May 2017, Adam took off for eight weeks of uninterrupted bar review study, an expensive full-day course. He left my office to avoid distractions, but made it to Christ the Redeemer on Sunday nights, where prayer and encouraging words bolstered him. I assisted Adam with his living expenses both times he took the bar exam.

Unfortunately Adam's second try at the Alabama bar exam in July did not work out, either. He was closer this time, but still a few points off. Soon he found a well-paying Lowe's security job in Montgomery, but two weeks before Christmas he decamped for Nebraska where he became a hearing officer on complaints involving inmates in that state's prisons. Later jobs took him to Minnesota and then Texas.

Adam agrees that, like the rest of us, he is a "work in progress." He has strengths, and he has areas to polish up. I enjoyed being his mentor, and expect to see him someday make a real contribution to the legal world. His initial dream was to develop a law firm in Selma, serving Black Belt counties. Whatever Adam eventually does, he has the capacity to impact this world, and I pray for him.

6

Alabama Prisons a Nightmare

Alabama leads the nation in many negative benchmarks, but its most notable eyesore is its prison system. America has the highest rate of incarceration among countries worldwide, and Alabama leads America. It is a nightmare.

One nefarious injustice after another spawns a high rate of assaults, rapes, stabbings, and killings within the prison system. The scope of the tragedy was documented in the 2018 report, *Alabama's Prisons are Deadliest in the Nation,* by the Equal Justice Initiative, which revealed that the state's correctional institutions had nineteen homicides in 2017–18 and that their rate of more than thirty-four homicides per 100,000 inmates was more than 600 percent greater than the national average from 2001 to 2014. The situation is a disgrace and a scandal, many times over, and is an outgrowth of an Alabama government so dysfunctional that top leaders of all three branches of government were ousted in 2016–17 (first the Speaker of the House was convicted of ethics charges, then the Chief Justice of the Supreme Court was suspended, and finally the Governor resigned to avoid impeachment.) Accordingly, badly needed prison reform languishes.

It is this vacuous leadership that causes the Alabama Department of Corrections to be continuously sued by inmates and employees. "Corrections" or "DOC," as the department is variously called, remains under frequent attack in court by the Southern Poverty Law Center and the Equal Justice Initiative, both of Montgomery, and the Atlanta-based Southern Center for Human Rights. The threat of a federal takeover of the prisons looms over the head of incompetent prison commissioner Jefferson Dunn. Meanwhile Alabama prisons disintegrate further into chaos and anarchy, as inmates in some institutions go on hunger strikes.

Surprisingly, innocent corrections officers have been bullied by DOC's administration, further decreasing morale among its own staff, which was at an all-time low in 2017–2019. Hard to believe, but true.

Two forms of "legal immunity" protect the state prisons and render its officials indifferent. The first is called "sovereign immunity," a blanket protection for all state agencies, deriving from the ancient English concept that "the king can do no wrong." The other, "qualified immunity," protects state officials in their individual capacities from lawsuits for violating prisoners' constitutional rights or employees' legal rights. Under this standard, unless a blatant violation of precedent occurs, state officials escape liability. Thus, the SPLC, the EJI, and everyone else challenging the prisons on behalf of inmate rights have mountainous hurdles to overcome, to succeed in litigation.

Employees nonetheless maintain under Title VII (42 U.S.C.; § 2000 (e)) the right not to be discriminated against on the basis of race, sex, national origin, or religion, and immunity does not exist. This gives me some room to negotiate a better outcome in a discrimination charged filed with the Equal Employment Opportunity Commission (EEOC) in Birmingham or in federal court.

Despite the barriers, I obtained a $100,000 settlement on behalf of one inmate, Derrick Calhoun, against a private prison in Uniontown in 2007. Calhoun had been beaten to a pulp and presumed dead, while prison guards stood by and failed to intervene. The monetary settlement was achieved largely because private prisons lack the immunity defenses that state-owned prisons have. That's what gave my case value. However the "profit motive" of private prisons works against inmates, as the privateers cut costs to enhance profits, resulting in reduced benefits and security.

In the last three months of 2018, I had three inmate stabbing cases come to my office via surviving, broken-hearted family members, two from the deadly St. Clair Prison in Springville and one from Elmore Prison near Wetumpka. All have been evaluated, but if we take any of them, it will require enormous resources to pursue them adequately, more than I have on hand. That is why I hope to get either SPLC or EJI to help.

Back in 2005, I listened to Elmore County Sheriff Bill Franklin brag to our Montgomery Lions Club that when he speaks to teenagers about avoiding drugs he tells them a good reason is to keep them from being raped or stabbed in either the county jail or state prison. "That's just part of the punishment," Franklin added. While Franklin's candor is commendable, the reality about which he speaks is abominable and really outrageous since it is tolerated by the authorities who should be stopping it.

Prison and jail officials forget that inmates are flesh and blood human beings like the rest of us. And believe it or not, lately the DOC has been bullying innocent correctional officers. Why has the DOC been persecuting its own officers? The answer that screams in my face is it makes the DOC "look better" in defending inmate lawsuits against it. This helps the DOC counter the criticism that it maintains too lax a control over its own correctional officers. There is a much better way for the DOC to treat its own officers; that is, with more respect and dignity. If the DOC did, it would also inure to the benefit of the inmates as more grateful and loyal correctional officers might work harder to prevent stabbings and assaults.

CORRECTIONAL OFFICERS TAKE ON BROKEN ALABAMA SYSTEM

The four amazing cases of officers Cornelius Simpson, Myron Chappell, Jeremy Hester, and Derrick Kelly, all in a twelve-month period, tell the story of the mistaken DOC overreach in prosecuting its own employees. In each case, the Corrections Department was misled by its Investigations and Intelligence (I&I) division. Sad but true. These officers have Gestapo-like arrest powers and often use them. Led by Latin American Arnoldo Mercado and his assistant David Gallew, its officers can intimidate the heck out of someone. According to officer Tony Lauria, the number of I&I officers has swollen from ten to thirty in the last five years. Ironically, this has proven counter-productive, giving inmates more opportunities to make up stories about DOC officers to take them down. Nonetheless, I respect Tony and I&I officer Susan Smith as two of the best.

Misguided I&I maneuvers include embarrassing DOC correctional officers by arresting them in open prison grounds in front of inmates. Ironically, such tactics encourage inmates to make false charges to try to gain advantage in the system. Yet in all four cases, between February 2017 and February 2018, I was able to get criminal charges dismissed, no billed by a grand jury, or acquitted before a judge or jury. "Four out of four ain't bad," I've been told.

Cornelius Simpson

Simpson, a forty-year-old African American correctional officer at Kilby Prison in Montgomery County, came to see me in May 2016. He was and is as humble, low-key, and honest as the day is long. Yet the DOC not only filed criminal charges against him for assaulting an inmate but fired him from his job of eight years. This was a job the single-father Simpson depended on to feed his family of four young children. In addition, Simpson was arrested for criminal assault.

He insisted he had not laid a hand on infamous inmate Bobby Campbell, other than putting handcuffs and leg irons on him to move him within Kilby. Simpson was backed up by eyewitness statements—six correctional officers and two inmates swore they saw Simpson and Campbell together at the time in question, with nothing happening. The only evidence DOC had of an alleged assault was the word of the alleged victim, "a notorious con-artist inmate." Indeed, Bobby Campbell had the worst record in the entire Alabama prison system for engaging in fraudulent activities and faking injuries. On top of that, Campbell worked "hand in glove" with I&I in setting up officers DOC wanted to get rid of. While the charges against Simpson were still pending eight months later, in January 2017, the "elusive Bobby" escaped from Donaldson Correctional Institute in Bessemer by faking release documents. This made statewide news. Nonetheless, I&I wouldn't back down against Simpson.

The DOC can be like a dog refusing to let go of a bone. It vaingloriously pushed the Simpson case. Meanwhile I fired off multiple letters to Commissioner Dunn and his attorney Jody Stewart between July 2016 and February 2017, requesting that the charges against Simpson be dismissed. Not once did I receive the courtesy of a reply, despite the weakness of the department's evidence! That simply made me work all the harder against the DOC.

In early February 2017, while Leslie and I were far away in Australia, the

Montgomery County Grand Jury "no billed" the charges against Simpson. I didn't discover this until two weeks after my return. Immediately, I filed a motion to dismiss Simpson's termination with the Personnel Board. In the alternative, I asked that the appeal be set down for a hearing before the Board. Judge James Jerry Wood scheduled a hearing for March 30, 2017.

The judge's scheduling order set precise dates for pretrial discovery, including an exchange of witness names and evidentiary documents. The Corrections Department screamed it didn't have enough time. I replied that Corrections had already had ten months since the May 2016 initiation of the charges, ample time indeed. Judge Wood agreed, denied the continuance, and ordered Corrections to produce its evidence to me and get ready for trial.

Last-minute drama ensued as Corrections filed a lawsuit in the Circuit Court of Montgomery County against its sister state agency, the Personnel Department, and Judge Wood himself, seeking indefinite delay on the pretext that the DOC had newly discovered evidence of criminal wrongdoing against Simpson. Judge Wood didn't buy it, and neither did Montgomery Judge Truman Hobbs Jr. Both denied the Department of Corrections a stay.

With client Cornelius Simpson in his case against the Alabama Department of Corrections in 2016–2017.

Amazingly, hours before the hearing was to begin, Corrections attorney Jody Simpson dramatically filed yet another motion for a stay, this time with the Alabama Court of Civil Appeals. That motion was also denied.

Accordingly, on Thursday morning, March 30, Mr. Simpson, law clerk Adam Andrews, and I headed over to the Corrections Department's main office at 301 South Ripley Street in Montgomery. After wading our way through tight security, we tried the case. Incredibly, most of the department's employees were on our side. That included twelve correctional officers from Kilby Prison, all testifying for Mr. Simpson. Under oath, their togetherness provided protection against the retaliation and implied threats from the DOC. The department had only two witnesses, namely Kilby's warden and a misguided I&I officer named David Gallew.

On April 10, 2017, we received a gratifying eighteen-page opinion and order from Judge Wood reinstating Simpson with back pay, worth about $75,000. Justice for Cornelius Simpson had finally arrived! After reading about our victory the next day in the *Montgomery Advertiser*, former U.S. Magistrate Judge Vanzetta McPherson called to congratulate us on winning a "rare victory from the Alabama Personnel Board."

Myron Chappell

Unfortunately, the Corrections Department's stupidity didn't end here. Myron Chappell, another Corrections officer with a good record at the Red Eagle Honor Farm, was the next victim of a misguided complaint by his own employer, the Alabama Department of Corrections. Chappell's misfortune was also stirred up by I&I officer David Gallew, who, only two years earlier, had been dismissed by the Town of Camp Hill for "conduct unbecoming an officer."

Myron Chappell's "sin" was that he allegedly misreported where marijuana was found on an inmate. What a terrible misdeed! Myron said the marijuana fell out of the inmate's clothes, while being shaken out, and fell onto the bed. "I&I" said no, the marijuana was under a mattress. Most relevantly, no one suggested that Myron Chappell had anything to do with the marijuana being with an inmate in the first place. The criminal charge against Mr. Chappell was "giving false information to law enforcement," because he allegedly misstated the precise location of the marijuana. Accordingly, Myron was terminated from his job of six years and was forced to defend himself against criminal charges in court in Montgomery, while also appealing his dismissal to the State Personnel Board.

On May 15, 2017, Myron received a much-deserved victory in Montgomery District Court, when Judge Troy Massey quickly found him "not guilty." The next day the *Montgomery Advertiser* trumpeted the result with a picture and big article.

On May 18, 2017, Adams Andrews and I took Myron to a second trial, this time to save his job at ADOC. The conflicting testimony of K-9 Officer Captain Welk could not be corroborated by the DOC. I&I agent David Gallew once again looked bad, admitting his case against Chappell was "full of inconsistencies and discrepancies." Not surprisingly but nonetheless amazingly, on June 8, 2017, Judge James Jerry Wood found the "preponderance of the evidence" in favor of Mr. Chappell, ruling that he should be reinstated with back pay. Judge Wood's thirteen-page opinion was the second in less than two months in favor of a state employee. In the old days, in front of younger Judge Randy Sallé, state employees virtually never won. That judge knew where his bread was buttered. Not so with the honest, independent seventy-six-year-old hearing officer Judge Wood. A former Ethics Commission member who calls 'em like he sees 'em, Judge Wood is either old enough or independent enough not to be swayed by undue influence.

Jeremy Hester

So "the times they are a' changing," but not enough. With word about my success spreading around the DOC, I was visited in May and June 2017 by two other DOC officers: Derrick Kelly, forty-year-old African American male, and Jeremy Hester, a forty-one-year-old Caucasian male. Both faced criminal indictments in Elmore County, charged with assault by inmates.

Hester was the brother-in-law of a talented young wrestler and protégé I coached at Montgomery's Catholic High, six-time state champion Zack Van Alst. This personal connection was an extra incentive. Hester was indicted in January 2017 over an incident occurring in June 2016. Yet neither he nor the DOC received word about the charge until months later. In April 2017, when stopped on a routine traffic charge, Hester learned from police about the outstanding assault indictment.

We immediately began a full-court-press defense. We discovered a letter signed by Commissioner Jefferson Dunn that confirmed how unfounded the charges were:

> On November 16, 2016, a hearing was held based on Warden Edward D. Ellington's recommendation that you be suspended without pay for a period of three (3) days for an incident that occurred on June 10, 2016. The Hearing Officer found you not guilty of all charges against you. Having reviewed the record of hearing and your overall work record, I do hereby approve the Hearing Officer's findings. Therefore, I am ordering all charges against you be dismissed and all paperwork pertaining to this incident removed from your file. You are a valuable asset to the Alabama Department of Corrections and hopefully your actions will continue to meet standards."

Hallelujah! Since the subject matter of the DOC suspension hearing was precisely the same as the pending criminal charges, I immediately filed a motion to dismiss. The DOC had already internally found Hester not guilty, I stated. Why bother again?

Judge Reynolds set a hearing at the Elmore County Courthouse on Tuesday morning, September 5, 2017. "The left arm of the DOC didn't know what the right arm was doing," I told the judge, who agreed and granted my motion, dismissing the case.

Derrick Kelly

Meanwhile, the amazing case of Derrick Kelly began well before he came to see me on May 26, 2017. This was just weeks after the Personnel Board victories of Cornelius Simpson and Myron Chappell.

The story Derrick told me was hard to believe. He was wrongfully accused of the criminal misuse of a chemical spray against an inmate who pulled a knife on him. At 6'2" and 325 pounds, Derrick was the same height but a little lighter than his 385-pound brother Gary, also a DOC officer.

The sad story began at Staton Correctional Facility on August 4, 2015. On that day inmate Jonathan "Bowtie" Caffee pulled out a sharp knife and flashed it menacingly at Kelly, who quickly responded by spraying Caffee with a chemical mace.

Bowtie was a Caucasian originally from Anniston. Tattooed from head to toe, he had a long conviction record, including burglary, robbery, receiving stolen property, and rape. Bowtie was cunning and took advantage of an inaccurate suspicion of Kelly by the "I&I division," which believed Kelly had brought contraband into the prison. Kelly adamantly denied that. The DOC had no solid evidence against Kelly, but fell hook, line, and sinker for Bowtie's tall tale that two different incidents occurred, about an hour apart. In the first incident Bowtie admitted pulling a knife, but said he dropped it, followed by a scuffle between him and Kelly. The second incident, said Bowtie, involved no knife. Therefore Kelly wrongfully assaulted him with the spray, the inmate asserted.

"Nonsense!" replied Kelly. "There was really only one incident. I was justified in using the spray in self-defense."

I obtained the DOC's investigation file and discovered that the only other employee eyewitness was DOC officer Willie Dudley, who gave two contradictory statements. The first was helpful to Kelly. It said Dudley called a "Code Red." That meant that an officer was in danger of his life. He was obviously referring to Kelly. After time passed and pressure was put on Dudley by the DOC, a second statement months later appeared to support inmate Caffey's contentions. Funny how that works . . . very suspicious, I thought.

In September 2017, I filed a motion to dismiss all charges based on a "Stand Your Ground" defense. Judge Sibley Reynolds presided at a December 7 hearing in the Elmore County Courthouse. Key state witness Dudley failed to show. My client took the stand, as did Bowtie and a few other non eyewitnesses. Bowtie, eyes darting menacingly, but now being rewarded by probation, and still basking in notoriety, said there were two incidents. He tried to minimize his knife-pulling, casually stating that all inmates at Staton had knives. Kelly insisted there was only one incident, but Judge Reynolds denied our motion, thus requiring us to go to trial.

Meanwhile, with the prosecutor's okay, I was communicating freely behind the scenes with the lead I&I investigator, Tony Lauria, exploring potential resolutions and evidence. Unlike my experiences with some other I&I officials, I found Lauria an honorable public servant. I hoped to work something out, leading to dismissal, but the best Ms. Peeples would offer was a plea to a class C misdemeanor of harassment. Kelly steadfastly refused the offer, insisting upon his innocence, and recognizing that even a minor misdemeanor could adversely affect his future employment.

There were many other cases ahead of us that cold January 22, 2018, day, including a murder, two DUIs, and a rape. Yet they all caved in at the last moment, accepting offers from the prosecution to lesser offenses with minimal punishment. Suddenly we were at the top of the docket, and the judge told us to strike a jury.

The *voir dire*, a process by which attorneys directly ask questions to

Celebrating in the Elmore County Courthouse with, from left, Derrick Kelly, his brother Gary Kelly, and a witness, Marlon Cole.

prospective jurors, is the first part of the jury selection process. Prosecutor Peeples looked sharp, mature, and much younger, as she questioned panel members. Trying to offset her charm, I employed self-effacing humor. My first statement, accompanied by a chuckle and smile, was "As you can see, I am no spring chicken." The jurors laughed, especially fellow seniors and septuagenarians. Picking a jury kept us busy until 3 p.m., after which we all went home. Derrick and Gary came to my house that night. I practiced my opening argument before them. We were all set to go the next morning.

Tuesday morning we showed up for trial. Strangely, the prosecution had doubted its case overnight and agreed to dismiss all charges. I negotiated that, in return for Kelly's resigning from the DOC, and we dismissed our appeal to the State Personnel Board. No big deal. Derrick had been working for the past two years as a truck driver, making much better money. He preferred his new profession and didn't want to go back. That was an easy choice.

So all charges against Derrick Kelly were immediately dismissed. The jury never heard the case. Shakespeare stated, "All's well that ends well." I agree with Shakespeare. Earlier I mentioned that Derrick weighs 325 pounds, and his brother Gary, also a DOC officer, weighs 385 pounds. In a picture at the Elmore County Courthouse celebrating our court victory on January 23, 2018, the two brothers, joined by our 400-pound DOC witness Marlon Cole, made me look petite. Surrounded by these three giants, I looked exuberant as the victory was huge!

OTHER CASES AND CONTINUED PRISON TURMOIL

As a result of the above four victories, which have echoed all around the walls and grounds of the Alabama prison system, numerous mistreated DOC officials have come see us. Many become clients. I can't be at the office all the time, so my partners Kenneth Shinbaum, Joe Guillot, and associate Chase Estes have picked up some of the cases.

In the spring of 2018, I was proud to represent Cedric Specks, a former assistant warden at St. Clair Correctional Facility, an unsung hero of helping to quell and calm St. Clair down after riotous conditions. Cedric had a warmth and charisma that caused inmates to believe he cared. Unfortunately, a consensual relationship with a nurse caused him to lose his job.

Yet, the greatest loss was the DOC's, after the Personnel Board refused to reinstate him. The DOC is woefully inadequate in expressing appreciation to its DOC officers in light of the perils they face every day. I fault Commissioner Jefferson Dunn and the "no holds barred" Investigations and Intelligence division for this.

Just before this book went to press, I began representing two more officers from Elmore Correctional Facility, Willie Burks and Leartrice Goodwin. Lt. Burks was terminated for failure to intervene in another officer's assault against inmates, despite his having told the officer to stop. Ms. Goodwin filed an EEOC charge of sexual harassment against a higher-ranked captain at the same Elmore facility.

As a firm, we represent many DOC employees, but we also represent several inmates stabbed to death or injured by other inmates. That is why it is so counterproductive, indeed outright stupid, for the DOC administration to so badly mistreat its own corrections officers. It diminishes their morale and lowers the number of officers available to protect inmates from other inmates.

The mental health of inmates has plummeted to an all-time low. Accordingly, in June 2014, the Southern Poverty Law Center (SPLC) and the Alabama Disabilities Advocacy Program (ADAP) filed a class action suit against the Alabama DOC, claiming the poor level of mental health care provided to prisoners violated the Eighth Amendment's prohibition against cruel and unusual punishment. In 2017, U.S. District Judge Myron Thompson agreed; he described as "horrendously inadequate" the poor level of mental health services provided by the DOC, and ordered the DOC to hire substantially more and better trained officers over the next three years.

The *Montgomery Advertiser* on January 24, 2019 also decried the increasing number of suicides in Alabama prisons statewide, saying that six inmates died by suicide in 2018, and forty more attempted it. This was probably the tip of the iceberg. When added to the number of prison deaths by stabbing, it is clear the Alabama prison system is in an epidemic stage.

In March 2019, reporter Andrew Yawn of the *Advertiser* wrote about a hunger strike by eight Alabama inmates in protest of what they alleged was unconstitutional placement in solitary confinement.

This grew out of a transfer on February 28, 2019, from St. Clair Correctional Facility, thirty miles east of Birmingham, to Holman Correctional Facility, in Atmore near the Florida line. Their great sin? According to the *Advertiser's* article, they were working to promote peace and prevent chaos within the prison system. A prison advocacy group, "Unheard Voices," criticized the solitary confinement as punitive, and serving no good purpose. Judge Thompson's 2017 opinion criticized such confinement as "deliberate indifference and widely acknowledged to elevate existing mental health issues to crisis levels and create mental illness in otherwise healthy people." "People need people," said SPLC attorney Maria Morris. "They rarely get to leave a small cell . . . with just a few feet to walk around in. The cells are dark and dank. Some don't have windows. Some have feces smeared on the walls that don't get cleaned. A living hell!"

On April 3, 2018, the U.S. Department of Justice issued a scathing fifty-six-page report on Alabama's prison system. Federal investigators detailed a myriad of incidents including sexual torture, violence, mismanagement, and suicides, and concluded there was "reasonable cause" to believe Alabama prisons were violating the Eighth Amendment guarantee against cruel and unusual punishment.

Not coincidentally, over the period April 8–10, 2019, Montgomery news media reported that three different sets of DOC correctional officers were brutally attacked by inmates and seriously injured within a twelve-hour period.

It is hard to know what is worse for the DOC's correctional officers . . ., the attacks from inmates or the attacks from their own boss, Commissioner Jeff Dunn, and his posse of I&I officers blowing things way out of proportion. Nonetheless the combination of the two answers the question in the April 24, 2019, front-page headline in the *Birmingham News*: "Why Can't Alabama Keep Correctional Officers?"

The Alabama DOC must vastly improve its environment if the state prisons are ever going to attract and retain good officers. There are many good people both in and out of the department who want to help but are stymied by DOC administration policies.

The Sunday, April 7, 2019, *Birmingham News* ran a lead story under the headline, "All Eyes on Dunn in the Wake of the Scathing."

Someday, somewhere, the insensitive Commissioner Jefferson Dunn of the world will be held accountable for the extremely inhumane conditions continually perpetrated in Alabama's prisons, a nightmare for both DOC officers and inmates.

Obviously more money will build bigger and better prisons. Yes it is paramount to attract, train, and retain good officers; this would have a domino effect of better treatment of inmates. Even more needed is dynamic, enlightened, and compassionate leadership. Also needed is the enforcement of better safety and security standards, to better protect everyone in the prisons. The DOC's top leadership, especially Commissioner Jefferson "Jeff" Dunn, absolutely must go. I heard Jeff Dunn, a retired Air Force colonel before he became commissioner, speak to the Montgomery Lions Club on February 1, 2019. Dunn displayed fancy charts on a power point about building and new and bigger prisons, and praised the protector of his job, Governor Kay Ivey. Unfortunately, he said nothing about the greater underlying problem of treating the DOC's own corrections officers better. Yes, they need more DOC officers, but no, Dunn has no idea about how much better the DOC would do if it afforded more respect and appreciation to its officers.

Dunn needs to be replaced for Alabama to dig its way out of this inhumane albatross. More inspired gubernatorial leadership is also absolutely necessary, although Governor Kay Ivey had, as of this writing, begun to take some steps in March–April 2019.

7

Ninety Years Old and Still Truckin'

How can a ninety-year-old like Marie Carastro seem so young and energetic? Her husband Bob is only two years younger. Both can be serious, but both know how to laugh spontaneously and deeply. She was eighty-six when they first came to see me in December 2015. I figured then they might teach me a thing or two or three. I was right. I have learned much and been inspired even more.

After sixty-five years as a professional dietitian in health care, Mrs. Carastro was truly an expert in her field. In her then-twenty-eight years at the Alabama Department of Public Health, she had become a legend to some and a burr under the saddle to others. She had an MS degree in foods and nutrition and was a certified specialist in gerontology, the "art of helping older people." Given her own advanced age, Mrs. Carastro well understood that field.

Mrs. Carastro combined a missionary sense of duty with high standards for keeping food safe to eat. Her inspections ranged throughout Alabama at independent homes, senior facilities, and homes for the disabled. All such facilities must meet the approval of the Alabama Department of Public Health. As the dietary leader, Marie would be one of three to four inspectors on survey teams fanning out across Alabama, without notice, to do their work. Yet inevitably she ran afoul of powers that be in the Public Health Office, bureaucrats uncomfortable with Marie's own elderly status. She sought my help.

Age and disability were the basis of Mrs. Carastro's first charge of discrimination, filed by me on December 22, 2015, with the Equal Employment Opportunity Commission (EEOC) in Birmingham. Pressure was being exerted on her by the Public Health Department to retire due to her age. While acknowledging her hearing was not perfect, Mrs. Carastro insisted she was otherwise "fully able to perform all the necessary duties of her job." Many of her younger co-employee surveyors marveled that Marie outworked and outperformed them, especially in the physical aspects of her job, given significant walking on hot days of the year.

In the first EEOC charge, Mrs. Carastro confirmed her "great heart for maintaining high standards for safe, sanitary food preparation, storage, and service."

Yet in October–November 2015, she was called in by Public Health's top management and instructed to respond to undocumented complaints from a survey she performed in Trussville. She asked for specifics, but the top brass refused.

Accordingly, paragraphs 11–14 of her EEOC charge read as follows:

11. I have been under such pressure lately that I have also prepared a grievance, which I am filing with the Alabama Department of Public Health. Although the administrators of the Department of Public Health, mindful of age discrimination laws, are careful not to openly criticize me due to my age, the very fact that they sometimes overly compliment me about how well I am doing because of my age, reflects their age consciousness about me.

12. From time to time, my supervisors and co-workers have suggested that I retire, or asked me when I am going to retire. Additionally, a supervisor told me that any problems management has with me are based on my age.

13. I have been told that staff at some of the nursing homes I evaluate have been told to call the Montgomery office if they "have a problem with me." Other nursing home facility staff have been told that "I have Alzheimer's and do not survey by myself anymore." I do not have Alzheimer's, and I believe these statements are further evidence of the Department's discrimination against me based on my older age, because Alzheimer's disease is typically associated with older people. It is also an indicator of disability discrimination, due to the alleged perception that I have Alzheimer's, when I do not.

14. Although I still have my job, I feel that the pressure I am being subjected to is for the purpose of making me resign. I therefore feel it important

to file this age and disability discrimination charge in order to protect me against further efforts to discourage me, and/or to influence me to resign because of my age, or because of a perceived disability (Alzheimer's) that does not exist, and/or due to an actual modest disability related to my hearing, which, although it does exist, does not prevent me from performing the necessary duties of my job."

After filing this charge nothing happened to Mrs. Carastro for the next nine months. But alas, in September 2016 she had to come back to see us. Associate attorney Chase Estes provided excellent assistance in helping me with her case, from the beginning to end. Accordingly, Chase prepared a second charge against the Public Health Department, alleging that Mrs. Carastro was "retaliated against" by Public Health management and subjected to a "cold and hostile working environment."

We all hoped the second charge with the EEOC would slow down the department's efforts to rid itself of Mrs. Carastro. But if that plan worked at all, it lasted for only a few months. By March 2017, Mrs. Carastro came to see us again, this time showing us the seven-day suspension notice she had received from State Health Officer Thomas Miller, M.D. This time Marie was cited for "engaging in inappropriate and unprofessional comments with dietary managers." She was also accused of "being argumentative." Oh, what a terrible thing! Yet the worst of her alleged shortcomings was that, in the northeast Alabama towns of Guntersville and Gadsden, she "touched managers on their hands." Oh, how bad!

I immediately requested a hearing on the proposed suspension. On April 20, 2017, Marie, her husband Bob, Chase Estes, and I drove over to the Public Health Department, located in the twenty-three-story RSA tower building in downtown Montgomery. A projected two-hour hearing morphed into six and a half hours. There was plenty of heat and no small amount of embellishment going on by the state's witnesses.

At the beginning, the state hearing officer announced she would be "fair and independent" because she was "not an employee of the Department of Public Health." She admitted coming from a law firm on contract with the Health Department for her to be a hearing officer . . . as if that made a difference. Rather than making her more independent, her words of protest smacked of "thou doth protest too much." It raised my eyebrows, and my concern proved founded.

The state's evidence in both cases was well orchestrated and rehearsed. A Guntersville food and nutrition manager, testifying by video link with a cigarette flopping from her mouth, said, "Oh, Mrs. Carastro slapped my hand." On cross-examination, I got the manager to concede that it was nothing more than a light tap, a handsy, folksy touch by Mrs. Carastro, emphasizing a conversational point. Unfortunately the kitchen manager was hypersensitive and hyperdefensive. "My kitchen is my baby," she volunteered. The Guntersville manager was posturing to strike back at Mrs. Carastro before being "tagged" on several issues. Those included (a) using cracked plates, (b) employees putting unclean fingers in drinking glasses, and (c) forcing an unwanted diet upon a hospice patient—all of which cause health problems, especially on seniors with weakened immune systems.

The Gadsden facility leader also moaned that she "felt defeated" before Mrs. Carastro even began the Health Department survey.

The hearing officer took copious notes when the facilities' witnesses testified, yet her pen barely moved when Mrs. Carastro and her two witnesses spoke. The hearing's outcome was preordained.

On May 23, 2017, the hearing officer issued a thirty-page opinion, repeating the rehearsed testimony of the Guntersville and Gadsden witnesses. The violations found against Mrs. Carastro were based on vague, esoteric standards.

The Health Department was surely pleased when the biased hearing officer concluded that "Mrs. Carastro's non-compliance with the Department's cited policies and procedures supported a suspension of her duties as a Licensure and Certification Surveyor in the Department's Long-Term Care Division." The penalty was a seven-day suspension of Mrs. Carastro without pay.

But even the hearing officer acknowledged that Mrs. Carastro is "tough and candid, and fair in the performance of her duties as a Health Provider Surveyor, and that her high standards had benefited the residents of nursing homes she had surveyed over many years."

By then, Mrs. Carastro had already filed three EEOC age/disability discrimination charges against the Health Department in Birmingham, but by July 3, 2017, it became necessary to do a fourth. This charge emanated from the unfair results of a May 2017 evaluation. Mrs. Carastro grieved that she was now being sent out alone, usually having to drive herself to destinations as much as three hours or more away. Then, at her destination, she was often inhibited by the State Health Department itself from doing her work.

If anyone could have the energy "to keep on keeping on," it is Marie Carastro. Every year, usually in late June, she used her vacation time to race as a pilot in the "Cross-Country Air Race." The last several years her co-pilot has been her fifty-four-year-old daughter Susan, the flight attendant her nineteen-year-old granddaughter Danielle. That totals 162 years from three generations of female family members flying together. In 2017, the forty-first annual race, they began a three-day zigzag in Frederick, Maryland, and ended in Santa Fe, New Mexico. In June 2018, Marie and her daughter flew from Sweetwater, Texas, hopscotching all the way to Maine. Many of the contestants did not make it because of the weather, but Mrs. Carastro and Susan did.

Where does Mrs. Carastro's amazing energy come from? I shake my head at this superwoman "still truckin'" on all cylinders as she entered her ninetieth year in 2019. What "fountain of youth" has Mrs. Carastro been drinking from? What kind of tea? I know she respects her Lord and Creator, and she says that helps. But . . .

Meanwhile, Mrs. Carastro was receiving honors and recognitions. One was a congratulatory certificate in May 2018 from Alabama's Secretary of State John Merrill. *Tuscaloosa Magazine* featured Mrs. Carastro in its summer 2018 edition as one of the "Six Most Intriguing People" in Alabama. It showed a 1948 picture of her as a nineteen-year-old quarterback throwing a football in an all-female game.

Mrs. Carastro finally decided that as of April 1, 2019, she would retire. In early summer 2018, I informally met Dr. Scott Harris, the new head of the State Public Health Department, and his attractive wife, Sandy, in the Old Cloverdale neighborhood, just before Scott assumed office. I spoke with him about Marie Carastro and thought I had persuaded him to allow Mrs.

Carastro to continue working until her retirement, then only six months away.

Turned out, I was overly optimistic, or maybe Dr. Harris didn't realize who he was dealing with. Somehow Mrs. Carastro's department managers persuaded Dr. Harris to terminate Mrs. Carastro, which Dr. Harris briefly did on September 10, 2018. Since there were only three days left on Mrs. Carastro's right-to-sue letter, the Health Department left us with no choice but to rush to file suit to preserve Mrs. Carastro's rights. We also filed a Notice of Appeal to the State Personnel Department. Long story short, after sending a letter to Dr. Harris, expressing our dismay, the Health Department reversed itself and reinstated Mrs. Carastro with pay and benefits until her agreed-upon retirement date on April 1, 2019, just after she was to turn ninety. The abrupt turnabout obviously required action by Dr. Harris. In return, a few weeks later, we let Dr. Harris out of the suit, but left Mrs. Carastro's supervisors in.

While Mrs. Carastro has been a champion against age discrimination, her case illustrates how tough it is to pursue such a case. 2017 marked the

Leslie and me at the ninetieth birthday party of "still truckin'" Marie Carastro.

fiftieth anniversary of the Age Discrimination in Employment Act. A half-century later, *USA Today* stated on September 2, 2018:

> "age discrimination in the workplace remains notoriously hard to prove . . . of the 18,376 cases filed with U.S. Equal Employment Opportunity Commission in 2017, only 2.2 percent were found to have "reasonable cause."

That is because age discrimination, unlike race and sex discrimination, is rarely "in your face." It is never shouted from the rooftop. It is nonetheless insidious and painful psychologically and financially. Yet in Mrs. Carastro's case, it was "in her face," as her accusers suggested she was in early Alzheimer's, which she was not.

Meanwhile, she retired as planned. For her thirty years of state service, Governor Kay Ivey and U.S. Congresswoman Terri Sewell both honored her with certificates of commendation and congratulations, which I presented to her at her ninetieth birthday party at the Capital City Club on March 28, 2019.

At the party, I just happened to sit next to Mrs. Carastro's ninety-eight-year-old sister Louise Crunk. What a lively conversation we had. Mrs. Crunk later performed some nimble dance moves on the floor, to everyone's applause. Then I was enthusiastically greeted by Mrs. Carastro's ninety-six-year-old aunt and many energetic cousins in their eighties. They claimed no special diet; it must be in their genes.

If Mrs. Carastro's case is tried, and not settled, she'll be a ninety-year-old plaintiff, which might be a record.

In conclusion, I greatly honor Mrs. Carastro, not only for standing up for clean food in nursing homes and other public facilities, but also for standing up for senior citizens who can still work, play, and live productive lives. There are increasing numbers of baby-boomers like me (born in the post-war 1940s) who fall into that category.

8

King of the DUIs

In legal parlance, "DUI" usually means "Driving Under the Influence" of alcohol, illegal narcotics, or even excessive prescription medication. If there is no accident, or no one hurt, and it's your first offense, the penalty is usually relatively light—a fine of $600 and a minimum ninety-day license suspension. A substance abuse court-referral program is also part of a "guilty" finding, whether by plea or trial.

If you're a repeat offender, or worse, if someone is seriously hurt or, heaven forbid, killed, then you're in big trouble . . . looking at jail time or an extended prison visit.

Accordingly, a true specialist in the field is what you need, even if it costs you a pretty penny to get the best in the business. In Alabama, at least, for many years that has been Montgomery attorney Tommy Kirk, known in some circles as the "King of the DUI's."

Like many good defense attorneys, Tommy started off as a successful prosecutor. I well remember Tommy back in the 1980s, when he ran the docket for the City of Montgomery in Municipal Court. He was then and remains today a gentleman. Please forgive the cliché, if I add the word "scholar," as in Richard Gere's famous movie, *An Officer and a Gentleman*. Substitute "scholar" for "officer," since Tommy has also been an officer of the court, which technically speaking, all lawyers are.

The scholar description, however, is especially appropriate if you enter into Tommy's building at 444 South Decatur Street in Montgomery, opposite the office where Tommy has long practiced law at 445 South Decatur. This "extra" building has eight rooms and contains approximately four thousand books of history, literature, and other eclectic topics. Tommy has an entire room devoted to the American Civil War and United States presidents.

Although Tommy is reserved in personality, he has a razor-sharp mind that is always clicking. His career has been a tapestry of interesting cases and a ministry of services to his clients.

Tommy sprang into this world on June 21, 1943, son of Edna Oswalt Kirk and James Floyd Kirk. His dad was the editorial page editor of the *Alabama Journal*, then Montgomery's afternoon newspaper. James Kirk died in 1947, at age forty-six. Tommy, only four at the time, remembers the funeral and wishes he could have known his father longer. Tommy's two older brothers, David and Paul, were both brilliant like their younger brother. David died in 1998, but Paul, eighteen months older than Tommy,

Conferring with "DUI King" Tommy Kirk at his famous book library.

graduated from Princeton and MIT, became a nuclear physicist, and lives in Baton Rouge. Good smarts in the family.

Tommy graduated in 1961 from Montgomery's Sidney Lanier High School, then at the apex of its high national reputation. Tommy attended Montgomery's well-respected Huntingdon College, graduating in 1966. He was ready to be launched, and after a couple of brief interludes, began his legal studies at the Jones School of Law in Montgomery, finishing in 1971 (the same year I finished Columbia Law).

After a first marriage in 1973 that lasted eight years, and a singlehood of four years, Tommy married the beautiful Rhea Cravens Alfreds, herself a divorcee with three young sons. Rhea specialized in teaching manners to young children, including my daughter Grace, at the Capital City Club in Montgomery. Tommy became a doting, caring father, helped raise all three boys, and now practices law with middle son Matt Alfreds, now forty-two years old. Besides being a great mother, Rhea is also the executive director of NCDD, the National College for DUI Defense.

There have been many dramatic "dodged that bullet" stories in Tommy's long and colorful career. In the following episodes shared by Tommy he has wisely changed names to protect the charged, who either imbibed too much alcohol or had drugs in their system. Somehow with Tommy's tactical navigation, they managed to avoid the hammer of the law.

One memorable case involved his client Ronny McDeal. During direct examination of a police officer, attorney Tommy noticed the officer used the word "alphabets."

On cross-examination, Tommy asked, "Officer, you expected him [McDeal] to do all the letters of the alphabet, correct?"

"Yes, sir," the officer responded.

"How many letters did you ask to be performed?"

"All of them" said the officer.

"Well, how many letters is 'all of them?'"

Then the police officer went silent—and for thirty seconds or so he was counting on his fingers. "Twenty-three," came the answer.

No response by Tommy. The jury appreciated Tommy's silence, and returned the wonderful two-word verdict of "Not Guilty."

In another case, Tommy was running late to a docket call in Selma's Circuit Court. He admittedly was speeding. Tommy came out of a curve and realized that a state trooper was coming from the opposite direction. The officer hit his blue lights immediately and started to cross the median. Tommy slowed and stopped, then sat on the side of the road five or more minutes before pulling off slowly. No trooper had come back around the curve. The night before a heavy rain had fallen—so much so that when Tommy drove back from Selma that afternoon, he saw the trooper's car still stuck in the soggy median. Tommy enjoyed imagining the trooper's colorful language over the turn of events.

Another time Tommy's client, Oscar Moon, was asked to get out of his car to perform field sobriety tests. Due to the angle of the roadway, the trooper asked Mr. Moon to go down to a service station's parking lot, some thirty or forty yards down the hill. The incline was pretty steep but Tommy's client ran down the hill without any trouble. The trooper fell down twice. The jury was impressed—finding Mr. Moon was better at balance and coordination than the trooper. Tommy made no small use of that fact in successfully defending Mr. Moon.

Another DUI defense involved client David Cantrell during mid-winter. It was exceptionally cold, certainly not short-sleeve weather. Mr. Cantrell was blue-lighted by a deputy for a minor violation: not using a signal to turn into a service station parking lot. When asked to step out of the car for field sobriety tests, Cantrell performed reasonably well. For any errors asserted, Mr. Cantrell replied humbly "I'm a skinny little dude," which he was. The jury must have been impressed because they found Mr. Cantrell not guilty of DUI. "The skinny dude" was a humble but successful explanation.

Another case Tommy Kirk cannot forget involved a Jeremy Bentz, who said he and three friends had shot pool over a time period of three and a half hours. Each had paid for a round of beer. Thus Jeremy and his friends each consumed four beers. Halfway through the time spent, they ordered pizza, and they consumed a large amount of it during their break from pool. When interviewed, Jeremy was asked what reaction, if any, did the combination of pizza and beer cause. Jeremy shared, "It makes me feel like a volcano—belching considerably and causing a need for a roll of Tums."

"Well," attorney Kirk said, "that's a great explanation, please explain that to the jury."

On the trial date, the question was again posed to Jeremy the client—"What reaction did you have from consuming so much pizza and beer?" Jeremy, with a deer in the headlights look and in absolute panic, replied, "It made me fart."

The trial judge had to turn his chair to the wall. However, all twelve jurors voted "Not Guilty" after the laughter ended. Tommy has learned well how to use humor.

Tommy's favorite case that he loves to share, in his own words, is:

It was in the spring of the year—turkey season had just begun—in fact, it was the first weekend of hunting the big birds. Caleb Hardy had packed the Jeep on Thursday afternoon and was headed straight to his hunting cabin. He had double-checked all the necessities before saying goodbye to his wife. He then headed to the interstate traffic to begin the two-hour drive. The last necessity was "Dusty," his family dog—a beautiful lab, jet black and absolutely the pride of his life other than his wife, Susan. Smart that dog was, smarter than the majority of the people Caleb knew and worked with. Now three years old, Dusty had all the makings of a true champion—that dog loved water more than dry land. Caleb's duck hunting buddies had become so enamored with Dusty that one offered Caleb $15,000, a huge amount compared to the true price Caleb had paid for this runt of the litter his brother's dog had produced. Yes sir—open the tailgate of the Jeep . . . Dusty would bounce right in, just with the "pop" sound of the gate. From that point on, however, until arriving at the cabin, Dusty was the absolute definition of quiet discipline.

Over the weekend Dusty remained at the cabin, while Caleb hunted the turkey. Sunday morning came, and Caleb packed up for the return trip. Dusty, as usual, jumped in his bed and drifted off to sleep. Caleb had about an hour's drive to Fairmont, a small town forty-five minutes north of the hunting cabin. Another twenty minutes took Caleb onto the Lake Davis area where, as he had for two decades, Caleb stopped at Talley's Marine Food Shop and purchased a case of Budweiser and some snacks. Also, he gassed up the Jeep and opened a delightful Bud.

Caleb knew he could easily enjoy two more as he drove home over the next ninety minutes or so. Some ten to fifteen miles beyond Talley's, a pothole caused that familiar tailgate "popping sound." Caleb remembered Dusty had bathroom duty back at Talley's, and the sound of the latch brought him to an emergency stop. Checking on Dusty immediately, Caleb discovered the worst nightmare—"Dusty, Dusty" he called—there was no response! Caleb turned around and began a search for Dusty—twenty minutes back to Talley's, and an hour back to Fairmont—what else could he do? Caleb searched by stopping every hundred yards or so, calling Dusty's name and praying he wouldn't see Dusty dead in the roadway. The case of beer helped Caleb, he thought, survive the fear and panic. "Dusty, Dusty" every stop took him all the way back to Talley's in the Lake area, and some fifteen or twenty miles back towards Fairmont. Sipping beer at every stop helped Caleb endure the anxiety and pressure.

Meanwhile, Colbert County State Trooper Holman was headed to a wreck scene and came upon a Jeep parked on the side of the road. The headlights were on, and the driver's left leg was on the ground. The interior lights were on by way of the open door. Holman thought the driver was on his cell phone—thankfully having pulled off the road. Trooper Holman had a call to check on, so he passed on by. Some 45 minutes later, trooper Holman returned to the same area—going back to his usual patrol. Holman noticed the same vehicle beside the highway, with door opened, lights on, and the driver's leg out the door but no cell phone being used or other excuse plainly in sight. There were some twelve to fourteen empties on the floorboard, passenger side. Caleb was sound asleep. An arrest took place and subsequently Caleb blew .23 on the breath test for the trooper. It was that bad—real bad! A .23—Caleb's second nightmare of the night!

After a jury trial, the verdict was returned. Not Guilty. However, the jury had a special question for the trial judge—"Did he find his dog?"

Summing up the King of the DUI's, it is fair to say that Tommy Kirk is one effective dude in the courtroom. He knows how to "get the ox out of the ditch," so to speak, whether on a Sabbath day, or any other day of the week.

9

Mendenhalls on the Mend

It's amazing how life brings you in contact with different people from different angles and different backgrounds. Just before my seventieth birthday on November 13, 2016, I bumped into new neighbors living catty-corner across the street on Felder Avenue in our historic old Cloverdale neighborhood. I first remember seeing and hearing Stanford calling out to me from Fitzgerald Park directly across the street from my home. He was friendly, sounded educated, and was a little difficult to see clearly in the shadows of dusk.

Soon I met his exuberantly friendly wife Linda, a fifty-six-year-old recently involuntarily retired attorney from Maxwell Air Force base. Blonde and originally from a liberal Jewish family out of Long Island, New York, Linda had met Stanford, the youngest of eleven siblings from a rural central Alabama family descended from slaves. It was a second marriage for both, a biracial couple sparking one another in the challenges of life while mending themselves.

They walked across the street to my birthday party in Cloverdale that Sunday afternoon in November 2016, the newest of friends. Linda raved about my two books, *The People's Lawyer* and *Civil Rights in My Bones*, proclaiming that we were soulmates with much in common. Soon we were invited into their apartment home for dinner. The next thing I knew I was representing Linda on two prior employment cases with the US Air Force, one with Maxwell AFB, the other with Keesler AFB.

The Maxwell case grew out of a transfer from Redstone Arsenal in Huntsville where she lost her job after she objected too strongly to her boss's calling her husband "a Negroid." She received a transfer to Maxwell AFB in Montgomery but was improperly placed on probationary status. Her young, first-time supervisor, though a lieutenant colonel, was narrow-minded and had unreasonable standards that Linda did not meet, causing her to lose her job after only six months in March 2017.

The Barksdale case arose out of an Air Force base in Shreveport, Louisiana, where Linda had applied for an attorney job in December 2015. Despite her far superior credentials over younger applicants (she was ranked No. 1 on the register), Linda was passed over, after being asked a number of aggressively age-sensitive questions. Hence Linda filed a complaint for age discrimination.

Stanford was a first responder and was injured on 9/11 when the World Trade Center was attacked. Later he lost eighteen close friends who sacrificed it all in Iraq and was lifted out of intense battle by helicopter, suffering severe physical and mental injuries himself. Stanford was declared one hundred percent disabled. He now draws about $1,200 per month from the U.S. Department of Veterans Affairs (VA), which is the only regular income the couple had for many months.

Linda survived an abusive first marriage, and so did Stanford. She first met Stanford, a mailman, when she was representing him in a divorce case in New York. She had a domestic private practice in Long Island but made only a modest living with no retirement or health insurance benefits. She later joined the Air Force as an attorney, but her involuntary termination in 2017 cut Linda just short of vesting in long-term benefits.

Linda and Stanford came to see me and paralegal Amy Strickland on a June 2017 afternoon to discuss both her cases. We signed attorney-client agreements, and started organizing numerous documents. Given their dire financial circumstances, my legal representation was "contingent," meaning that I would only get paid if I won.

Meanwhile, Linda, excited about my two books, volunteered to start promoting my literary efforts. That was encouraging. Linda put great energy and enthusiasm into the effort, much to my appreciation, setting me up with speaking engagements in different parts of Alabama. She says that working on my books has been good medicine for her. She appreciated the opportunity and gives me more credit than I deserve.

After losing her job at Maxwell, the Mendenhalls moved in April 2017 one and a half hours southwest to Camden in Wilcox County in the heart of the Black Belt. Both U.S. Attorney General Jeff Sessions and Alabama Governor Kay Ivey grew up in that county, developing their right-wing views in the former plantation area. Leslie and I were invited down in May 2017 to the Mendenhalls' new habitat: an antebellum, Greco-columned mini-mansion in need of repair. That weekend the four of us and Linda's son Ryan floated on the celebrated ferry at Gee's Bend, voyaging several miles down the Alabama River. Once docked, we rolled down the plank onto a rough paved road where several older African American women in a shack were piecing together colorful quilts. We bought an original patchwork of criss-crossing designs and installed it as an honored piece of art at our Lake Martin cottage.

The Mendenhalls indulge in no pity party. They embrace their Christian faith at Saint Wisdom Baptist Church in Camden. They (or she) can laugh one moment and be on the verge of crying the next. They've also started to pick up a little extra change by renting Airbnb stays at their antebellum home.

By early 2018, Linda's web of applications netted a fish, when she was hired on a $25-an-hour basis, doing contract legal work on a major corporate project in Jacksonville, Florida. Before the year was over, she had moved on to a similar job in North Carolina. Meanwhile Stanford remained at home in Camden, but occasionally popped up to Montgomery to do volunteer yard work at the Scott and Zelda Fitzgerald Museum. Although there is no quid pro quo or bartering agreement, but because he cannot afford legal services, I in turn helped him pro bono on a couple of legal concerns, one civil involving his gas meter, the other a frivolous class C felony criminal charge of theft by deception that ought to be dropped by the prosecution. Linda and Stanford maintained daily contact by phone and email and got together on a regular basis, and Stanford pops up at my law office without appointment, often when I am quite busy on other matters.

What makes this eclectic couple from such diverse backgrounds so interesting? More than anything, it was and is how resilient they have been. They are survivors. Being human, they get rattled and tossed by the winds of life, but they keep on keeping on, and usually land on both feet. They have not let setbacks or misfortunes get the worst of them. Wounded but not defeated.

10

Nigerian Students Take on ASU

In 2014, not long after Success Jumbo met and married fellow Nigerian student Chichi Oji, Success came to my law office to enlist my help about shortcomings in how Alabama State University was administering Nigerian government scholarship money, to the detriment of Success and forty other Nigerian students. They said ASU was overcharging them for many things, and siphoning off scholarship money for other independent school needs not related to the students.

Success's wife Chichi became close to my wife Leslie and me after staying with us four months from January–April 2006. We had met her months earlier in 2005 in Benin, West Africa, as part of an Alabama delegation that included Leslie and me. Chichi was the travel guide for our Alabama-Benin Reconciliation Conference.

Success said ASU was not paying for his modest off-campus apartment expense needed for Chichi, his newborn son—Success Jumbo Jr.—and himself. Thus I sent a first letter to Provost Leon Wilson and a second one later to then-President Dr. Gwendolyn Boyd. Neither letter received the courtesy of a reply. I soon learned why.

By 2015, other dismayed Nigerian ASU students had also come to see me. They said they also were being shortchanged and subjected to inflated prices for books, food, lodging, etc., when compared to non-Nigerian students. In this regard, I was shown and acted upon letters from Mr. Kingsley Kuku, the high-level Nigerian government official who originated the scholarships. Further, a former senior ASU professor, Dr. David Iyegha, who helped bring the students over from Africa, showed us facts and figures reflecting how badly ASU was ripping off the Nigerian students.

Finally, since Success and most of the other Nigerians had no money of their own to pay an up-front attorney's fee, I agreed to take their case on a contingency basis.

A first suit was dismissed on jurisdictional grounds, but I quickly filed a revised national-origin discrimination complaint in August 2015. That complaint survived a Motion to Dismiss, with U.S. Chief District Judge Keith Watkins expressing a favorable ruling on five different causes of action.

By late summer 2016, ASU attorney Kenny Thomas and I were close to settling the case for approximately $200,000. While that wasn't nearly the $800,000 the students thought was owed them, it was a good chunk of money. Instead, the students independently consulted with Nigerian-born attorney Anthony Ifediba in Birmingham, and they came to see me in Montgomery, ultimately persuading me to associate Ifediba in a shared leadership of the case and continue on.

The next thing I knew ASU attorney Kenny Thomas was insisting on deposing all thirty-seven of my plaintiffs. We in turn noticed the depositions of four to five top ASU officials, with Ifediba and his associate Ron Jackson being present for all depositions. Ifediba also agreed to pay for the cost of those depositions, no small consideration in my agreeing to his association in the case.

Various discovery disputes, not unexpected, kept things sparking as both sides geared up for pretrial battles in the summer of 2017. In early August 2017, after two contentious days in court, we hammered out an agreement to protect ASU from mishandling $201,000 of unused Nigerian settlement money. Given what had happened to scholarship money from 2013–15, that was a real concern for us. Another client of mine, ASU professor Dr. Delilah Dotreman, testified in court that ASU president Gwendolyn Boyd shocked the faculty on November 1, 2016, by declaring that "ASU didn't have enough money to pay for toilet paper." Her testimony was also very damaging to Provost Wilson, suggesting he had mishandled the scholarship money.

Depositions began in earnest in July 2017. At times verbal missiles fired by ASU attorney Kenneth Thomas towards my co-counsel Ifediba were so sharp they were humorous. Kenny directed some colorful, profane

Outside the U.S. District Court with, from left, Nigerian student Jimmy Iwezu, Nigerian-American co-counsels Anthony Ifediba and Patricia Ojakovo, and students Kenny Batiste and Success Jumbo.

language toward my Nigerian partner, which I thought was excessive. When I defended my colleague, Thomas would laugh it off, saying it was only used "for effect." I enjoyed being the calm voice between the two as summer moved into fall.

In April 2018 Alabama State filed a motion for summary judgment. We worked hard and prepared a thorough reply, astutely showing how, compared to other ASU students, the Nigerians were truly discriminated against on the basis of their national origin, causing the loss of large amounts of funds that otherwise should have come to the students.

Meanwhile, Judge Watkins, due to a crowded docket caused by not enough federal judges to handle the caseload in the Middle District of Alabama, allowed our case to be transferred to a south Mississippi judge, Keith Starrett. His competence level was much less than that of our Alabama judges. In an exceedingly misguided, short memorandum issued May 3, 2018, just one week after we submitted our summary judgment response, Starrett granted summary judgment for ASU. This prevented us from taking the case to court. His opinion looked like he had barely glanced at our brief, ignored our strongest evidence, and misinterpreted many other facts. We were dumbfounded. It was like Starrett resented the Nigerian students. We filed a post-judgment motion that Starrett denied on July 23, 2018.

On September 17, 2018, we filed a notice of appeal to the Eleventh U.S. Circuit Court of Appeals in Atlanta. I associated lawyer David Sawyer to assist Chase Estes and me in preparing the brief. A strong case was made that the Mississippi judge badly abused his discretion in two different regards: (a) failing to apply the proper equal protection standards to the plaintiffs' Title VI claims; and (b) by refusing to consider the Nigerian students' affidavits and exhibits as evidence of discrimination. We cited ample case law in our favor, which is supposed to guide a court in its ruling, but the judge ignored it.

To my surprise and that of ASU counsel Kenny Thomas, a mediator from the Eleventh Circuit tried to schedule a mediation by long-distance telephone. We finally did so on November 26, 2018, but it was a wasted effort.

To my amazement, we received an opinion on January 31, 2019, denying our appeal, saying that while ASU may have discriminated against the Nigerian students, and even wrongfully taken their money, it wasn't proven that ASU "intended" to discriminate against the students based on nationality. Only in Alabama do folks get away with such, even if the opinion was written in Atlanta, Georgia.

Especially undermining our case was the indecisiveness of the Nigerian government, named by us as a necessary party defendant. The Nigerian state did enter an appearance but otherwise did not help us. My co-counsel Anthony Ifediba, a Nigerian citizen himself, attempted to persuade the Nigerians to reassert the strong pro-student stand they had once taken on the money. Unfortunately, influenced by a continuing change of leadership in their national government, the Nigerian representatives failed to do so, thus diminishing our claim against Alabama State University.

In mid-February 2019 we filed a petition for a rehearing en banc. That means we were asking the entire Eleventh Circuit to look at the case, not just the three-judge panel that made the initial decisions. On April 2, 2019,

Press conference outside the U.S. District Court in Montgomery, 2017.

the Eleventh Circuit denied the relief. Accordingly, we were left with either appealing to the U.S. Supreme Court in Washington or dropping the case. As this book went to press, that was undecided.

Let me add that I have much respect for Alabama State University generally. I live only one long block away and am frequently on its campus for civil rights events, dramatic performances, or the Friendly Supper Club the first Monday of the month. However, I am happy to represent both faculty and students who feel aggrieved by ASU's policies or practices, and have done so fairly frequently over the last forty years.

11

Police Misconduct

Wrongful Police Killings

The period of 2014 to 2019 in the U.S. experienced a terrible epidemic of innocent, unarmed civilians killed by police officers. Sadly, there have also been too many law enforcement officers killed in the line of duty. When will it stop? Will we ever become more like our sister Anglo-tradition countries of Canada, Australia, New Zealand, and Britain, where the percentage of killings is a miniscule one percent or less of what happens in the USA? When will our country legislate and enforce tougher gun control laws and protect its innocent citizens?

UPDATE ON EMERSON CRAYTON CASE

Alabama's record on innocent civilians wrongfully killed by police is as bad or worse than that of any other U.S. state. My 2016 book, *Civil Rights in My Bones*, described the wrongful killing of Emerson Crayton, a twenty-one-year-old unarmed African American man killed by an Alexander City policeman in 2014. The shooting happened in a Huddle House parking lot, as Emerson was heading home. In 2016, Huddle House had just paid $100,000 on our negligence claim, but the city was still fighting us. Shortly afterwards, in a non-confidential settlement, Alex City caved in and paid $500,000.

A total of $600,000 is still way short of what a human life so wrongfully taken away is worth. A father's life so needlessly snuffed out, leaving a two-year-old daughter and her young mother, Kolea Burns, scrambling for help. The entire settlement by law went to the young daughter, with a *guardian ad litem* appointed by the court to represent the child's interests.

And Crayton's heartbroken parents by law received nothing other than $10,000 in funeral expense reimbursement that my co-counsel and I gave them out of the attorney fees portion of the settlement.

THE ALICE SIMMONS CASE

You'd think law enforcement officers in another Alabama community only two years later would have learned from Alex City's bad experience, but another police shooting in 2016 of a thirty-seven-year-old white female reflects otherwise. The problem is that guiding precedent from similar cases establishes "qualified immunity" defenses—a legal doctrine providing a wide umbrella of excuses for police to escape liability—at both the state and federal level. All a policeman has to say is *"I thought the person was going to kill me if I didn't kill him first." So don't indict me, or sue me. I was just "standing my ground,"* which is another state-law defense.

Due to a confidentiality clause in the thirty-seven-year-old female's case, the names of the city and victim have been changed. Otherwise the following facts are true and accurate.

Life had for a long time been a struggle for Alice Simmons. Unlike her sister Amy, Alice suffered from bipolar episodes, depression, and related mental health issues.

One spring day in 2016, Alice told her caring parents, Mark and Teresa Simmons, that she had a pocketknife and was going to drive off, cut her wrists, and die.

The Simmonses were quite upset and decided they couldn't sit idly by. Sister Amy had earlier installed a GPS on Alice's car. With this computer assistance, Amy located where Alice was driving on I-65 in central Alabama.

The Simmonses called 911 in Rockville, told them about Alice's suicidal mindset, and asked for the help of the Rockville police. The parents told the 911 dispatcher that their daughter had a pocketknife and intended to cut her wrists. The parents then jumped into their car and drove to within two miles of their daughter on a federal highway. At that point Alice was being trailed by a police convoy led by two unmarked cars. Frightened, Alice pulled off the highway and sped down a back-country road.

Finally, Alice stopped. Not knowing the identities of the non-uniformed officers behind her in the unmarked cars, Alice jumped out of her own car, and displayed a closed pocketknife in her hand, according to evidence later obtained from police.

Unfortunately, the Rockville police, in defiance of training standards just received in their department the preceding week, overreacted, opened fire, and killed Alice.

Alice's heartbroken parents and sister Amy came to see me a day later, unable to control their sobs. They were also dealing with an enormous burden of guilt. After all, it was the parents' telephone calls which led to the Rockville police trailing Alice and ultimately shooting her.

Through discovery information obtained from Rockville police, we learned that the policeman who shot Alice had other nonlethal devices available, which he easily could easily have been used to contain Alice.

Due to conflicting schedules, organizing depositions was difficult. Notwithstanding, my law partner Kenneth Shinbaum helped significantly, and we associated another crackerjack attorney down the street, whose assistance was critical. Research assistance came from my associate attorney Chase Estes, with paralegal Lill Neace organizing tomes of evidence. The insured City of Rockville was geared up with four high-powered defense lawyers to battle us.

The City of Rockville, as was its right, fought us tooth and nail, claiming the police acted in self-defense. The "qualified immunity defense" was our biggest legal hurdle. Under this defense, unless there is a bright, clear, redline precedential case saying the police conduct violated constitutional standards, the police escape liability. The issue boiled down to this question, "did the Rockville police have a reasonably objective basis for believing that, if he (the policeman shooting and killing) did not use deadly force first to protect himself, then he (the policeman) might himself be killed?" If so, the policeman would be justified in using deadly force.

There were also big legal battles over venue, namely in what county should the trial be held. One county was good for us; another county was much better for the defense. The Rockville defense lawyers also threw in a "stand your ground" defense and novel "pursuit" theories as additional defenses. An unsuccessful mediation set the foundation for a later settlement. In the end, a substantial settlement was a pittance, when compared to the value of a life but, after knocking at each other for over two years, both sides were willing to put it behind them. There was also a significant risk of adverse rulings by the nine Republicans sitting on the Alabama Supreme Court, especially on the immunity and venue issues.

POLICE BULLYING PEOPLE BUT NOT KILLING THEM

Not all police excessive force cases result in killings, but they can be very painful nonetheless. Despite the true stories described below, I know that, on many occasions, Montgomery police officers under dangerous circumstances courageously help citizens in distress. I join in saluting and expressing gratitude to the many good officers who are not bullies, and who risk life and limb in protecting the public.

Tyannis Lawrence (Lowndes County, Alabama)

On May 23, 2016, Sententa Lawrence, the young African American mother of eighteen-year-old Tyannis Lawrence, came to see me. They lived in the small Tyler community in southwest Lowndes County, Alabama. Sententa was accompanied by her older sister, Hattie. They had an incredible story. They described how slightly built Tyannis, still handcuffed, appeared before a local judge at the Lowndes County Courthouse in Hayneville. After addressing Judge Adrian Johnson on a bond issue, Tyannis was brutally attacked and beaten in open court by deputy sheriff Christopher West. The deputy, a 6'2" 275-pound African American male, didn't like the "smirky look" on Tyannis's face and decided to "wipe it off."

Unbelievably, Deputy West reached out over a rail in the courtroom, grabbed Tyannis, picked him up into the air and over the rail, slammed Tyannis to the floor, and started pounding away at him. That attack was so blatant and outrageous that West himself ended up being criminally prosecuted . . . just barely and briefly. Lowndes County prosecutors claimed a conflict, and let neighboring Montgomery County send two deputy district attorneys to Hayneville to prosecute. Testifying against Deputy West were Hayneville police chief Kelvin Mitchell and many other eyewitnesses. In 2016 Chief Mitchell even came to my office with the Lawrences to express how upset he was and offered to help. Despite the overwhelming testimony against him, Deputy West had a trump card in his pocket—the district judge assigned to the non-jury case, who acquitted West. At a later deposition Deputy West admitted he and Judge Tom Sport were friends.

To paraphrase Paul Harvey, this was "not the end of the story." We filed suit on September 14, 2017, against Christopher West and Lowndes County, alleging violations of Tyannis's constitutional rights under the Fourth, Eighth, and Fourteenth amendments, as well as negligence. In the fall of 2018, I associated a new of-counsel attorney, David Sawyer, to help prepare a plaintiff's motion for summary judgment. He did an excellent job. Before the judge could rule, a mediation was conducted by former Montgomery County Circuit Judge Randy Thomas on March 18, 2019, and the case resolved on a basis highly pleasing to my client.

Tracy Tye (Abbeville, Henry County, Alabama)

On June 15, 2017, Tracy Tye came in from southeast Alabama with a shocking story.

Three weeks earlier, the forty-eight-year-old Tracy and her husband Kent Tye came cruising in a Mercury Grand Marquis down a main street of Abbeville on their way to grocery shop. Kent was driving; Tracy was in the passenger seat. Suddenly Abbeville police lieutenant Kevin Randolph stopped Mr. Tye in front of a school. Randolph ambled to the passenger window where Mrs. Tye was sitting. She handed over her husband's driver's license and registration, though neither was requested. Lt. Randolph found no problem with either. However, he demanded that Mrs. Tye step out of the vehicle. She complied. Her husband was not asked to step out.

Lt. Randolph immediately berated Mrs. Tye, saying, "You look bad, so you must know where drugs are in the car." Mrs. Tye replied there were no drugs on herself or in the car. Her husband was asked if he had anything illegal on him. Mr. Tye responded, "I have a blunt" (a makeshift marijuana cigarette). Lt. Randolph tore the blunt up and stomped it under his feet, but did not charge Mr. Tye with possession of drugs, only with driving without a seatbelt.

What happened next to Mrs. Tye was a woman's worst nightmare. After patting her down, Lt. Randolph called for a female jailer to come and search Mrs. Tye . . . publicly. Six other police officers also showed up with flashing lights, enhancing the public spectacle.

The worst was yet to come. Lt. Randolph and the female jailer forced Mrs. Tye to raise her shirt, exposing her breasts. Embarrassed and humiliated, she insisted she was clean. Adding insult to injury, Lt. Randolph forced Mrs. Tye do a "squat and cough" procedure. That required her to pull her shorts all the way to the ground, again exposing herself in front of a fast-growing public audience. Mrs. Tye couldn't believe what she was being subjected to. It was surreal. It was all happening so fast.

The squat procedure caused Tracy to leak urine. People were riding by, gawking, and laughing. The officers were smiling at each other, winking, cutting jokes, and enjoying the spectacle. Lt. Randolph wise-cracked to Mrs. Tye, "Don't pee on my truck."

No drugs were ever found. The entire incident shook Mrs. Tye to her soul. Months later, she was still suffering nightmares and headaches, afraid to go out in public, fearing she would be recognized and laughed at in downtown Abbeville. She has received psychological counseling, but needs more.

We filed a claim for Mrs. Tye with the City Clerk of Abbeville, citing her Fourth, Eighth, and Fourteenth amendment constitutional rights and adding state claims of negligence and wantonness. Her claim was presented to an executive session of the Abbeville Town Council and were denied. Although ample supporting legal precedent from the Eleventh Circuit Court of Appeals exists, prideful Abbeville could admit no wrong. Nonetheless, in a letter to the town council's attorney, I cited two similar federal cases from Georgia, where the qualified immunity defense was denied and a municipality held liable.

Months later, after a bad spat with her husband, who would have been a necessary and key witness for her, Mrs. Tye decided not to pursue her case.

Montgomery Cases

In my two earlier books, *The People's Lawyer* and *Civil Rights in My Bones*, there is much discussion about my cases with the Montgomery police department. In 1986, I also had two landmark federal cases involving the

Montgomery police department. The first, in a non-jury trial, challenged the practices of Mayor Emory Folmar in awarding high promotions to police officers who were his bodyguards and political band members. U.S. District Judge Myron Thompson ruled in our favor three years later. The second was representing policeman Steve Eiland, who wrote a satirical poem about the mayor. With the able assistance of co-counsel Vanzetta Penn McPherson, that case was finally won in the Eleventh Circuit Court of Appeals. In 1990, the police officer who stopped me for speeding, when he saw my name on my license, laughed and said, "You don't know how much your name is cussed and discussed at the police department. The top brass, they hate you. The rest of us, we love you."

Well, maybe not all of the rank and file officers did.

My peak for handling brutality and excessive force cases was around the year 2000, when then Mayor Emory Folmar was just leaving office. I easily had more than a hundred such cases during his twenty-two-year tenure as mayor. I didn't always win or settle, but I had a solid $50,000 result in one case and lesser significant amounts in other cases. It wasn't about the money—they usually panned out less well than other types of cases, and the self-insured City of Montgomery preferred to fight them tooth and nail. But I felt a mission and a calling in taking these cases. I know that my cases in the 1980s to 1990s made the MPD top brass refine their roughhouse tactics. Who knows? Some lives might have been saved as a result.

Despite butting heads with Mayor Folmar publicly and privately, I had one humorously memorable moment with him in 1991. At a "celebrity waiter's luncheon" to raise money to fight leukemia, Emory dressed up as an Arab sheik and I was there dressed as a wrestler, which I had been in my younger years. At one point, I picked Emory up, twirled him in the air, and gently put him down on the floor, pinning him. Especially funny was that Emory was surrounded at the time by his usual hand-picked police security detail. Gasping with open mouths as this was happening, they didn't know what to do. Fortunately, they did nothing.

The City of Montgomery took a positive step forward in 2016, hiring an African American police chief, Ernest Finley, with a friendly demeanor. Yet even Finley can't keep police misconduct from reasserting its ugly head.

*My "wrestling"
encounter with
the late Emory
Folmar during
a charity event
in 1991. This
is the first time
these photos
have ever been
published.
Emory was
the mayor of
Montgomery at
the time, and
we frequently
wrestled over
serious matters
as well.*

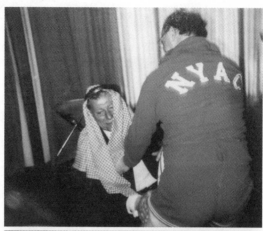

The following incidents experienced in 2016–17 by clients Linda Saffold, Anfeney Hoskins, and Devarious McQueen are real-life human stories of Montgomery citizens, bullied by police, who have also come to see me.

Linda Saffold

On September 12, 2016, Linda Saffold, a forty-two-year-old African American woman was sitting in her Montgomery home, tending to her children, and helping her son Andre with his homework.

Suddenly the front door to her home sprang open. A shining light beaming in from outside revealed the Montgomery police. They didn't bother to knock. She said, "Yes . . .?"

One of the officers asked if she were "Amanda Staffold." She replied "No, I am Linda Saffold." Another officer asked to see her ID. Linda cooperated but asked, "What is this all about?" The officer then ordered her to put her hands behind her back. Linda politely asked again what this was all about, adding that she was a "mental patient under medical care."

Ignoring her comment, one policeman snatched Linda's right arm, pulled her close to him, and placed his other arm around Linda's neck. Another officer started squeezing her very hard, causing her neck to sting painfully.

Joining the fray, yet another officer came up behind Mrs. Saffold and snatched her left arm. Both officers threw Linda onto the sofa in her living room. Soon four more officers barged into her house, helping the first two pick Mrs. Saffold up again, and slam her onto the floor, onto her chest. The heavy officers dug their knees into her back and neck. Her horrified children were looking on.

Mrs. Saffold kept bellowing that she was a mental patient with medical problems. The officers would not listen. They finally pulled her up off the floor, placed her legs in shackles, and proceeded to tear up her house, looking for a gun she didn't have. Mrs. Saffold had no idea what was going on or why the police were there.

The Saffold family was devastated. Not only did Mrs. Saffold suffer back, neck, and head injuries requiring treatment at Jackson Hospital, but she also overdosed afterwards, because she "was hurting so badly inside." Meanwhile her twelve-year-old daughter couldn't control crying seizures, and her oldest son, fourteen, "used the bathroom on himself," she said. Her youngest son also received medical treatment for stomach pain related to anxiety about police mistreatment of his mother.

Unfortunately for the police, the case turned out to be one of mistaken identity. Yet the police never apologized. Accordingly, Mrs. Saffold hired us to pursue a claim. That we did on February 21, 2017.

To Montgomery's credit, it paid Mrs. Saffold a five-figure sum, in return for a release by her of her legal claims. Even that settlement amount was surprising, given the self-insured and self-satisfied City of Montgomery's usual reluctance to admit any wrongdoing. As I mentioned earlier, Montgomery is known for fighting most police misconduct cases "tooth and nail." At least this has been my experience multiple times.

Anfeney Hoskins

Another case of mistaken identity involved Anfeney Hoskins, a forty-one-year-old severely disabled African American male. Legally blind since birth, Mr. Hoskins also has cerebral palsy. He was too infirm physically and mentally to make a claim himself against the City of Montgomery police, but his mother, fifty-eight-year-old Kathleen Hoskins, did so for him.

Exactly what happened? On February 20, 2016, the Montgomery police were looking for a suspect wearing a red jacket and black pants. Mr. Hoskins, sitting on his uncle's steps on Hill Street, met that description. Several Montgomery police came up to him and asked if he had been on Maple Street. Mr. Hoskins spontaneously replied, "No, I have not been, and we did not call y'all."

Never mind. These officers decided to show the local Montgomery blacks who was boss. Despite shouts from neighboring citizens protesting Anfeney's disabilities, the officers grabbed Mr. Hoskins, lifted him up, and shackled his feet. After handcuffing his arms, they dug their knees into his back. Mr. Hoskins was hysterical, frightened, and hurting. He could not see who was attacking him, or beating him up. He kept screaming, "Don't kill me, don't kill me. I ain't done nothing."

The onlookers also repeatedly told the police that Anfeney was handicapped and had committed no offense. Nothing stopped the Montgomery police who continued to beat up on this disabled middle-ager. Yet Anfeney was not arrested. Indeed, there was nothing to arrest him for. Still, he had to go to Jackson Hospital to receive medical treatment for swollen joints and shoulder pain. Anfeney has also experienced great psychological injury, bad dreams, and mental anguish.

We filed a claim for him on May 17, 2016. The City of Montgomery stonewalled as usual. Accordingly Mr. Hoskins filed suit with our help in August 2017. A defense motion to dismiss was denied by Circuit Judge Truman Hobbs Jr., who ordered that the case be mediated. Mediation never happened but the case was still settled in October 2018, with a modest settlement approved by Hobbs at a pro-ami hearing in November 2018.

Devarious McQueen

I was contacted by eighteen-year-old Devarious McQueen's devoted grandmother, Shirley Foster of Selma, in June 2017. Her Montgomery grandson, a senior at Jefferson Davis High, had been charged with attempted murder of a police officer.

I studied the facts and carefully watched a video taken by one of two girls in the car with Devarious at the time of the incident. The Montgomery police had yanked Devarious out of the back seat and beaten him unmercifully.

Fortunately, the girl's video preserved the unmistakable truth that the officers wanted to distort when they accused Devarious. A high bond was set on the attempted murder charge. The officers embellished the case, claiming that Devarious tried to grab their gun. The video showed otherwise. Amidst the scuffle, at one point Devarious's hand was close to touching an officer's holster, but that never happened. Contrary to the police claim, Devarious never tried to pull the gun out. Instead, the officers beat Devarious and then hid behind their badges, with false charges of wrongdoing.

A monumental victory was achieved on May 5, 2017, when Judge Troy Massey heard the evidence in a preliminary hearing and found no probable cause that any offense was committed. Judge Massey dismissed all charges against Devarious. People were shaking their heads in amazement in the courtroom. This was highly unusual. The police were not happy, but Devarious's family was beyond ecstatic.

I knew the DA's office could still submit the case to a grand jury. By September 2017, I learned that was happening and contacted Montgomery district attorney Daryl Bailey, requesting that Devarious be allowed to testify for himself before the grand jury. That normally is only a privilege, and not a right. The old saying is that a DA can indict a ham sandwich, if he wants to. Yet Bailey is more honorable than that; unlike many DAs, he is more interested in justice than in convictions. Devarious, prepped by me in advance to display a proper attitude, demeanor, and provide good answers, handled himself well. Two weeks later, an indictment dribbled out of the grand jury. It was only for a class C misdemeanor of "disorderly conduct." This was a victory for my client. Later I helped Devarious get a pre-trial diversion, which would have given him a clean record upon completion. Unfortunately, Devarious missed important appointments and was taken off. He later pled to the misdemeanor of resisting arrest, was given no fine but required to pay modest court costs and receive a short probation, completed when court costs were paid.

Merrill Todd

Another interesting case in this vein involves Merrill Todd of Chambers County. See Chapter 21.

Mother/Son Duo Grapple with Hospital Security Guards

On April 19, 2018, Newt Higman called me about his wife, Britt, and son, Zack, who had been arrested by off-duty City of Valley police serving as hospital security guards.

Turns out Mrs. Higman was called by her twenty-two-year-old cancer-suffering son, who was doubled over in an east Alabama hospital emergency room, fighting off unrelenting sharp pain. Like a mother bear rescuing her cub, Mrs. Higman rushed to the E.R., where she questioned authorities about why her son was not receiving attention and treatment.

When she refused to leave her son's room, the security guards arrested and handcuffed her, and dragged her out. Responding, Zack said, "Take your hands off my mother." Whereupon the guards slammed Zack backwards.

Both were hurting when they came to see me.

With Newt and Britt Higman and their son, Zack, of Dadeville, Alabama.

Zack was not charged, but Mrs. Higman was charged with trespassing. We prepared to defend and file suit. After several months of vigorous legal activity, the hospital dropped all charges and took other measures. My clients felt vindicated via a confidential settlement.

UNFORTUNATE ADDITIONAL KILLINGS/EXCESSIVE FORCE CASES

Just as we finish certain cases, others flare up, including some recent police killings. Our office has talked with family survivors who are prospective clients while our own investigation ensues, leading to likely claims for damage, in the following cases.

Wrongful Death of Cedric Mifflin Resulting from Shooting of Phenix City, Alabama, Police on May 7, 2017

In mid-2018, this case was brought to us by his mother, Mrs. Pochya Sanders, as a result of her son Cedric Mifflin being shot in the back and killed by a Phenix City police officer following a high-speed chase through the streets of Phenix City. Law partner Kenneth Shinbaum is assisting me.

Wrongful Death of George Crenshaw in Hayneville, Alabama, on November 14, 2018, from Shooting of Hayneville Police Officer and Lowndes County Deputy Sheriff

This case was brought to us by family members on November 29, 2018. It involves a shooting of George Crenshaw, a mentally disabled man, at his home, by a Hayneville police officer and a Lowndes County deputy sheriff. Crenshaw had a knife in his hand but was defending himself in his own home following the unwelcome entry of the two law enforcement officers. Former Hayneville police chief Keldrick Mitchell is incensed about this incident, believing it could have been totally avoided. Law partner Shinbaum is working with me on this case as well.

Wrongful Death of Melissa Boarts off Interstate 85 in Macon County

Another case taking ample time of Julian's in 2016-2017 involved the wrongful police shooting of Melissa Boarts. Julian represented her parents in pursuing a case that was subject to a tight confidential resolution agreement in 2018. Hence nothing further will be stated.

Attorney Julian McPhillips, center, discusses the lawsuit he filed Tuesday against the city of Auburn on behalf of Michael and Terry Boarts in Tuskegee.

TODD VAN EMST/
TVEMST@OANOW.C(

Newspaper article reporting the filing of a wrongful death case.

Wrongful Subjection of Ulysses Wilkerson to Excessive Force by Troy, Alabama, Police Department

On December 23, 2017, seventeen-year-old Ulysses Wilkerson was beaten so badly and kicked in the head by the Troy police that his head was disfigured. The case soon attracted national attention, with an investigative reporter from Oakland, California, working on a documentary about it. In addition, the *Troy Messenger*, the local newspaper, repeatedly ran front-page headlines about the case from December 26, 2017, through January 5, 2018. Ulysses's mother, Angela Williams, sought legal help from a Dothan attorney on the obstruction of justice and resisting arrest charges against Ulysses, and explored a civil claim representation with a prominent Florida attorney.

Frustrated by a lack of progress, Ms. Williams came to see us in early 2019, spending substantial time with me and Kenneth Shinbaum about the case. I soon also associated David Sawyer, and we began aggressively to gather evidence. Although brutally beaten to a pulp, young Ulysses hurt his case by activities in Decatur (in north Alabama) he was later involved in. This one is a daunting challenge and is still in the early stages. I thank brilliant Montgomery lawyers Bobby Segall and Griffin Sikes Jr. for their occasional assistance on some of these cases.

12

A Holley First
Amendment Result

Camp Hill is a town in the southeast corner of Tallapoosa County, Alabama. It is just north of U.S. Highway 280, running from Alexander City, the largest municipality in the county, toward Dadeville, the county seat. Camp Hill is in a rural setting with a predominantly black population in a majority white county. Auburn University is eighteen miles southeast. The Georgia state line is fairly close.

General Andrew Jackson, well before he became president, defeated the Cherokee Indians in 1814 at the Battle of Horseshoe Bend, twenty miles from Camp Hill. About twenty-eight miles northeast is Goldville, the center of a short-lived gold rush in the 1840s. Famous former governor John Patterson, now in his nineties, lives on a farm in Goldville.

During my forty-four years of practicing law in Montgomery, I have had many clients from Camp Hill with employment cases, personal injury claims, criminal cases, and, most recently, a good constitutional law case involving the right of free speech.

The sad truth is that the First Amendment has been watered down considerably since the mid-1980s. At that time, the U.S. Supreme Court ruled in *Connick v. Myers* that to be constitutionally protected, speech must be on "a matter of public concern."

During the 1980s, I made headlines with several successful First Amendment cases against Governors George Wallace, Fob James, and Guy Hunt, mostly on political-association issues. These were landmark constitutional law cases with much news coverage. Given the recent more conservative shift of court decisions, this type of case occurs less often. In 2016, besides this Camp Hill case, I had only one other First Amendment case, involving the town of Valley, in Chambers County, adjacent to Tallapoosa County. That one, too, still pending, involved a political-association claim. Associate attorney Chase Estes has been a great help in both cases.

The Camp Hill case came to me on January 22, 2016. It involved former Camp Hill mayor Frank G. Holley. Born December 6, 1938, Holley was seventy-eight when he first contacted me, mentally quite sharp though "hard of hearing." Holley's office intake sheet said, "Injured after being wrongfully arrested." I quickly diagnosed that Mr. Holley's real problem was much more than a simple personal injury, and it was not my usual employment dispute. As facts unfolded, it developed into a classic First Amendment case.

Mr. Holley, an African American man, was elected mayor of Camp Hill in 1976 and subsequently served four terms in office. He was eventually defeated for reelection by another African American citizen, Danny Evans.

Upon leaving office, Mr. Holley remained an active, interested citizen of Camp Hill. He attended town council meetings to address various issues of public concern. One was to rename a street in honor of President Barack Obama. Another was to contact the Alabama Department of Transportation to replace street signs. Another was to strengthen Camp Hill's dog leash laws. Mr. Holley also addressed issues related to public investment. That involved the taxpaying citizens of Camp Hill. Holley also criticized the lack of a town audit for approximately three years, and he questioned whether Mayor Evans was receiving excessive pay.

Not surprisingly, Mayor Evans did not welcome Mr. Holley raising these issues, especially at council meetings. In a deposition, Mayor Evans admitted this. The new mayor "felt intimidated," he said, by former mayor Holley coming to town council meetings. So, what did Mayor Evans do? The answer was classic retaliation.

And Frank Holley wasn't alone. The new mayor developed a pattern and practice of targeting citizens he did not like. Affidavits from former police chief Roosevelt Finley, from officers Nathan White and Morris Greathouse, and from citizen Douglas Heard confirmed Mayor Evans's habit of targeting people he disagreed with.

On September 4, 2015, my client Frank Holley wrote Mayor Evans a stern letter:

I have been informed that you have broken "Federal Law" by direct-
ing "Police Profiling" aimed at certain individuals including me. This is no
surprise because of my addressing important and sensitive issues at council
meetings which has drawn attention to your incompetency, and your inability to compete intellectually. I have knowledge of authentic evidence
supporting my claim.

For your information, if I am confronted with Police Profiling, I am
coming after you and the police with all legal means available.

You have wrongly gone after Douglas Ray Heard on three unsuccessful
attempts. You have fabricated lies to get Former Chief of Police Roosevelt
Finley terminated in 2000 and 2014 mainly because he refused to break the
law as directed by you, Former Police Officer Eric Kelly left the department
for the same reason(s), you unjustly terminated Former Police Officer Nathan
White for a second time and Former Police Officer Dave Gallew, Former
Reserve Officer Morris Greathouse, Former Recreation Director Carolyn
Harris Davis, Former Maid Maxine Morgan, Former Attorney John Allen
Fulmer and Former Utilities Superintendent Josh Travis left because of you;
this is only a partial list.

So what happened to public-spirited citizen Frank Holley after he raised
these questions? Ten weeks later, on December 14, 2015, Camp Hill police
chief Johnny Potts, directed by Mayor Evans, began following Mr. Holley
on an unstriped county road, hoping to catch him for something.

Eventually he stopped Holley and asked for his driver's license and proof
of insurance. Potts also noticed a pistol in Holley's vehicle and asked Holley
about a permit. Holley displayed paperwork justifying receipt of the gun
from the sheriff of Tallapoosa County. Chief Potts also asked Holley if he
had been drinking, to which Holley replied, "No." Nonetheless, the chief
still arrested Holley for DUI, but he later dismissed the charge when Holly
blew a "zero" on a breathalyzer.

At no time during the stop did Chief Potts inform Holley he was receiving a ticket for improper lane usage. In fact, there was no striped lane on
the county road. Yet Holly was later charged with improper lane usage and
with the absence of a pistol permit. Arrested, Holley was physically hurt

when Chief Potts, driving him to the police station, recklessly ran off the road, injuring Holley's previously painful shoulder.

On March 23, 2016, our McPhillips Shinbaum firm filed suit against the Town of Camp Hill, Mayor Danny Evans, and Chief Potts for violating Frank Holley's First Amendment freedom of speech rights. A state law claim of negligence, related to the shoulder injury, was added.

The case proceeded with depositions in Montgomery and Camp Hill. The defendants' February 17, 2017, motion for summary judgment was taken under advisement by U.S. Magistrate Judge Charles Coody. Chase Estes and I worked hard to prepare an opposition response, which we submitted on March 8. A trial was scheduled for September 2017, but Judge Coody postponed it, stating that more time was needed to consider the issues on summary judgment.

Nine months later, on May 31, 2018, two-and-a-half years after suit was filed, we received a sixteen-page opinion and order from Judge Coody. He detailed the history of free speech violations by former mayor Evans,

Enjoying a victorious moment with former Camp Hill mayor Frank Holley, his wife, Frances, and associate attorney Chase Estes in 2018.

discussed applicable case law, and ruled in Holley's favor on his First Amendment claim. Judge Coody denied our state law claims, but we really didn't care about them as much. We won what mattered most, the federal First Amendment claim.

By this time, June 2018, my client Frank Holley was eighty years old. He was still ticking and still mentally sharp. I talked with defense lawyer Brad Everhardt of Hill, Hill, Carter, Franco, & Cole about final resolution. Instead Brad filed an objection to the district court judge, Myron Thompson, to which we filed a response. But I didn't get my favorite judge.

Instead, the case was reassigned to Chief Judge Keith Watkins, whom I also respect but who is much more conservative. Hooray again. On October 29, 2018, Judge Watkins upheld the Coody opinion and recommendation in the most important respect, ruling in a twenty-three-page opinion for Holley against the Town of Camp Hill, but letting defendants Evans and Potts out of the case. Still, it was a huge victory in Alabama for free speech on issues of public concern, protected by the First Amendment. Frank Holley, Chase, and I were gratified by the result, one we felt would have been more likely in a more liberal state. Yet even in Alabama, a more conservative state, a respect for freedom of speech exists.

On January 14, 2019, a mediation took place. Brad Everhardt represented the Town of Camp Hill and its insurance company. Associate attorney Chase Estes joined me in representing Frank Holley, who was present with his attractive wife of fifty-five years, Frances Holley. The agreed-upon mediator was the highly respected former U.S. magistrate judge Delores Boyd. A brilliant legal mind sharpened by time off the bench, Ms. Boyd peppered both sides with the vulnerabilities of their case and astutely helped steer a great result. While the terms of the settlement, as in most cases, were confidential, Mr. and Mrs. Holley left my office at 5:30 that afternoon, smiling, having achieved a good measure of civil justice.

The aging Frank Holley may no longer be mayor, but, as Judge Boyd stated, he should be very proud of his many great years of public service. To which I add that he should be honored beyond that small town for having stood up for, and won, on the important civil liberty of free speech.

13

The Ghee-Whiz Gang of Eight

Doug Ghee is the father of six daughters and one son, in that order. Born in 1945, graduating from the University of Alabama in 1968, and beginning his career as a schoolteacher, Doug switched gears, went to Cumberland School of Law in Birmingham and graduated in 1973.

This young lawyer soon returned to his hometown of Anniston and connected with fellow attorney Henry Agee. They formed a two-man general practice firm with the musical name of Agee & Ghee.

I met Doug and Henry in 1977. At age thirty-one, I had just launched my long-shot campaign to become Alabama's attorney general. I considered myself exceedingly blessed to have the enthusiastic support of both lawyers. Doug soon took the lead. Thanks to him, my campaign did well in his hometown in 1978.

Forty years later, in 2018, I am looking at a picture of the eight attorneys in his family law firm. There are four good-looking daughters, three sons-in law, and Doug himself. How do they all get along, I wondered? Who must referee and settle differences of opinion that must inevitably exist? Who else could it be but Papa Doug?

Daddy Ghee didn't complete his family early. After six daughters (two pursued other careers), Doug's persistence on having a son finally paid off. In 1994, Brenda Ghee gave birth to a boy. They named him Marshall. And guess what? Surprise, surprise. Marshall is a student at Cumberland Law School, expected to graduate in 2020, and he's considering joining the family firm. Why miss out on all the fun?

There are numerous grandchildren in the family, and one, a junior at the University of Alabama, has shown interest in a legal career. Doug recently said, "I certainly will encourage my grandchildren to pursue the law. Short of the ministry, there is no better service to humankind."

Doug reminds his children what a big blessing it is to be a lawyer, serving people. Doug and his children see their law practice as a ministry, and that spirit and attitude blossoms in their practice. Thinking like this may not be "only in Alabama," but it is in great abundance at the Ghee firm.

IN SEPTEMBER 1978, I finished second in the nine-man attorney general's primary election, five thousand votes ahead of the president of the state senate. Unfortunately for me, vote theft and fraud in several Alabama counties caused a ten thousand-vote shift, costing me my spot in the run-off election. The great consolation prize, however, was the many friendships that I made statewide. No better friend was made than Doug Ghee. This fellow literally sparkles with goodness and kindness. Yet he retains an inner toughness that enables him to repeatedly stand up to injustice.

In 1990, Doug was elected to represent Anniston in the state senate; he served until 1998, making a great name and reputation for himself. A long boardwalk through the woods at Mt. Cheaha State Park is named for him. When I ran for the U.S. Senate in 2002, Doug graciously agreed to be my Calhoun County coordinator again. He gave me good advice that I failed to follow, to my detriment. That is, if I were going to run, I needed to take off full time to do it. I gave my campaign plenty of time and energy, but I kept getting sucked back into an ever-demanding law practice. I lost the race, of course.

Over the years Doug and I have referred cases back and forth to one another. We've also mutually enjoyed each other's company, including that of wives and children. When I turned seventy in November 2016, Doug and Brenda joined Leslie and me at Mt. Cheaha State Park to celebrate the occasion.

Doug's daughter Wendy stayed in our Montgomery home's basement apartment for about six months in the early 1990s. She became great friends with us and our daughter Grace. Wendy reflects the best of both parents. We knew Wendy's future husband, Jack Draper, at St. James School, which my children attended, before Wendy met him. Jack's father, Fred, and mother,

Susu, taught history and English, respectively, at that school for many years. After moving to Wendy's hometown, Jack became mayor of Anniston in 2016. Doug's guiding hand, and Jack and Wendy's charm, were instrumental in his electoral success. Jack's parents soon moved up to the Anniston area.

In the late 1800s and early 1900s, Anniston rivaled Birmingham as a rapidly growing industrial base. Anniston is not a small town today, but with economic struggles, it is no longer one of Alabama's larger cities. As its steel industry faded as part of nationwide economic shifts, many poverty-stricken people were left in Anniston, especially folks of African American descent. Many are Doug's clients; some have been referred to me.

Anniston retains remnants of its earlier historical significance in two interesting local museums. One is the Anniston Museum of Natural History, a pet project of Doug's and one of the top seven natural history museums in America. The other is the Berman Museum of World History, with such diverse artifacts as Josephine Bonaparte's dresser set; Jefferson Davis's dueling pistols; and Adolph Hitler's silver set.

Doug's initial partner Henry Agee moved on to Tennessee in 1982. By the 1990s Doug's firm had regrouped as a three-lawyer firm consisting of Doug, Wendy, and Jack. Over the next twenty years the Ghee Draper firm

From left (with year of admission to the Alabama bar), Lindsay Ghee (2016), Bruce Downey IV (2006), Laura Ghee Alexander (2006), David Alexander (2006), Jennifer Ghee Downey (2003), Jonathan Draper (1998), Wendy Ghee Draper (1998), and Doug Ghee (1975).

added three more Ghee daughters and two sons-in-law. They are Jennifer Ghee Downey and her husband Bruce Downey Jr.; Laura Ghee Alexander and her husband David Alexander; and Lindsay Ghee, the last to join the firm in 2016. The firm is now known as Ghee, Draper, and Alexander.

Doug summarized their divisions of legal work. Oldest daughter Wendy handles bankruptcies, debtors court, adoptions, and select family court matters. Daughters Laura, Jennifer, and Lindsay handle family court matters, but Laura also does probate work. Jennifer engages in criminal law and personal injury. The youngest daughter, Lindsay, also does criminal law and child custody. (In October 2018, Lindsay, showed Leslie and me around the firm's historic offices in Anniston, as we became better acquainted with her. We were honored to attend her Anniston wedding in March 2019.)

Son-in-law Jack's major duties are now mostly those of mayor, but he still practices business law. Son-in-law Bruce Downey Jr., son of a prominent Montgomery attorney, does mostly personal injury cases. In a recent medical malpractice case arising out of nearby Gadsden, Bruce obtained a $20 million verdict, the largest ever in Etowah County. At this writing that verdict was on appeal to the "chop 'em and reduce 'em" Alabama Supreme Court, now consisting of nine pro-business ultra-conservative Republicans. Son-in-law David Alexander handles criminal and family court cases.

Son Marshall, soon to graduate from law school, says he "wants to do everything" and "loves it all." His inclusion would thus grow the firm to nine lawyers, all closely related by blood or marriage. Obviously the only nepotism rule at Ghee Draper is to practice it. The main point is the family members have fun practicing together.

And they do have some interesting cases. Doug laughed as he told me about one the firm handled in the early 2000s, referring to it as the most expensive blow job ever (as the father of daughters, Doug was hesitant about using the term "blow job," suggesting the more polite "oral sex").

In any case, an upset female visited the firm, complaining about how she was forced at Big B Pharmacy, as a customer, to engage in oral sex with the store's manager. How did this happen? It occurred when she went to the store and shoplifted a greeting card. The manager saw her, captured it on tape, and said he was about to call the police. But he said he wouldn't press charges if she would have oral sex with him. The customer complied, and the manager said he had never felt so good. The customer got ready to leave, but the manager backtracked, "You must come back tomorrow and do it one more time, or I will call the police." She agreed to come back.

But first she went to see the police on her own. The police wired her up for sound and video. When she did go back, a plainclothes officer was not far away and arrested the manager. A lawsuit was filed against Bruno's, the corporate owner of Big B pharmacies. A jury returned a verdict of $1,500,000. Big B, however, appealed to the Supreme Court of Alabama in Montgomery, and the verdict was reduced to $250,000. Doug said that proves that blow jobs are worth more in Anniston than in Montgomery.

All I can say is thank you, God, for the Ghee family. There's no telling how many people in Calhoun and the neighboring counties of Jefferson, Talladega, Etowah have benefited from their gifted legal services.

Interlude

Travel is Good for the Soul

Not only in Alabama but everywhere "travel is fatal to prejudice, bigotry, and narrow-mindedness." To these famous words of Mark Twain, I add, "It is also good for the soul."

This realization is not profound—surely most would agree—but many avoid travel, citing cost, glitches, and homebody instincts. While travel in faraway places may not be for the faint of heart, voyages by air, sea, and land restore—and sometimes strain—my scattered resources. Trips are usually energizing, eye-opening, and stimulating. Generally the farther I get away from home, the more relaxed I become. Usually our return is with a fresh perspective, plus mental and physical relaxation. Please forgive me if I incite envy. My hope is the opposite—to kindle your sense of adventure to see more unknown places.

In my 2016 book, *Civil Rights in My Bones,* "Traveling With Leslie" is a chapter in which I shared adventurous trips to all seven continents and many countries. Other trips we've taken over the past forty-five years included forays to Antarctica, Israel, Scandinavia, Latin America, and many parts of Europe and Asia. We also traveled by water with our three children on the Mediterranean Sea, and in Alaska, Hawaii, Norway, and the Caribbean. In all these journeys we have seen historic and breathtaking sites, and have enjoyed meeting diverse, colorful and interesting people. We've strengthened family bonds, and return with batteries recharged.

Give Leslie the lion's share of the credit; she not only speaks four languages including Spanish, Portuguese, and French, but she makes travel arrangements and keeps a lid on the kids. My gratitude to her is unlimited. I joke that she is like my American Express card . . . "I won't leave home without her."

My gratitude to God is even greater, because He made us all, and introduced Leslie and me to one another in Manhattan on March 30, 1973.

Leslie was raised in Brazil and studied in Switzerland, and I traveled extensively through India during 1967–68, where my family was then living, as well as through Europe, and the Middle East en route to India, and the Orient on the way back. These experiences were foundational to our mutual love of travel. Yet returning in 1975 to the Alabama where I grew up from 1946–59 only increased my enthusiasm for travel.

My focus in this new book is on the past three years, starting with a 2017 cruise in Asia and Australia, then a 2017 father-son trip to Iceland, followed by a 2018 camera safari to Africa, and finally 2019 trips to the Caribbean and to the Galapagos Islands. As in previous trips, I kept a travelogue. This chapter draws from that writing.

I. Southeast Asia-Australia Cruise, January–February 2017

On January 13, 2017, Leslie and I flew from Atlanta to Toronto, and then popped over the North Pole to Hong Kong. This former British island city had lost some of the colonial charm I enjoyed when I first saw it in 1967, coming back from India, and again in 1986 while on a trip to China. The airport was now on an adjacent island. There was less sparkle, and nightclubs were not as apparent. The rainy, overcast, low-60s smog of Hong Kong and jet lag made all the more inviting our boarding a Norwegian Star ship three football fields long.

Our first day on the South China Sea was pleasant, with a balcony to take in the sights and sounds. Fifteen restaurants were scattered around the ship. This was a culinary treat but not a weight-loser's delight. The Stardust Theater sparkled with entertainment.

Eclectic, diverse people were on board, of many talents, making the voyage all the more fun. We delighted in meeting a threesome of beautiful young female dancers: Meagan from Ireland, Catherine from New York, and Addie from Alabama.

There were at least fifty different nationalities on the ship, counting employees from many third world countries of Africa or Latin America. The three leading nationalities on board appeared to be Brits, Germans, and

Americans, in that order, but there were numerous Australians and Asians, especially Filipinos. We also enjoyed a family of two Mexican brothers and their mother, and Leslie took pleasure in speaking Portuguese to Brazilians.

Our first stop was in Vietnam, a country whose history has penetrated my inner consciousness for many years. We disembarked at Nha Trang, busy with swaths of population traveling by motorcycle or bicycle, punctuated by Buddhist monuments, some of ancient reddish-pink rock. Another was a big white Buddha the size of the Lincoln Memorial in Washington D.C.

Quoting from my travelogue of January 19, 2017:

> Vietnam touched me in myriad ways. My reaction was deeply emotional, and spiritual, summing up memories of the late 60s and early 70s in America, when protest of the war was a centrifugal force, spewing out casualties at home, and in Southeast Asia. The undertow sucked up my brother David, leaving my parents and me wounded and radicalized. My siblings, Sandy, Betsy, and Frank were also hurt. I was in a prayerful mode, asking God to forgive me and our country.
>
> Another reaction about Vietnam was discerning the mixture of poverty and prosperity, existing side by side, not unlike America in that regard . . . Why did we ever try to convert them, by bombing, to our system or government? . . . Vietnam's peasant communism to our free enterprise system? We didn't bomb Communist China or Communist Russia. 58,000 young American lives later, and 2 million Southeast Asian lives later, we realized we made a mistake. And what a costly mistake. And I lost my dear brother, David. Please God forgive us.

We arrived in Singapore on Sunday, January 22 and stayed over the following Monday, while mechanics restored one of the ship's two motors. We'd heard about Singapore all our lives, but now finally, we were actually seeing and enjoying it.

We avoided the excursion buses and negotiated with Ray, a burly but friendly and intelligent forty-year-old Indian-Singaporean minivan driver. He drove us all around Singapore, from 9 a.m. to 6 p.m. The first stop was the breathtakingly sculpted and recently completed "Gardens by the Sea."

High artificial trees served as rain-catchers and solar panels, while baskets brimmed with vines and vegetation. The landscape architecture was powerful. Chinese New Year's ornaments colorfully adorned the vegetation. Odd-shaped rocks artistically shaped the landscape.

That Sunday morning Ray waited for us while we attended the spiritually uplifting Anglican Church of Our Savior. Despite a downpour we also enjoyed walking thorough the Singapore Botanical Gardens, especially the Orchid Garden. Other exciting locations were Indiatown, Chinatown, the Parliament, and St. Andrew's Cathedral. The next day we took a Christmas card picture of Leslie at Jurong Bird Park, with chirping birds perched on her shoulders and head. Her facial expression is priceless.

On January 24, we crossed the Equator. We joined the many passengers celebrating with a King Neptune party at the swimming pool, with music and pageantry. I received a certificate from King Neptune stating that I was an official member of those that had crossed the equator (Leslie got hers in 1951 when she was three, on the way to or from Brazil).

Two more days at sea, and we landed in Bali, Indonesia. Tenders zipped us to the mainland. An excursion bus bounced us to a bird and reptile sanctuary about an hour away. Along the route Hindu and Buddhist statues stared at us from amidst the rice paddies and stores. A bird sanctuary chirped at us from colorful fine-feathered friends. Most of us appreciated a ten-foot Komodo dragon, since engine troubles eliminated our ship's planned stop at Komodo Island, where these creatures abound. Other sites in our excursion included a Hindu compound where several generations lived, a Hindu temple more than a thousand years old, and a boutique. We also enjoyed an hour-long Thai dancing show, where a dragon and fierce warriors engaged in combat. We made it back to the ship's tenders by mid-afternoon and were back on the Norwegian Star within minutes, scarfing down a late lunch.

The last country of our ship's voyage was designed to include five stops in Australia, ending in Sydney. Although Singapore mechanics fixed one engine, the other soon went on the blink, thus eliminating scheduled stops at Brisbane and Airlie Beach (Great Barrier Reef), both in Australia. We still made it to Darwin and Cairns, with a final three-day sea stretch to Sydney, the ultimate destination.

On Sunday, January 29, 2017, the Norwegian Star docked early in Darwin, preparing us for an excursion into this historic town. Stopping at historic WWII action points, we also enjoyed the Museum of Art and National History, the Botanical Gardens, the Northern Territories Parliament house, and the state Supreme Court. We learned that Typhoon Tracy demolished Darwin on Christmas Eve Day, 1974. Only three buildings were left standing, yet amazingly only sixty-six people were killed. The population of Darwin at that time was fifty thousand. In the aftermath, thousands evacuated by plane and ship, and many never returned. Today, Darwin has more than doubled its pre-Tracy population. A funny thing happened at the Botanical Garden when a "praying mantis" jumped on Leslie's head and refused to leave. Good pictures captured this incident and many other scenes.

Given the extra days at sea, I was thrilled with the time to read a plethora of interesting books. And my travelogue is replete with stories of interesting fellow travelers we met, many over meals.

We especially enjoyed a family of three siblings and their spouses from Michigan. Led by older brother Cass Connolly, an attorney, they were involved in a minor insurrection to hold the ship accountable for our five lost excursion stops. An interesting Irish-Italian Catholic bunch, they were fun to hang out with. We also related well to Glen and Susie Stewart, missionaries from Texas stationed in Guatemala.

I ran daily on the thirteenth-floor track, taking in the picturesque view on all sides. In doing so, I became acquainted with two multi-talented entertainment brothers Yuri, fifty-seven, and Constantine, sixty-four. Their Greek father and Russian mother escaped from Communist Russia when the brothers were kids. They settled in a Russian colony in Manchuria, northern China. Now Australian nationals, the two brothers and their wives had been entertaining travelers on the cruise circuit for years. They spoke excellent, articulate English with an Australian accent, and sparked the passengers with wit, humor, and good cheer.

On February 2, the cruise ship parked itself several miles out in the harbor, and we were up early to tender to the shore. Our tour excursion was named "Cairns, Kuranda, Aboriginals, and Army Duck." We visited an amazing rain-forest nature park, and interacted with Aborigines in all their historical glory. Dressed and painted in native garb and color, they showed us how to throw boomerangs. They accurately threw spears great distances, and they posed with us for pictures. Located in one hundred acres of World Heritage Rainforest, local Pamigirri aboriginal dancers entertained us. Afterwards we boarded an amphibious Army duck for a land-water ride, enjoying our guide's narration about the wildlife and vegetation we encountered. From there we proceeded to Kuranda, a village nestled in the heart of the rainforest. The Koala bear sanctuary was a sight to behold, oc-cupied also by kangaroos, wallabies, crocodiles, and exotic birds and snakes.

We returned to the ship to pursue the final leg to Sydney. Our cruise balcony provided a view of many beautiful, sculpted islands along the Australian east coast on a sunny but windy day.

There was much merriment on board. An Australian quartet, the "Aus-tralian Boys of Motown," inspired us the last night. From our perch over an atrium, we sang to Motown tunes. The songs included "New York, New York," "My Way," "Delilah," "Hey Jude," and "Sweet Caroline." Balloons dropped from a higher floor, giving the gala a festive Happy New Year's Eve spirit.

On the last day of the twenty-one-day cruise, Sunday, February 5, we enjoyed the beauty of the sea and vistas of setting suns, other ships, and cresting waves. Yet we were ready to hit the dry land of Sydney the next day.

And so we did. Taking a taxi to the Hotel Stellar off Hyde Park in central Sydney, we caught the decisive last quarter of the American Super Bowl on T.V., as Tom Brady led the New England Patriots to a come-from-behind victory over the Atlanta Falcons. Alas!

We spent two more days in the Sydney area, enjoying a panoramic tour of this world capital, its harbors, tall buildings, historic churches, and green parks. The last day was a picturesque journey to the Blue Mountains, amidst a heavy rain and fog. One set of mountains and valleys echoed the Grand Canyon. When the clouds parted, the famous "Three Sisters" rock formation was a wonderful sight to behold.

The next day, February 8, we flew fourteen hours across the Pacific Ocean to Vancouver, Canada. From there we jetted back three hours to

Toronto, and two and a half more to Atlanta. What a trip! We were a bit tired, but elated!

II. Father-Son Iceland Adventure, August 2017

In recent years Leslie has encouraged me to take a trip to Iceland with our son, David. We have enjoyed several other father-son trips, most notably in 2009 after David's high school graduation, when we traveled to Colorado, stopping at many places along the way. Such shared adventure strengthens bonds and broadens our mutual horizons.

A column I published in the *Montgomery Advertiser* on September 3, 2017, nicely sums up our trip:

"Iceland" the name conjures up daunting images of cold weather, Viking influence, Artic winds, and too much ice. Surprisingly the country, only 884 miles northwest of Ireland, has had nowhere near the influence on America as has the Emerald Isle.

Yet this vast expanse with a modest population of only 300,000 has a captivating geography, history, and culture increasingly attracting world attention and tourists. Largely shaped by volcanoes, some ancient, many still simmering, Iceland was a visual feast, amidst a myriad of experiences, and pleasantly crisp air for my son David and me, embarking upon a week-long father-son trip in mid-August 2017.

We landed at the Keflavik International Airport after an overnight flight. Following an afternoon nap, we popped the short distance (45 km) into the nation's capital Reykjavik and enjoyed its Annual Music Festival spread over four stages across green meadows and the inner city.

The next day we visited the Blue Lagoon, the famous geo-thermal pond surrounded by miles of charcoal-colored lava fields. We also enjoyed several spectacular Reykjavik sites, from an observatory-style Perlan museum, to its Settlements Museum, preserving the building remnants of the earliest 800–900 A.D. inhabitants.

Also enjoyed was the iconic Hallgrims Church with its 246-foot high tower, an architectural wonder and the most photographed emblem in Iceland. An elevator scoot to the top provided a panoramic view. Other highlights in Reykjavik included the Einar Jonsson Museum, with its breathtaking sculptured exhibits and the National Museum of Iceland.

Once on the Golden Circle road, the geological wonders of Iceland bounced out at us, from the Niagara-like waterfalls at Gullfest, to the exploding geysers at Geysir, and the amazing Continental divide at Pingvellir, with tectonic plates visible above the surface, dividing Europe from the Americas. David and I enjoyed a long hike in this rustic location, soaking up the beauty, history, and fellowship.

The first Icelandic parliament convened at Pingvellir in 930, and remained there until 1798. Meanwhile in 1000, King Olaf of Norway (also known as St. Olaf) brought Christianity to Iceland. The faith was further developed, first by the Catholics, and then the Lutherans.

We much enjoyed the Medieval Museum in Reykholt, with its emphasis upon the fabled Snori, father of Icelandic literature. The multiple lava waterfalls at Hraunfosser, descending into a volcanic cave at Viagelmir, and bouncing on endless gravel roads continued our adventure.

We made it to Borgarnes by mid-week and enjoyed the best of our five

With David in Iceland, 2017.

Air B&B lodgings and the town's famous Settlement Museum. David's electronic savvy connected us each day with our next Air B&B, and usually interesting fellow travelers and native Icelanders. Overall, the natives were polite, well educated, and versatile in English. The modern Icelandic tongue is similar to the "Old Norse" of the country's earliest settlers, unlike modern Norwegian, which has evolved.

It was a treat to see the Snaefellsnes peninsula, its rugged shorelines, seals sunning in the bay, and ample birdlife, juxtaposed against snow-covered mountains. One morning we caught a ferryboat from Stykkisholmor and soaked in the North Sea scenery, navigating to Flately Island. There we enjoyed a vigorous perimeter hike through sheep pastures and potholes.

Iceland today relishes its distinct identity, low crime, and growing prosperity. Immigrants are well received, and tourists are loved. Proud they are that Leif Ericson, a native Icelander, discovered America in 930 A.D. The USA gave Iceland a large gift statue of Erikson in 1930, installed in front of Hallgrim's Church.

The downsides of Iceland are the high costs of everything and the vast, treeless expanses of lava fields and rocky mountain roads. Although the weather was pleasant during our trip, the winters can be brutal with snow, ice, and Artic air.

If you yearn for adventure, tarry no longer in exploring this intriguing land, its hospitable people, and geological wonders. After a week we were renewed, refreshed, and full of family lore.

We have many great pictures from the trip and our father-son bond became even stronger.

III. Botswana, Zimbabwe, Zambia, and South Africa, March 2018

Africa! Africa!

The name evokes different images and rings different bells for different people. For me, since I began collecting stamps in the 1950s and learned the name of D'Ahomey for what later became Benin, the continent has symbolized intrigue, mystique, adventure, misadventure, tragedy, and opportunity.

And history . . . given the vast proportion of the American population with roots in that continent, which has profoundly impacted my professional and spiritual life. And still does.

Given also our travel bug, Leslie and I have now visited Africa five times.

The first trip was in March-April 1975 as we were leaving New York but before moving to Alabama. We enjoyed a month-long tour of the continent, starting with Egypt and the pyramids. We then flew to Nairobi for a two-week camera safari of Kenya and Tanzania, enjoying Treetops and Ngorongoro Crater. A week in South Africa followed, including taking the Blue Train from Johannesburg to Capetown, and finally a brief stop in Angola before hopping over a short Atlantic span for a week in Brazil.

The second time was in 1988, when Leslie, Rachel, Grace, and I spent a week in Morocco, taking a private car tour from Tangiers to Fez, to Marrakesh to Casablanca. Grace especially enjoyed the camels, and we all breathed in spectacular desert beauty.

The third time was in 1995, when, as part of a Mediterranean cruise, Leslie, Rachel, Grace, four-year-old David, and I spent a day in Egypt, traveling by tour bus from the harbor of Alexandria to the pyramids of Gaza. The next day we were in Israel.

The fourth time was in 2005, when Leslie and I, sans kids, traveled with an Alabama delegation to Benin as part of a Reconciliation movement with the part of Africa from which the last slaves were sent to America in 1859.

The fifth time was March 16–31, 2018. I kept a 33-page travelogue. Some tell me it's a good read. However, this chapter recaptures the highlights.

Southern Africa

Not only South Africa, when one uses the above term, but the countries of Botswana, Zimbabwe, Zambia and Namibia, and most powerfully the country of South Africa itself, make up the region called "Southern Africa." You could also throw in Madagascar, which we didn't see.

In response to a Columbia University alumni solicitation in the spring of 2017, Leslie signed us up for the trip. We figured the mailing went to thousands, so we expected a good crowd to be part of our excursion. Not so!

As 2018 began, we discovered that only three alums had signed up. They were Leslie, me, and Guillermo Strauss of Buenos Aires, Argentina.

In fact, the trip was almost called off by the New York agency organizing it.

As the date drew nearer, I developed a little foreboding myself. My law partner Joe Guillot reminded me there were "mean people over there." Associate attorney Chase Estes expressed concern about terrorism and kidnapping. Even I wondered about the safety of the small aircraft we'd be flying in. The least of my worries was the wild animals we'd be encountering.

The day of departure finally arrived. On March 16, we boarded a nonstop Delta flight from Atlanta to Johannesburg. Fourteen hours later we arrived. We overnighted in the fancy Hotel D'Orlean near the airport, and the next day we flew to Maun, in the northwestern delta country of Botswana, not far from Angola and Namibia.

Botswana

Our guide, Ishmael, quickly quelled any apprehensions. His enthusiasm, warmth, and abundance of knowledge about where we were headed were most reassuring. We boarded a small airplane piloted by an Afrikaner, rose to about five thousand feet, and had a bird's-eye view of many elephants on the ground. We soon arrived at a thatched-roof camp known as Le Roo La Tau, on the banks of the Bogeti River adjacent to a delta. Upon arrival, we jumped into a jeep, drove down to the river, and stepped onto a small outboard vessel. We immediately encountered several groups of elephants drinking. Not far away was a group of twelve to eighteen hippopotami.

At a candlelight dinner that night on the river's edge, a wild noise erupted. Ishmael reassured us there was nothing to worry about—it was only two nearby lions courting.

Our first full day in Mukgadikgadi National Park was a winner. Big and majestic elephants were everywhere. We learned there are 120,000 elephants in Botswana, a country the size of Texas or France. We also learned that of all the countries of southern Africa, Botswana has had the most peaceful history, having escaped the civil wars, unrest, and apartheid of others.

That same first day, from our Land Rover vehicle, we took in two prides of lions with mother lionesses protecting their cubs, one set of three, the other of four. They lived in nearby thickets of bushes. Our jeep got too close for my comfort.

Other highlights involved seeing gracious giraffes traipsing through the brush, antelope, kudu, springbok, and numerous species of exotic birds.

The next day we sped through rough country until we arrived in Nxai Pan National Park. Its primitive roads were mostly loose sand or hardened, deeply rutted clay. Even at modest speeds of thirty to forty kilometers per hour it was like riding a rollercoaster. We encountered many zebra, giraffes, elephants, springboks, and eagles. Leslie's camera was constantly snapping.

The next day, Wednesday March 21, we boarded another small airplane, arriving in an hour at Camp Okavango, operated by Desert and Delta Safaris. The boardwalk from the airfield was raised six feet above a marshy area. Our cabin was a long way from the main camp, but we enjoyed the company of many other nationalities at lunch. That afternoon we were off in dugout canoes on tributaries of the marshland. This was the afternoon when Leslie caught a magnificent picture of a giraffe sprinting across the canal, kicking up water.

At each lodge we received a special bottle of champagne to celebrate the forth-fifth anniversary of our meeting on March 30, 1973. At Okavango we shared the bottle with a Chinese delegation at dinner. Through an

A magical moment in Botswana, March 2018.

English-Chinese speaking guide from Zimbabwe, we toasted the Chinese and wished them and their country well. They erupted in applause and reciprocated the good spirit. Someone joked that I should have been a diplomat.

Before leaving Okavango, we rode a small outboard boat up the delta channels. Animals galore. At one moment, however, a drizzle turned into a downpour, with thunder and lightning crackling all around us. With speed and prayer, we made it back to the base alive. Just in time. The tin roof on our cabin was pounded with the cannon-booms of falling crabapple-like balls from a large Marula tree overhanging our cottage.

More field excursions took us into interesting terrain, including an island dominated by baboons. What fun! We also kept meeting interesting fellow travelers from all over the planet.

Our third two-day bush camp was Camp Xakanaxa, near the Moremi Game Reserve. Lions, zebra, giraffes, elephants, and other wildlife were all around, often reflecting a pristine elegance. One night a big hippopotamus wandered up from the channel and foraged around the small wooded area between our tent cabin and Ishmael's. The hippo could easily have knocked over both cabins, Ishmael later shared with me. Thanks again, Lord, that he did not.

The next day we again bumped, swayed, and bounced around deeply rutted dirt roads and curves. We plowed through several large puddles (more like little ponds) as we persisted in our search for God's bountiful creatures.

Leslie's eagle eyes spotted animals and sights we otherwise would have missed. One was a deadly "black mamba" snake. Its head ducked into a hole midway up a tree to ferret out eggs to eat from a burchellis' (starlings') nest. Suddenly the parent birds discovered the intruder and, amidst screeching sounds, started diving at the snake like two kamikaze jets. In response, the snake reared up, with its head cocked like a cobra, to defend itself. It was all a sight to behold.

One noon hour we pulled into a site by a hippopotamus lake where three similar jeeps were parked. There in the middle of this jungle was a long table with ten chairs on each side. A picnic feast was prepared, with wine included. An enchanting interlude. Everyone was amused.

Upon our return to Camp Xakanaxa, the anniversary of our meeting one another was honored for the third time. We gladly shared the champagne with two Australian couples, a Swiss-German couple, Guillermo, and Ishmael. Unfortunately our great guide announced that he would be leaving us, having been called back to Maun to escort other tourists, probably a much larger contingent than our threesome. We exchanged gifts and email addresses with Ishmael and promised to stay in contact.

A few hours later we were off to our fourth and final stop, traveling by small plane to Kasani International Airport and Chobe National Park. The Chobe Game Lodge was more hotel-like than our previous campsites. We encountered many interesting fellow tourists. On a river voyage we visually feasted on a herd of fifteen elephants, some engaged in playful head knocking, with tusks extended, others taking a bath. Impalas, springboks, warthogs, and hippopotami were also enjoyed. At night we enjoyed a dinner under the stars, with an African band, sounding very Jamaican or Caribbean-like, livening up the evening with their music.

Zimbabwe and Zambia

We were soon off to the final portion of our trip, an excursion to Zimbabwe and Zambia to see the mystical Victoria Falls. This is one of the seven UNESCO wonders of the world. We were drenched but blown away by the magnificence, the natural architecture, the near constant mists, and the surrounding rainforest. Raincoats were absolutely necessary. Riding the rutted highway from Victoria Falls, Zimbabwe, to Livingstone, Zambia, while crossing the bridge over a deep gorge—the sum total was breathtaking. We were also hit by street vendors who wouldn't give up.

We finally made our way, via an ambling dirt road and an unimpressive entry, into another breathtaking location called the Lookout Restaurant. This human watering hole was perched on a cliff overlooking a gorge that resembled the Grand Canyon. Incredibly some people were fearlessly engaged in zip line trips and bungee jumps off the edges. The mere sight preyed on my nerves.

We returned to the Elephant Camp, on the Zimbabwean side, a five-star facility run by the fifty-nine-year-old Ashley Pearson and his wife. A former private security services contractor who grew up in the British protectorate of

Leslie and me at Victoria Falls with Guillermo Strauss of Buenos Aires, left, and next to him our Zimbabwean guide.

Rhodesia, now Zimbabwe, Ashley was a tough hombre but with a pleasant personality. Leslie and I stayed in the most distant of his tent cabins and again enjoyed the interaction with other foreign tourists and the natives. One, a Zimbabwean driver, curiously named "Bornface" took us to the harbor for a sunset cruise on the Zambezi River. Along the way Bornface expressed a deep resentment about the double standard in Zimbabwe, whereby whites were paid much more than blacks for doing the same work. In a country with over ninety percent unemployment, and most people living off the land, Bornface was still grateful to have a job.

Leslie and I also enjoyed meeting Sylvester, a grown cheetah discovered as a three-day-old cub barely alive after a lion had killed his mother and siblings. The cheetah grew up domesticated and became the "big pet" of the Elephant Camp community, a star attraction for incoming guests.

South Africa

On Thursday, March 29, we flew back to Johannesburg to catch our trans-Atlantic flight back to Atlanta. The clockwork smoothness of our prior schedule finally developed a serious glitch. After waiting in line for hours, the 350 passengers were told the flight was canceled. Anger, groaning, and pandemonium broke out. Where was anyone to spend the night? There were only one or two Delta agents to help. The cattle-car effect was worsened by the lateness of the hour.

We finally ended up at the Premier Hotel, a rundown two-star abode for overflow passengers. Delta rebooked us for a 3 a.m. Saturday flight. We took advantage of the extra day to enjoy the many positive changes in Johannesburg, a city Leslie and I first saw forty-three years ago. We especially enjoyed Gandhi Square and attended a Good Friday service in "Joberg," with an outdoor Passion play, including Jesus and the two thieves on crosses, and a loudspeaker repeating the Gospel narrative. We also toured Soweto, fascinated by seeing so much of South Africa's civil rights history.

We returned to the Premier Hotel, only to discover that our next-morning Delta flight had also been canceled. We made a mad dash to the airport, hoping to find the next best way home to America. After multiple times of pushing our baggage cart up and down escalators and across several hundred yards of airport, we finally secured, at the last moment, a South African Airlines flight to London, with a connection by Virgin Atlantic to Atlanta. We had heartfelt prayers of thanksgiving to the Lord for a great adventure despite the somewhat harrowing return trip. We made it back to Montgomery late Saturday night, in time for Easter service the next day. Again, thanks be to God and praises to our Good Lord, whose resurrection we celebrated well.

IV. Tortola, St. Thomas, and the Bahamas, December 2018–January 2019

On my seventy-second birthday, November 13, 2018, Leslie announced her surprise present to me, namely a Norwegian Cruise line trip to the Caribbean Virgin Islands from December 29, 2018, to January 5, 2019. Accordingly, after driving to Atlanta through a blinding rainstorm on December 28, we caught a Delta flight to Orlando. The next day, we enjoyed a stimulating hour and a half visit with second cousin Michael Smith, his interesting wife Peggy, a former West Virginia legislator, and Michael's thirty-eight-year-old daughter, Caroline.

Then we shoved off from Canaveral Port on the Atlantic Ocean. This Norwegian cruise ship had more than double the passenger capacity of the one on our Orient trip of two years earlier. Yet it was "free" to us, due to a good will offering from the cruise line after the elimination of half of our scheduled Orient stops during the earlier voyage.

The first two full days at sea, December 30–31, were just that, "at sea," cruising only. Leslie and I had a fourteenth-floor cabin with a balcony—a peaceful milieu for reading, working on this book, and enjoying the ocean scenery. Watching the Alabama-Oklahoma football game on a computer late at night at sea was exhilarating but challenging, as the screen occasionally blinked off and on.

A visit to Tortola on New Year's Day, with its steep hills and picturesque harbors, was a great way to kick off 2019. Especially uplifting that night was a Beatles impersonation act, bringing back many memories of their hits from the 1960s–1970s. Amazingly, the performers were an Italian foursome whose voices accurately mimicked the Beatles. We also enjoyed a comedy show.

While this trip had many redeeming features, almost everyone felt there were too many people on board—about five thousand. Many were seniors, some older but quite a few younger than our seventy-two and seventy-one. Almost all were retired, but that did not spur me yet to quit working, especially when I saw some sad faces and distant looks. Another negative reinforcement was the number of obese people in their middle ages. It motivated me to eat less.

On January 2, we landed in St. Thomas of the American Virgins Islands for a short stay. A highlight was a gondola trip up a steep hill; the top offered a picturesque vista of the harbor, ships, catamarans, shops, and people. We also enjoyed gift shopping for our brood of eight.

Another day at sea on January 3 introduced us at breakfast and at dinner to an interesting California couple, Don and Ray Jones, sixty-two and forty-seven, only married two years, but each with interesting stories. We had many other interesting short visits with fellow travelers.

The highlight of January 4 was a stop in the lower Bahamas at a private island owned by Norwegian Cruise Lines. We enjoyed snorkeling and time on the beach. We packed that night for leaving the ship the next morning. A flight back from Orlando to Atlanta Saturday brought us to daughter Grace's home in time to celebrate her thirty-eighth birthday with her, our son-in-law Corbett, and our granddaughters Nanette and Emmanuelle.

V. Ecuador and the Galapagos Islands, February 2019

It has been forty-eight years since the first and only other time I visited Ecuador. I had just finished Columbia Law School and taken the New York bar exam. After a month camping in the Rockies with my sixteen-year-old brother, Frank, I landed in New Orleans, where I was inspired by Uncle David before launching on a month-long solo journey around South America.

All I remember about Ecuador from 1971 was a rustic trip to the high-lands, seeing some of Quito, and a road trip to Guayaquil. Traveling alone I was more outgoing in meeting people, but that is all I remember.

The Delta flight on February 11 from Atlanta to Quito was shorter than expected, just under five hours. We arrived at 11 p.m. and were transported by tour bus with fellow travelers to the Marriott in downtown Quito.

Tuesday the 12th had our Gohagan of Chicago group traveling to the Old City. Especially memorable was the Street of Seven Crosses, with its many major churches within a mile of each other. We ventured into the Church of La Compania de Jesus, which dazzled us with its gold-covered monuments. We also enjoyed the Santa Cruz Square and the amazing archeological collection in the Casa del Alabado Museum.

The next morning our three twenty-passenger buses caravanned to where the equatorial line is marked in the village of Mitad del Mundo. Our guide, Vanessa, whose ancestry was a mix of Spanish and indigenous Indian, took us through a variety of straw and mud huts used by early ethnic inhabitants. Pictures were taken of the Equator line, and most of us ascended a tower museum about three hundred feet high. At the top we enjoyed a spectacular view of the surrounding scenery of ancient volcanoes at altitudes of about eight thousand feet.

Ecuador is the only country in Latin America that uses American currency as its own, including the one-dollar coin that is shunned in the

USA. Not surprisingly, despite its diverse population of indigenous Indian, Spanish descendants, and other immigrant influences, it is one of the most economically and politically stable countries of the lower Americas. Also, like Costa Rica and Panama, Ecuador attracts many expatriate Americans as permanent residents.

Our first evening we had a welcoming reception and a lecture by Brevard College geology professor Jim Reynolds, a board member of the Galapagos National Trust. Although his lecture dealt primarily with the volcanic origin of the Galapagos Islands, he described his life-altering involvement with these islands. When I questioned Jim about what he meant by "transformational," he described having been captivated by the pristine and protected nature of the islands and wildlife.

The Galapagos Islands, 724 miles due west of Ecuador in the Pacific Ocean, are where three ocean currents come together. Teeming with thousands of marine species, the islands are secluded from the South America continent by ongoing volcanic and seismic activity. As a result, exceptional animal life has developed through the millennia, including giant tortoises a century old. Also abundant are iguanas, seals, sea lions, penguins, sea turtles, and amazing species of birds and fish. Indeed, the name of the islands comes from the humongous giant land tortoises, which include eleven subspecies. Each of the major islands has a different type of iguana, and these overgrown lizards are all over the place.

The Galapagos Islands gained world attention when the famous English scientist Charles Darwin visited in 1835. Of course, what he saw there inspired his theory of evolution.

This magnificent archipelago and natural reserve is home to one of the world's largest ecosystems. In 1959, it was declared a National Park of Ecuador, and in 1979 a World Heritage site by UNESCO, terming it a unique "living laboratory."

Visited for many years mainly by pirates and sea lion and whale hunters, today the islands attract tourists whose numbers are controlled with the use of state-required permits. On Valentine's Day, February 14, we flew from Quito to Baltra, the only airport in Galapagos. Upon arrival, we transferred to Zodiacs, inflatable motorized dinghys, for transport to the *Santa Cruz*

II, a relatively small cruise ship. There were only sixty-two passengers, with about an equal number of crew members. We arrived in time for lunch.

Our first afternoon we voyaged by Zodiac to Dragon Hill on Santa Cruz Island. It was primarily hard black lava covered with sand. Our twenty-year-old Ecuadorian guide, Sabastian, introduced us, in articulate English, to the local wildlife, primarily iguanas, and the diverse vegetation. The most memorable event, unfortunately, was the slip and fall of professor Jim Reynolds, our first-night lecturer in Quito. In his early sixties, slim, and athletic-looking, Jim's walking gait was unsteady due to a stroke in his twenties, necessitating his use of a cane. Yet this was Jim's thirteenth time in Galapagos. His stumble on the uneasy lava footpath bloodied his face and leg, but left no broken bones or concussion. I helped shoulder-carry Jim to a pickup spot and medical attention by a Zodiac crew.

Sparkling conversation at dinner that night was enjoyed with a mixed couple, Algin Garrett, an African American dermatologist now teaching at Penn State, and his long-time girlfriend, Mary Griffith.

The next day, February 15, was Leslie's seventy-first birthday. We enjoyed two ventures, the first an hour-long Zodiac exploration of wildlife in the bay of Fernandino Island. The steep banks reminded us of Ireland's Cliffs of Moher. At mid-morning, snorkeling gear enabled us to swim closely with sea turtles, sea lions, penguins, and iguanas, amidst a background of colorfully arrayed fish.

On February 16, the *Santa Cruz II* was anchored in the bay outside Puerto Ayora, also on Santa Cruz Island. We minibused to the Charles Darwin Research Station, observing tortoises of all ages and sizes. We then drove to a sugar and coffee plantation, where the process of developing both products was demonstrated. After a hearty lunch in an upper-plateau country, we hiked across a farm with several hundred giant tortoises, the largest about six hundred pounds. Leslie snapped some amazing photos, but the equatorial heat and humidity got to us and everyone else. We returned to the town and back to the ship.

In the late afternoon of the 16th, I read the last six pages of *Hard Rain,* Frye Gaillard's 704-page history of the 1960s. It was an incredibly good read, especially with its highlighting of the civil rights and anti-war movements of that decade, both bringing back emotional memories.

At dinner, Leslie and I were a part of a table of six that celebrated her birthday with cake and a "Happy Birthday" serenade. That evening a rousing Galapagos male sextet, playing great Hispanic music, accompanied by three beautiful dancing girls, entertained us. The young ladies pulled me and other passengers away from our chairs to dance. A great thrill. We applauded and appreciated the musicians and the colorful dancers.

Sunday the 17th was devoted to snorkeling and ferrying by Zodiac from the ship to the remote islands. Observing a band of pink flamingos and a family of sea lions were among the best moments, but battling horseflies was the worst. In the morning I finally met on board a seventy-five-year-old still active trial judge named Joe Huber from Palo Alto, California, traveling with a Smithsonian group. Leslie and I enjoyed his good company and even met several others for the first time during our last day at sea.

Monday, February 18, was the last day of our joyful journey. Feeling rested and reenergized, we expressed our goodbyes to fellow passengers and crew. The Zodiacs zipped us back to Baltra Island for flights to Guayaquil and Quito. We reached Atlanta on Tuesday morning, February 19, at 5 a.m. It was our granddaughter Nanette's third birthday.

14

Roy Moore

The most misunderstood figure ever in Alabama politics was, or is, Roy Moore. Reviled and demonized by many (and treated like the "devil incarnate"), Roy Moore is equally admired and defended by many others who believe he is a "saint," paying the price of discipleship (as in Dietrich Bonhoeffer's *The Cost of Discipleship*).

On May 25, 2018, I dashed in from a downpouring Montgomery rain into the Cahawba House restaurant. There I discovered Robert Vance, an unopposed Democratic candidate for chief justice of the Alabama Supreme Court finishing his lunch. Young Bob graduated from Princeton in 1982, was later elected circuit judge in Birmingham, and ran Roy Moore a very close race for chief justice in 2012. The younger Vance is therefore a darling of the state's liberals. His opinion carries great weight with me, as do his family ties (his father, the famous Bob Vance, was the Alabama Democratic party chairman in the rough civil rights days, was a good friend to my father and me, and became an Eleventh Circuit U.S. Court of Appeals judge before his assassination by mail bomb in 1985).

Yet I was surprised, but then not too surprised, to hear young Vance describe Roy Moore as the "most liberal Alabama Supreme Court justice by far when serving on the court, and that applies to not only civil cases but also to criminal cases." Bob further volunteered that in his 2012 race he "never heard even a hint" of Roy Moore mistreating any woman he dated.

Thus in one fell swoop, Robert Vance validated for me why I still like Roy Moore, despite his being unfairly tarred and feathered by a liberal national and state press and a liberal elite in the 2017 U.S. Senate race. I have been a good Democrat for fifty years, am a longtime member of the

State Democratic Executive Committee and a four-time delegate to the Democratic National Convention (1980 for Jimmy Carter; 2000 for Al Gore; 2012 for Barack Obama; and 2016 for Hillary Clinton), a 1978 candidate for Alabama Attorney General and a 2002 candidate for the U.S. Senate. I am known for being liberal myself. But because I am a trial lawyer, I know that Moore was the best friend my underdog clients ever had on the Alabama Supreme Court. Moore was also the best friend on the high court that minorities and the lower socioeconomic classes in Alabama had among the nine Republican justices when he was on the court. Moore proved that in numerous cases.

Roy Moore has always had a heart for the "little guy" and so do I, both professionally and personally. And the beating and pummeling of Moore in 2017 caused my heart for the underdog to sympathize with him all the more. I also knew that much of what was printed and said about Moore was exaggerated and embellished. Some accusers sported a "jump on the pile" mentality in claiming sexual harassment. Except there was no umpire to blow a whistle.

There are three types of conservatives: religious; economic; and racial. Moore is surely the first, but not the other two. That happens to be where I am also. In the 2012 Republican primary, Moore won without a run-off against two much better financed Republican candidates for chief justice of the Alabama Supreme Court. He thrashed former Alabama attorney general Charlie Graddick and Chuck Malone, then the presiding chief justice. Something of a folk hero, Moore enjoyed exceedingly strong support statewide, and that included from blacks. African Americans were part of his base and knew Moore was a real friend on the Alabama Supreme Court. His support was strongest among black ministers and churchgoers. They had no problems with the Ten Commandments.

Those villainizing Moore ascribed to him only the most impure of political motives . . . saying his support for the Ten Commandments, and against abortion, was purely politics. Having come to know Moore personally in recent years, first on the campaign trail and then in the courtroom, I believe his views on moral issues were deeply genuine, even if they hurt him politically, which was the case with some voters. There was even a quiet humility about Moore, surprising for a supposed politician, but earnest and contrary to the public image projected by the press.

Moore's opponents, especially extreme liberals, tried to paint Moore as a "backwoods bumpkin," or a throwback to dumber pioneer days of Alabama when Biblical values were still important. This annoyed me because of evidence to the contrary. Moore is a graduate of the U.S. Military Academy at West Point, a university with very high academic standards. He is also a Vietnam veteran and has been a public servant for most of his life. Moore's Alabama Supreme Court opinions, whether you agreed or not, reflected a well-educated ability to write. Moreover, I agree that Biblical values are relevant today, despite a secular ethos spewing otherwise.

The Ten Commandments are also important, and, many Hindus and Muslims have told me they agree with Christians and Jews in believing the Commandments need to be more widely emphasized, if not for religious reasons, then for moral, ethical, and legal reasons. Indeed, the Commandments underlie much of America's criminal and civil law.

I remember the famous sermon by my father, the Reverend Julian L. McPhillips Sr., that is framed in the Rosa Parks Museum in Montgomery, about "Thou Shall Not Commit Murder." Dad preached this in 1965 at St. Luke's Episcopal Church in Mountain Brook, Alabama, after the acquittal of the murderer of Episcopal seminarian Jonathan Daniels, a civil rights martyr. Dad said that of all the Ten Commandments, the one you'd least think you'd ever need to preach on was "Thou Shalt Not Murder." Dad added that in 1965, the chances of being murdered in Alabama were great, whether you were white or black, if you were involved in civil rights.

Those who initiated the Ten Commandments lawsuit in federal court challenging Moore's placement of the monument in the Alabama Supreme Court building were most unhappy about the burdens of the seventh commandment, it appeared. "Thou shalt not commit adultery" runs starkly against modern secular values of some.

Then there is abortion. For many years it has been the most sensitive and delicate issue in American politics. It represents a clash between two ostensibly worthwhile goals: (a) the preservation of innocent unborn human life; and (b) the right of a woman to make decisions about her own reproductive needs. Coming out of liberal New York in 1975, the pro-choice option seemed right and convenient to me, yet my pro-life view (discussed at more length in both my earlier books, *The People's Lawyer* and *Civil Rights in My Bones*) started developing before our son David came to us by adoption in 1990. He was twice saved from an abortion when his biological mom was first three months pregnant and then five months. I recognize exceptions, like the life of the mother, and I certainly favor contraceptives. Accordingly, Roy Moore's views on the abortion issue didn't bother me. Regrettably I recognize how people of different views could demonize Moore, proclaiming other reasons (such as sexual harassment allegations) to go after Moore, when the real, underlying motivation was their strong opposition to Moore's pro-life stands.

By the time the December 2017 Moore-Jones U.S. Senate race was over, Moore's name had become "radioactive," especially in liberal circles but even among some Republicans. I've never in my life seen such a vicious, biased and unfair journalistic attack from the national, state, and local press. It was unmerciful. The media totally lacked the journalistic independence it normally aspires to maintain. Pro-Moore letters to the editor were ignored, while the least little negative about Moore was blown up out of proportion. John Archibald of the *Birmingham News* was unrelenting, scorching Moore every day of the campaign. Did it gain Archibald anything? Well, yes—the Pulitzer Prize.

Meanwhile, Alabama Media Group editorialist Kyle Whitmire was constantly attacking Moore in snide, sanctimonious columns and repressing Moore's positions. Archibald and Whitmire were a one-two punch. They never spoke a single good word about him, falsely portraying Moore as a sexually predatory monster, which he absolutely is not and was not. It was the worst case of biased journalism I've ever seen, and I say that as a good loyal Democrat.

What really galled me was when a prominent attorney, whom I know personally but choose not to name here, introducing Cornel West at the 2018 Durr Lecture in Montgomery, called Moore "a pedophile" and repeated a dastardly lie pushed by his political opponents, attributing to Moore the false statement that "blacks were better off during slavery." An exasperated

Moore fumed in his ardent denials, insisting he had never said anything remotely like that. Moore is nowhere near a "pedophile," an ugly, pernicious insult, if ever there were one. The attack on Moore was an attempt to strip him of his moral authority. Unfortunately, with some independents and many voters, it succeeded.

Meanwhile, the attorney accusing Moore proved the vulnerability and hypocrisy of making such accusations, when on October 22, 2018, he himself was involuntarily removed from his employment at the University of Alabama, due to allegedly sexually harassing a female employee under him with sexually explicit and inappropriate text messages and emails. What goes around comes around.

Speaking of Cornel West, an African American scholar who has taught at both Princeton and Harvard and been known as a civil rights firebrand, he made a most appropriate statement when he said, "We are all 'broken vessels,' in need of healing, and in need of Jesus as Lord." West is a liberal civil rights Christian evangelical. I can identify with that.

Back to Roy Moore. He didn't like losing a U.S. Senate campaign, especially one he felt he should have won. Far more hurtful to Moore was the personal attack on his integrity. The allegations involved events of forty years ago that had never appeared in five previous campaigns. Moreover, none of the women ever claimed Moore had sex with them, only that he was too aggressive. None ever filed any civil or criminal charges that could have corroborated their 2017 stories. Although Moore repeatedly insisted their stories were untrue, he was irreparably tarnished, sullied, and hurt.

More than most plaintiff's lawyers, I have handled many sexual harassment cases, mostly for women. Yes, there is often truth in their allegations, but there is also a "me too" embellishment for some who jump in. For others, if financial or personal gain is perceived, stories tend to puff up out of nowhere, hard to disprove, given they happened forty years ago. Of all the accusations slung at Moore, the worst was minuscule in comparison to women's complaints against Donald Trump or Bill Clinton. These two presidents were, and are, more experienced and skilled at blowing things off, or away. On the other hand, Moore was like "an innocent deer in headlights." He didn't know what hit him, when the allegations first erupted. Yet, aided by

$37 million in advertising and an unprecedently biased press, it is amazing that the margin of Moore's defeat was as small as it was.

Moore denied it all vehemently. Yet for doing so he ends up getting sued by one of the accusers, Ms. Leigh Corfman. Amazingly, Ms. Corfman didn't sue Moore over an unwanted sexual contact, for which a statute of limitations passed away decades ago, if he ever did anything actionable. Instead Ms. Corfman sued him because Moore denied what she said. She claimed in a lawsuit that Moore's denial made her look like a "liar," or slandered her. How could a woman of such modest means afford to pay for two attorneys flying in from San Francisco and another attorney coming down from New York? All three came to Montgomery to represent Corfman on a simple venue hearing in April 2018. I spoke in court with each of the three, who admitted where they came from. But who is really behind Corfman's lawsuit, and why? Is someone of high financial resources afraid that Moore might rise phoenix-like from the ashes and threaten America with his moral values?

Given my strong Democratic Party orientation, and yet not enthused about either Doug Jones or Roy Moore, I refrained from saying anything publicly about either during that campaign, and I did not contribute financially to either campaign. I especially disliked Roy Moore's pulling a gun at a campaign rally to emphasize his opposition to gun control laws. I also felt the Democrats nationally were better on other issues important to me, including immigration, the environment, education, and criminal and civil justice.

My issues with Jones, going back to my 2002 campaign for the U.S. Senate, were detailed in the 2005 second edition of *The People's Lawyer*. However, I credit Jones for a smart campaign in 2017, and I especially credit him for his leadership in prosecuting in the early 2000s the last two bombers of the church in Birmingham in 1963. Of course I credit Bill Baxley for convicting the first bomber in the more difficult era of the 1970s. In any case, when the Jones-Moore election was over in December 2017, I wrote Jones to congratulate him and say that any past misunderstandings between us I considered "water over the dam."

Shortly thereafter, Roy Moore called me about helping defend him in the lawsuit filed by Corfman. My subsequent work on Moore's behalf, and that of my partner Kenneth Shinbaum, was primarily on venue issues, seeking to change venue from Montgomery County to Etowah County. It started with an adverse ruling by new Montgomery County Circuit judge Roman Shaul, but we filed a petition for a writ of mandamus to the Alabama Supreme Court, denied by that court in August 2018.

Judge Moore is being defended by attorney Melissa Issak on the merits of the case. She is smart and hardworking. (I also teamed up with Melissa on October 25 and November 1, 2018 in bringing charges against Attorney General Steven Marshall to Montgomery County D.A. Daryl Bailey over Marshall's violation of Alabama's ban against Pac to Pac transfer contributions.)

A videotaped deposition of Roy Moore took place at my law office on October 8, 2018. Moore handled well his grilling by New York attorney Neil Roman. Two other attorneys, one from New York and one from Birmingham, also represented Ms. Corfman at the deposition table. Moore was represented by Ms. Isaak, Kenneth, and me.

As we entered 2019, Moore's motion for change of venue was denied by both the Montgomery County Circuit Court and the Alabama Supreme Court. It has become increasingly likely that Melissa and I will be representing Moore in a December 2019 trial on the merits of the case in Montgomery County. Judge John Rochester from Clay County, two counties northeast, has now been assigned to handle the case. He is a fair jurist whom I have known for forty-two years. On January 11, 2019, Melissa and I squared off in Montgomery before Judge Rochester with attorney Harlen Prater of the Lightfoot Franklin firm in Birmingham over a multitude of discovery disputes. That articulate lawyer is one of about seven attorneys representing Ms. Corfman. Again, the literal million dollar question is where did she get that kind of resources from?

On January 10, Melissa and I filed a "Renewed Motion to Dismiss." Citing ample case law, our brief said that Moore has a "qualified privilege" to defend his reputation against defamatory attacks. That is, he has a right to say he is innocent, deny what is said, and defend himself against attacks on his character, without being sued for doing so. We argued this motion orally on March 4 in the Montgomery County Courthouse library. At this writing, we are awaiting a ruling. Nonetheless, in addition to arguing Moore's privilege to defend himself against a defamatory attack, without subjecting himself to liability, I added that he could not be responsible for statements others made in coming to his defense. Finally, I argued the relief Corfman sought, namely a retraction, apology, and injunction against future speech, was unconstitutional and unavailable as a matter of law.

My own experience as a U.S. Senate candidate in 2002 was not nearly as bad as Moore's in 2017. No one ever accused me of sexual harassment. Yet a *Birmingham News* sabotage article, cleverly written for effect, made me look "gender-insensitive," when I was not. Having broken glass ceilings for women in cases all over Alabama, I didn't appreciate this unfair characterization. My objection was more personal than political. Nonetheless, I can empathize with Roy Moore being made to look "gender-insensitive" and worse. It hurt him deeply. I know somewhat how he felt.

On November 6, 2018, in a statewide election with a million people going to the polls, Alabama voters overwhelmingly supported an amendment to Alabama's 1901 Constitution, authorizing public displays of the Ten Commandments. More than seven out of ten voters backed the measure. Moore must have felt vindicated.

In the same election, with a record-breaking 1.7 million Alabamians casting their votes, Republicans defeated Democratic candidates by a 60–40 margin in most races. That included competitive and energetic candidates for governor (Walter Maddox), attorney general (Joseph Siegelman), and chief justice of the Supreme Court (Bob Vance Jr.). In the latter, despite running against Vance's better-funded and -organized campaign, Republican Tom Parker (often accurately portrayed as being close to Moore politically) defeated Vance 58–42.

What this also proved was that, had Roy Moore been on that same ballot in November 2018 rather than in a special election in 2017, his outcome likely would have been far different. This was because so many election contests at that time all across the other forty-nine states, at federal, state, and local levels, would have siphoned away Jones's campaign money from Alabama. The crucial fact is that the Moore-Jones contest was the only campaign in the entire USA in November–December 2017, with Doug

Jones also receiving great assistance from Moore's Republican rival Luther Strange, darling of the Big Business Republicans, whom Moore had defeated in the August 2017 Republican primary.

In late December 2018 news media also reported that "online fakery" was used on social media to attack Roy Moore. Interestingly, the news reports about these misleading online tactics came from the *Washington Post* and *New York Times*, both newspapers that editorialized and wrote daily news reports against Moore during the fall 2017 campaign. Doug Jones was quick to say that he had nothing to do with the fake social media; some attributed them to Russian sources.

In any case, the rare electoral "perfect storm" had developed twelve months earlier. The unprecedented circumstances generated an incredible record $37 million in contributions to the Jones campaign to defeat Moore in his Senate bid.

The pile-on by the accusing females, never heard from publicly before in forty years and across five campaigns, tarred and sullied Moore's reputation. Soon thereafter many other prominent men in the political, entertainment, and media worlds were hit by similar allegations in a fad gone wild. What this bodes for America is unknown. Roy Moore's future also remains to be seen.

15

Baking the Wrong Flower

It is refreshing to meet personalities whose good character traits echo an earlier era. That is precisely what sixty-four-year old Caucasian male Charles Gilmer modeled when he came to my office on January 9, 2017.

Known more casually as "Chuck," this sparsely bearded but gray-haired denizen of rural Lee County, Alabama, quickly captured the good will of my office staff. Chuck frequently brought sausage and honey to my firm from his Salem farm, together with pictures of deer he fed and coddled.

Chuck absolutely didn't deserve the legal problems he encountered from his employer, Flowers Baking Company of Opelika. Flowers, a business with many plants spread across the Southern states, bakes bread, cakes, and other delicacies purchased by wholesalers and retailers alike.

But Chuck did no baking. He was the building maintenance supervisor of the Opelika plant, which employed two hundred workers. Chuck was extraordinarily handy—the exact opposite of this author. Chuck could fix, build, or pave almost anything.

Unfortunately for Chuck, after forty years on his job, in December 2016 Flowers terminated Chuck, saying he was "insubordinate." They also accused him of violating company rules by using "profane, threatening or abusive language and/or behavior directed towards a supervisor." Truth be known, Chuck's language was only directed at an underling, though not an African American or a female, the usual targets of suspect behavior in most plants. Instead, his words were directed towards a young white male, William Nelson, whose parents and grandparents had long worked for Flowers. Gilmer admitted he chewed the immature Nelson out, and said he did so for good reason after Nelson recklessly slung a long, sharp piece of metal across the premises.

Not coincidentally, Gilmer's termination occurred amidst a Flowers's youth movement, which encouraged older employees to resign and be replaced by younger employees. Gilmer had been repeatedly encouraged to retire by his superiors, notably chief engineer Daryl Funderburk. Chuck's standard reply was, "I plan to work until I'm seventy, about six years away."

In wrongfully pushing Chuck Gilmer out, the company, in a punny play on words, was "baking the wrong flower."

Many of Gilmer's fellow employees were upset by his firing and sent him supportive written statements. They described Chuck as "passionate," "a man of dedication," "a better man," and even a "perfectionist." The compliments were plentiful. "He will be truly missed" echoed his co-employees.

Older white males are not my usual clients in civil rights case. However, Gilmer is no shrinking violet. He was ready for a fight and willing to pay for it. Soon, on Chuck's behalf, I became engaged in two courtroom battles, one in state court, the other in federal.

Our first salvo was filing an age discrimination charge at the Equal Employment Opportunity Commission in Birmingham. We articulated the disparity between the way younger employees received less discipline for greater offences at Flowers, when compared to Gilmer's termination. In particular, the thirty-nine-year-old Nelson was not disciplined at all, despite his dangerously throwing the sharp object across the plant floor, nor was Nelson even chastised for disobeying Gilmer's orders.

We also articulated the hypocrisy of several Flowers executives, who violated the rule against using company resources for personal gain unrelated to company employment. This, too, was supposed to be a firing offense, but went unenforced.

The EEOC requires that a complaint be investigated for at least six months before a right-to-sue letter can be issued, providing a ticket to federal court.

Meanwhile, in the second legal battle, the Alabama Department of Labor denied Gilmer's unemployment compensation. Chuck had filled out paperwork early in December 2016, and he called weekly to inquire about Labor's determination of his charges. In mid-February 2017, the Department said it had mailed Gilmer's "determination" weeks earlier. Unfortunately, but typically for Alabamians, Mr. Gilmer never received it, and his time to appeal had expired.

The State Labor Department could not have been more indifferent or less gracious. The State's hard-line mantra is that the mailing of a letter constitutes service. It doesn't matter whether the employee receives the letter or not. The state abides no excuses. At a deposition I took of state witness Ashley Newcomb, she admitted there were numerous ways the Labor Department could have lost, misplaced, or never even mailed Gilmer's unemployment determination.

So our law firm filed suit for Chuck in the Lee County Circuit Court against both the Labor Department and Flowers Baking. We drew the renowned Judge Jacob Walker. He tried the case over two days in May and July 2017. Several witnesses, including my former client Roy McMullen, insisted they also had never received notices of termination in their unemployment cases. Neighbors on Gilmer's rural postal route testified about how poor the mail service habitually was for them. Judge Walker's order reinstated Gilmer's right to seek unemployment compensation. This was no small slight for the Labor Department, but it was a significant courtroom victory for Gilmer, despite his legal expense.

Meanwhile, with our age discrimination case rocking along in federal court, the usual discovery procedures began. We requested a right to inspect the Flowers's premises in Opelika, to make photographs, and to depose employees. Not surprisingly, Flowers objected.

A mediation was held in Montgomery on December 20, 2017. We sparred back and forth; Chuck wanted an amount well above the six-figure threshold. Experienced employment mediator Debra Leo exhibited her usual good technique, and it was helpful. Yet at the end of the day Flowers remained entrenched, and settle we did not.

Accordingly, I sent a letter the next day to Flowers's lawyer, Christopher Deering of Birmingham. I summarized Gilmer's points and insisted on inspecting the plant and deposing twelve witnesses. At first, Chris and Flowers dug in their heels. Similarly Chuck was all fired up, as we spun out epistles, back and forth, over our respective positions.

After a January of ice, snow, and intransigence, but with prodding from the skillful Ms. Leo, Flowers and Gilmer agreed on February 2, 2018, to a mutually acceptable outcome. The resolution is subject to a confidentiality agreement, but my unwavering new friend, no wallflower himself, was happy, believing he had achieved civil justice. Accordingly, Chuck's flower is no longer being baked. Thank you Lord.

16

The U.S. Air Force Challenged

The U.S. Air Force is full of good, competent, and well-qualified people, for the most part. Its military arm is strong. Along with the Navy, it probably draws more people from the better-educated echelons of American society than other military branches. Yet it sometimes does strange things that defy fairness and hurts its civilian personnel, and sometimes vice-versa.

My law partner, retired Lieutenant Colonel Joe Guillot, is one of the Air Force's best. He champions the Air Force. He is highly intelligent and has a good moral compass. We first became good friends at Christ the Redeemer Episcopal Church. At the age of forty-three, Joe, while still employed by the Air Force, started attending Jones School of Law in Montgomery. He graduated three years later at the top of his class. Joe handles the broadest range of legal cases in our office of the eight attorneys, including employment law, my specialty. Joe also monthly audits our firm's financial books and records, a valuable service.

Yet Joe would agree that his former employer, Maxwell Air Force Base in Montgomery, has endured a plethora of complaints involving unlawful employment discrimination from its civilian personnel. With the consent of my clients, I highlight in this chapter three sets of bad experiences of former Air Force civilian employees. These are cases I was still handling as 2019 began. They've caused me to conclude that the U.S. Air Force could do much better in how it treats its civilian employees. Notwithstanding, the two Air Force bases, Maxwell and Gunter, contribute much to Montgomery's economy and attract many great people like Joe and his wife Maria. Yet the sum total of the following clients' cases, each raising serious questions individually, tell a story bigger than either David Sanchez, Shirley DuBose, or Linda Mendenhall.

I. David Sanchez

A white Hispanic fifty-four-year-old male, Dr. David Sanchez, came to see me on December 8, 2017. A reasonable man accompanied by his supportive wife, his sad story left me shaking my head. I soon prepared, and David signed, disability and age discrimination complaints against both the U.S. Air Force and its civilian contractor, MEDS (Management Enterprises and Development Services), through whom David had recently been serving the U.S. Air Force as a physical therapist.

Sanchez had been a licensed physical therapist since 1997. After first obtaining a master's degree in physical therapy, and later a doctorate degree, David was employed from 2005–11 as an active-duty person with the 42nd Medical Operations Squadron at Maxwell. Our local Air Force base does much through independent contractors, or I should say "quasi-independent" operators, as Maxwell maintains much control over its civilian help. Sanchez began working in 2011 for a contractor named "Up and Running." In 2012 he moved to MEDS.

Whether paid directly by the Air Force or by a contractor, Mr. Sanchez's work was directed and managed by the Air Force, which also determined his hours and duties.

During his later years in the military, Sanchez developed some orthopedic issues of his own, involving spine pain and arthritis in his arms and legs. When David left active duty in 2011, the Department of Veterans Affairs (VA) determined he was significantly disabled. Yet with discipline and strategy, he could still fully perform all the duties of his job. Accordingly, he continued working as a civilian employee through the two contractors.

The quality of Sanchez's work was actually so good that many of the top brass at Maxwell became his clients. That included multiple general officers and other Air University impresarios at the 42nd Air Base Wing.

Unfortunately for Sanchez, a muscular thirty-two-year-old female triathlon athlete, Major Erin O'Conner, arrived at Maxwell in October 2016. She was appointed the officer in charge of physical therapy. Within months,

David started encountering problems from O'Conner, subjecting him to caustic, cynical remarks, including the sometimes ageist term "a scatterbrain."

O'Conner also increased Sanchez's workload to treating more than one hundred new patients a month. This was in addition to his already established clients. O'Conner flashed by Sanchez frequently, throwing darts at him with her eyes and subjecting him to increasingly hostile and sarcastic remarks.

O'Conner even criticized him for the lower amount of weights he used with his patients, as if that made Sanchez a weak, older man. "Is that all?" she would ask in disdain, or "Is that it?" O'Connor insisted, "You should be using heavier dumbbells," and she barked while flexing her own biceps. Topping off her bravado and macho manners, O'Conner repeatedly shook her fist at Sanchez, as if to threaten him. Although Sanchez never felt physically threatened by her, Major O'Conner continuously, and unprofessionally, undermined his competence in front of other staff and patients.

Another Maxwell officer, Lieutenant Colonel Ryan Mihata, told Sanchez that O'Conner "is fresh from school and may have the newest and best information" and "that you and I may be out of touch with new concepts." Such remarks smacked of age discrimination, Sanchez believed.

On November 16, 2017, Sanchez was terminated. He wasted no time in coming to me. We filed age and disability discrimination charges against both MEDS and the U.S. Air Force, outlining the above wrongs against O'Conner, among other contentions. Sanchez and I attended a prerequisite informal meeting with Maxwell's EEO office on the cold morning of January 10, 2018.

The wheels of justice turn slowly in EEO arm of the U.S. Air Force, so slowly that justice is often denied, as will be seen below. Ominously for Dr. Sanchez, it may be a long time before his case is resolved.

We did, however, receive a right-to-sue letter from a different body, namely the EEOC in Birmingham, on February 22, 2019. Hence, we filed suit in the Middle District of Alabama on April 16 against both MEDS and the U.S. Air Force.

II. Shirley DuBose

Shirley DuBose is an African American female, born in June 1959. With true grit, she worked hard and obtained a doctor's degree in nursing. She became clinical nurse case manager for four years at Maxwell AFB, from February 3, 2010 until she was terminated on November 1, 2013. What happened to her?

Like Sanchez, DuBose also worked for the 42nd Medical Group through a contractor, ERP International. Yet, as with Sanchez, the 42nd Medical staff and officers managed and supervised DuBose, determining her work hours and duties. This gave us jurisdiction against both the U.S. Air Force and the private contractor under federal employment laws. The following facts were alleged by Ms. DuBose.

DuBose worked under Major Perdue, a white female who harassed her. When she first came to see us on August 18, 2014, she said age, color, and race were all involved. Since this involved the Air Force, I quickly associated partner Joe Guillot to help.

Dubose's troubles began with her supervisor Major Perdue questioning her credentials with the insulting question "Are you an RN?," as if she didn't look like one. Perdue then dispatched another officer, Caucasian female Lieutenant Colonel Heather Bland, to audit DuBose's files, digging at her in an incessantly demanding, angry, and condescending tone.

Perdue also bombarded DuBose with age-related and racially offensive remarks, calling her "Grandma" and "Old Lady." When DuBose asked her to stop, Perdue's curt reply was, "Don't you know by now that whites run things, and I am in charge now."

Perdue demeaningly told DuBose to "eat your banana," adding, "black people are no good and can't be trusted." DuBose also quoted Perdue as saying, "I will get rid of you because your kind is useless anyway!" Perdue denied saying she would fire DuBose.

Unfortunately, the racist attitudes of too many Maxwell managers and contractors kept taking their toll on DuBose. She said she was enduring at least three significant age and/or racially hostile incidents per month in her final year of employment with the 42nd Medical Group. She cited other Caucasian female officers, particularly Lieutenant Colonel Kimberly Manning, for harassing and threatening her with racially offensive and age-sensitive remarks.

On November 14, 2014, Joe Guillot prepared an excellent ten-page "Complainant's Stipulation and Finding of Facts" detailing age, color and/or racial harassment/discrimination and reprisal against DuBose.

Afterwards, we learned, and then learned again and again, that "the delay tactic" is a major way the Equal Opportunity arm of the U.S. Air Force fights cases. Justice delayed is often justice denied.

Despite several conferences with varying judges and Air Force counsel, and despite judges always urging us to settle, the case remained unresolved for over four years. It was obvious the judge didn't want to try the case, but the Air Force refused to offer even peanuts. DuBose understandably didn't want to give her case away.

For the next four and a half years, Joe and I would periodically touch base, file motions, or attempt to get the case back on track, with little success. By late January 2019, fifty-four months had passed since DuBose first visited us. We had no trial or mediation and only lame excuses from the bench.

Finally, a trial date was set for March 19, 2019, and the Air Force finally caved in.

After much internal discussion and additional trial preparation, on March 5, 2019, Joe and I settled the case with Major Emily Wilson of the U.S. Air Force, for $45,000, including attorney fees. In doing so, we helped reestablish Shirley DuBose's good name, reputation, and integrity. She was vindicated, and she and her husband, Adolph Gerald DuBose, a retired Army chaplain, were relieved.

III. Linda Mendenhall

This energetic lady who has inspired my literary work was written about earlier in Chapter 9, "Mendenhalls on the Mend." The following expounds her particulars.

Linda landed at Redstone Arsenal in Huntsville, Alabama in February 2009. She and her husband, Stanford, moved from Huntingdon, New York, for Linda to accept a contract attorney position at Redstone Arsenal. Stanford, an African American man, is 100 percent disabled from combat wounds suffered in Iraq.

The first five years of her Redstone job went well for Linda until the day

Chief Counsel Fred Allen called Linda's husband a "Negroid." Mrs. Mendenhall, understandably, didn't take too kindly to that, so she expanded an already pending race discrimination charge filed with the EEOC. In the end, Linda was willing to drop the entire charge if Allen would simply apologize to her husband. Allen refused, so Linda pursued her case.

Not surprisingly, the devoted wife and wounded warrior ended up getting herself fired! The U.S. government finally settled her case by offering Linda another Air Force legal job in Alabama's historic state capital, Montgomery. Not realizing what was ahead, in accepting this offer, Linda jumped from the frying pan into the fire.

Linda and Stanford traversed down I-65 to Montgomery's Maxwell Air Force Base in September 2016. For the next six months, she worked very hard, coming to her office early on most days. At first Linda had to drive daily from Camden, ninety minutes southwest, but she routinely opened up the office at 7:30 a.m.

Mendenhall didn't realize that her new Maxwell job had a probationary status attached. That designation usually exists for new employees, not a long-term one like Mendenhall who had been with the Air Force since 2009.

She was shocked to discover from day one that her new boss, Colonel Michael King, defied Air Force protocol in being highly disrespectful to her. It was "worse than that," she said. "He was cruel."

King began undermining her right and left, peppering her with ugly comments about her appearance. Mendenhall had a diagnosed genetic condition of lipedema, causing severe pain in her extremities. That gave her the appearance of obesity, primarily in her legs. King frequently compared her to other disgustingly overweight people, sending her into orbit.

Adding injury to insult, King also denied her the reasonable accommodation of being able to sit at her desk. King told Mendenhall that she needed to stand on her feet more of the time.

This was more that any self-respecting person could take. Mendenhall had her human limits. King was "baiting" her, she believed. To the end, King got his "sick jollies" by making fun of her, Mendenhall added. On March 1, 2017, she received the axe. King gave her a quick thirty minutes to "grab your personal items" and skedaddle out the door.

Mendenhall wasted no time in filing a disability discrimination charge against Maxwell and King. The wrongful termination greatly anguished her, sinking her into a depression difficult to shake for many months thereafter. Having just met me at my seventieth birthday party in our Old Cloverdale neighborhood, Mendenhall subsequently asked me to be her attorney. I agreed to do so.

After many emails back and forth, and many telephone conversations with Air Force counsel, the case is still pending for trial.

Mendenhall also filed an age discrimination case against Barksdale AFB near Shreveport, Louisiana, after interviewing there for a job in December 2015. At this time, she had applied for many jobs but obtained only a few interviews. Barksdale AFB invited her to come visit. When she arrived, she was immediately asked many blatant age-related questions, including when she planned to retire.

She lost that job opening to a much younger, less experienced attorney.

She asked me to help her on this case, too. We settled it in February 2018, for a mere $3,500. Yet that was better than nothing for the age discrimination she suffered in the application process.

Five months later, not a penny had arrived. We then discovered that "getting the settlement in" required our law firm's jumping through numerous hoops. The USAF referred us to the Defense Department. The red tape there has discouraged me from ever taking another Air Force case again in my life, if I can help it.

Just to receive the settlement, my office manager Amy Strickland had to register our firm with a nine-digit number in the U.S. Government's System for Award Management (SAM). In addition, Amy had to provide a TIN (Taxpayer Identification number) so the IRS could conduct a validation of our TIN and taxpayer number. In addition, our registration had to be sent to the Defense Logistics Agency (DLA) and the Commerce and Government Entity (CAGE) Code System for assignment to the CAGE code. There were several other stupid steps. It is aggravating to think about and boring to tell about. Now I can now see why Donald Trump campaigned so successfully for eliminating government red tape. It's enough to discourage the Russian army.

17

Selma in Turmoil

Selma is one of the birthplaces of the civil rights movement. My protégé Terri Sewell, the first African American congresswoman from Alabama, humorously says I pulled her out of the "cotton patch of Selma," upon recruiting her to Princeton in 1981. Her words, not mine. No disrespect intended for this once great city.

More decaying urban than rural, and with a proud antebellum history among its Caucasian descendants, Selma is better known worldwide for its civil rights history. In 1965, the infamous beating by state troopers of marchers on the Edmund Pettus Bridge, and the Selma-to-Montgomery march that followed, were thunderclaps echoing around the globe.

Martin Luther King Jr, Fred Shuttlesworth, Frederick Reese, Amelia Boynton and her son Bruce Boynton, L. L. Anderson, James Bevel and Diane Nash, Bernard and Colia Lafayette, John Lewis, C. T. Vivian, and James Orange all left deep footprints in Selma's civil rights history, yet the brightest Selma legal light ever in this arena was native son J. L. Chestnut Jr. (1930–2008).

An attorney with the courage and tenacity of a lion in defeating injustice, Chestnut could also double you over with his humor and wit.

In the early 1970s, J. L. helped my brother Frank McPhillips, then a Harvard student researching civil rights, and in 1972 assisted my parents with the McGovern campaign in Alabama. Our family ties run deep.

The highest professional compliment I ever received was during a 1984 trial in Selma when my co-counsel, J. L. Chestnut Jr. spun around in front of judge and jury, and proclaimed: "I'll be damned, McPhillips, if you ain't the white J. L. Chestnut." I was humbled and honored when his wife and younger daughter Vivian asked me to be one of three eulogists for J. L. at his 2008 homegoing celebration in Selma.

Selma's fame has continued to grow even in the twenty-first century as the subject of two significant movies: *Selma, Lord, Selma*, portraying the life of the youngest marcher beaten on the bridge in 1965, namely Sheyann Webb-Christburg; and the 2015 blockbuster, *Selma*, with David Oyelowo playing Martin Luther King Jr.

Meanwhile, the subject matter for new movies about Selma seems to continue to develop.

The French word "drôle" means "funny strange," a word archaically existent in the English dictionary. Thus I felt "drôle" when J. L. Chestnut's oldest daughter, Ms. Gerald Chestnut, came to see me on May 31, 2017, seeking legal help.

Gerald's problem was Darrio Melton, Selma's newly elected mayor, thirty-eight years young. A former state representative, Melton defeated two former mayors, George Evans and James Perkins, in 2016. The new mayor did so with agile assistance from, among others, Gerald Chestnut and another Selma female, Dorita Clay. Yet after his election, Melton un-gratefully dumped both from their jobs.

Chestnut and Clay were not his only female victims. They were soon joined by city treasurer Ronita Wade and city recreation department em-ployee Carneetie Ellison, both of whom also became my clients.

The charming and outgoing Gerald's story is beyond sad. She had been living for many years in California. Melton cleverly lured her back to Selma to work in his campaign so he could attract a significant set of Selma voters, black and white, to whom Gerald's ties, and her father's ties, were strong. Melton promised Chestnut the moon, a cabinet-level job as planning and development director.

Melton was elected in November 2016. Three months later, in February 2017, Chestnut became the city's new planning director, and relocated home from Los Angeles, at great expense to herself. She performed well, but she soon recognized that Melton's near total inability to communicate with the city council members was hurting both Melton and Selma.

Accordingly Chestnut, more as a public-spirited citizen than as an

*With Selma clients, from left, Carneetie Ellison, Ronita Wade, and Jeff
Hardy, outside our law firm office in downtown Montgomery.*

employee, advised Melton that he needed to get along better with the
council. Unfortunately Melton took great offense and retaliated by firing
Chestnut on April 18.

I filed notices of claim with the City of Selma relating to contract,
fraud, and a violation of Chestnut's First Amendment right to free speech.
Then, while I was at an October 2017 meeting of the Selma city council,
representing Selma treasurer Ronita Wade, it finally dawned on me that
one major problem for Melton was his great discomfort with strong African
American women whose opinions differed from his. A pattern and practice
of sex discrimination appeared in Melton's termination of Chestnut, Wade,
Ellison, and Clay, although the "strong" personality part is not necessarily
covered by federal anti-discrimination laws.

Selma City Councilman Sam Randolph was right on the money as he
spoke boldly and clearly to about fifty people at that October meeting:

> Mayor, all of those things you have stated about Ms. Wade are bogus.
> You know that they are bogus. You have a problem with strong women and

you need to admit that you have a problem with strong women. You fired Ms. Chestnut and replaced her with a weak man. You fired Ms. Wade and replaced her with a weak man. You fired Ms. Val Jones and replaced her with a weak man. You told the council that you had NOT hired a replacement for Ms. Wade's position when you know you had already hired a replacement. You continue to lie to the council.

Ronita Wade herself had been fired by Melton only a few weeks before. At the hearing, I helped persuade the city council to reinstate her by a 5–4 vote.

The reinstatement, however, was never accomplished. Melton then placed Wade on administrative leave. Two months later, in December 2017, he fired her a second time.

In the fall of 2017, I filed sex discrimination charges on behalf of Chestnut, Wade, and Ellison with the Equal Employment Opportunity Commission.

Wade's situation had long been brewing. A seasoned professional with much finance experience with the City of Atlanta, this native Selmian returned to her family home a year before Darrio Melton was elected. She was and is careful, conscientious, and honest, to the Nth degree. It has been my honor to represent her.

After her second termination, I returned to the Selma city council on Wade's behalf in February 2018. Mayor Melton failed to show up for the hearing. Some Selmians, including several city council members, said the mayor was afraid to face my cross-examination. I was allowed to make an opening statement. That included the following two of ten points that I made:

Mayor Melton is seeking complete control over the city finances and does not like the idea that the council is responsible for the city finances. He has complete control over the finances as long as the city treasurer, voted in by you, the city council, is not in office. Thus he has continued to hold the city finances hostage, while Ms. Wade is out of the office.

The mayor discontinued communication with, and isolated himself from, Ms. Wade, cutting off responses once he obtained draft copies of the proposed budget. He used the draft copies to modify and create a budget separate from the one they (the mayor and Ms. Wade) had collectively developed with the department heads to create. This was just another part of his premeditative plans to destroy Ms. Wade's creditability, so he could remove her as city treasurer."

I also shared with the council about the cold and hostile working environment Mayor Melton had subjected my client to.

This time the city council voted 6–2 to reinstate Ms. Wade.

As 2018 wore on, Wade and Ellison maintained regular contact with me on adverse developments in their jobs. This unfortunately included a third time Wade was being placed on administrative leave by Melton, this time on September 26, 2018. I shot a letter the same day to Mayor Melton, demanding he reinstate her. In October 2018, I appeared a third time for Ronita Wade before the Selma city council to restate the obvious: the council was allowing the mayor to ignore its decrees and strip away its authority. Alas, the council was not sure what to do.

The council's only attorney, Jimmy Nunn, soon left to become probate judge. He was not getting involved. I suggested a declaratory judgment action in the Dallas County Circuit Court. On November 21, the day before Thanksgiving, I filed one on behalf of Wade against Melton. The city council was included as a necessary party defendant. We suggested the council realign itself as a plaintiff against Melton. I subsequently recommended to Council President Cory Bouie that the council consider hiring the brilliant Bobby Segall as its attorney, and they did.

Meanwhile the dysfunction of the City of Selma was being noticed far and wide. On December 19, 2018, the *Birmingham News*, Alabama's largest newspaper, published a front-page feature article under the headline, "Shrinking Selma." The subhead was "Dramatic decline: Iconic civil rights city's population falling faster than any other 10,000 plus city in Alabama." The feature took up two-thirds of the front page and the total of page three. The article stated that Selma's 2010 population was 20,756, but by 2017 it had shrunk 11.5 percent to 18,370. The Selma public school system had dropped from 4,055 students in 2000 to 2,854 in 2018.

Another theme was that the declining population was making it difficult to fund basic services. And this, of course, tied into the controversy between my client, the city treasurer, and Selma's mayor who wanted to allocate Selma's shrinking budget in ways suiting his personal interests.

The *Birmingham News* article also highlighted Selma's serious crime problem—the highest crime rate in the state. Selma resident Lula Dean told the *News*: "They're shooting, stealing, robbing. I'm afraid to be out at night. I hate to say it. It's dangerous here."

All this was background to the bombshell announcement on November 2, 2018, that three of Selma's finest police officers, Sergeants Jeff Hardy and Kendall Thomas and Lieutenant Toriano Neely, had been indicted by the Alabama attorney general for allegedly giving false information to AG's office investigators.

The bogus, frivolous nature of these charges echoed the massive dysfunction of Mayor Melton and his weak chief of police, Spencer Collier. Meanwhile, the morale of the Selma police department plummeted to an all-time low. When I showed up on Thursday, December 6, to represent another client in Selma's municipal court (located inside Selma's rundown, antiquated police building), the court was an hour late in opening up, and the building was sparsely occupied.

The three officers, Hardy, Thomas, and Neely, had first come to my office in early October 2018, seeking legal representation after being involuntarily placed on administrative leave. The officers were flabbergasted, as no information had been given them as to who allegedly did what or when. I sent letters to the mayor and chief, demanding to be so informed. That was like throwing a rock into the Grand Canyon. The mayor habitually never replies and did not this time. I finally caught up with Chief Spencer Collier by phone. Not surprisingly, he pretended not to know. "Pretended," I say, because a day later he told the *Selma Times* it had something to do with missing guns, which was a mystery to my clients.

My assistant attorney David Sawyer and I quickly filed motions to dismiss the indictments, due to the total absence of information in the indictments as to specifics of wrongdoing. Even more frivolously—after we had pushed the State for a month to obtain information, the State finally provided a thumb drive containing thirty thousand documents, but with none specified. Alas, bad faith knows no limits! It would have taken us months to wade through this dung heap. Another motion was filed with the court.

At a hearing on December 21, 2018, Judge Collins Pettaway—having rarely seen motions like ours—displayed a reluctance to grant the motion but agreed to certify its questions to the Alabama Court of Criminal Appeals in Montgomery. Accordingly, we filed a mandamus petition pursuant to Rule 21 of the Alabama Rules of Appellate Procedure with that appellate court on January 16, 2019, but it was later denied. Only in Alabama.

In February–March 2019, David and I filed a battery of additional motions to dismiss—challenging the lack of *Garrity* warnings as to all three officers, Hardy, Neely, and Thomas, and also challenging improprieties in the Dallas County grand jury, on constitutional grounds.

We all gathered before the court in Selma on May 9 to argue the motions. On May 22, we received an order from Judge Pettaway dismissing all three cases. Hooray, this was a huge, enormous victory. Our clients, terribly damaged, breathed a big sigh of relief.

On another front, both Ms. Wade and Ms. Chestnut received "right to sue" letters in September 2018 from the Equal Employment Opportunity Commission in Birmingham, both dealing with sex discrimination charges.

At a press conference following the big victory after dismissal of criminal charges against Selma police officers, from left, Tory Neely, Jeff Hardy, and Kendall Thomas. At right is my fellow lawyer, David Sawyer.

Chestnut also has a First Amendment free speech case and Wade a First Amendment freedom of political association claim.

Meanwhile, my representation of Wade has continued with the declaratory judgment action in the Dallas County Circuit Court. We decided not to pursue the EEOC charge lest our case be removed by petition to federal court in Mobile, two and a half hours drive away. Also the "strong black woman" claim has a "personality dimension" that is not illegal under federal law. In filing the state court suit, we reserved the right to tack on later a First Amendment claim arising from Melton's solicitation of financial information from Wade when she was city treasurer under former Mayor Evans, which she promptly refused while Darrio Melton was a candidate. This was before the new young mayor first removed Wade as treasurer in September 2017.

On May 6, 2019, Judge Don McMillan of the Dallas County Circuit Court issued an order reinstating Ms. Wade as city treasurer and ordered the mayor not to interfere with her duties. Hooray again. A week later, on May 13, we filed a motion with the court to order Mayor Melton to show cause why he shouldn't be held in contempt of court for further interference with Ms. Wade and her duties. We held his feet to the fire. The mayor soon caved and started allowing her to do her job.

Despite all the shenanigans and dysfunction described above, I believe there is much hope for a better Selma in the future. One group in particular making some waves in the Selma area is the Black Belt Community Foundation. My close friend and fellow Princetonian Daron Harris '96 is one of its most energetic leaders. He tells me that this organization is doing much to inspire improvement in Selma on numerous fronts.

Every year in early March, Selma also attracts renewed national attention with its annual Bridge Crossing Jubilee, organized by Hank and Rose Sanders. Jesse Jackson still makes an annual appearance, and the dignataries often include candidates or potential candidates for the Democratic nomination for U.S. president. For instance, on Sunday, March 3, 2019, U.S. Senator Corey Booker of New Jersey and former candidates Hillary Clinton and Bernie Sanders were all present.

To quote the late Saturday Night Live comedian Roseanna Roseannadanna, "things happen." That is especially true in Selma. Trying to wipe egg off their prosecutorial faces after a Dallas County Circuit Court dismissed indictments against Selma police officers Hardy, Neely, and Thomas, the Alabama Attorney General's office assembled a new grand jury on June 7, 2019 and rushed a re-indictment of the three. The alleged crime? Interfering with the AG's investigation, an absurd charge since these three were investigators themselves.

"Skullduggery at its worst," and a "blatant political prosecution," I proclaimed at a Selma news conference the following Tuesday, June 11. Firm attorney David Sawyer filed new dismissal motions we expect to be granted again. Afterwards speaking to the Selma City Council that evening, I slammed Selma police chief Spencer Collier for not supporting these officers, and added that Selma badly needed a new chief. Before the night was over, Collier agreed, and resigned.

Yet Selma lives on!

Most of all, my longtime dear friend, U.S. Congresswoman Terri Sewell, is always doing something to help Selma and the entire Black Belt area. So does her mother, Nancy Sewell, the first black female city councilwoman in Selma, also known for encouraging Terri and others to "bloom where you're planted."

No doubt Selma shall rise again! And bloom again!

18

Auburn University Defending

Auburn University is an honorable institution. It means well and often does many things exceptionally well. It graduates future leaders of Alabama and America. Just look at Tim Cook, who heads up the industrial giant Apple corporation. One of my sons-in law, Jules Plucker V, is an Auburn grad and does excellent work in Huntsville for the Army Corps of Engineers. Being an Auburn man or woman means something special.

Yet even so, as big as it is, the former Alabama Polytechnic Institute sometimes has difficulty curbing certain excesses and teaching managers and academics not to violate federal laws against race, sex, age, and disability discrimination as well as the Family Medical Leave Act. This failure has sometimes cost it dearly. The constitutional rights of due process, freedom of speech, and so on have sometimes tripped Auburn up as well.

As described in my earlier books, I have represented or counseled more than three hundred Auburn faculty members from the early 1980s on. The past few years covered in this volume were no exception to the Auburn cases knocking on my door in yesteryear. No doubt some Auburn deans or department heads can't help stepping on toes. Other leaders care, but don't realize they have a problem. I respect Auburn greatly, but like any educational institution, especially one of its mammoth size, it has difficulty controlling all its arms and legs.

This keeps employment lawyers like me in business. I generally represent the plaintiff's side, ably assisted by partners Kenneth Shinbaum, Joe Guillot, and associate attorney Chase Estes, and also, more recently, by two attorneys of counsel to the firm, Tanika Finney and David Sawyer. Meanwhile, Auburn's lawyers, both in-house and external, do their best to guide and steer this land grant university "against the tide" (pun intended) of problems.

Auburn is very well represented by a stable of Balch & Bingham attorneys, led by veteran attorneys David Boyd, Dorman Walker, and Kelly Pate, all of whom are professional, polite, and effective. I love to joke and kid around with Kelly about the famous time she jumped in a pool, fully clothed, to help save a couple of struggling children. And Dorman Walker, despite his effective opposition on the issues, has always been a prince of a fellow to work with. We, too, laugh about things.

"Legislators and judges make the law," I tell many clients, "and we attorneys only interpret it."

I have to wonder, however. Sometimes, legal potholes at universities like Auburn are difficult to foresee or navigate; sometimes they are so wide open, one must be blind or insensitive not to see them. At least that's what some of the following cases reflect.

VERONICA CHALOUPKA

Let's start with Veronica Chaloupka, a fifty-five-year-old black female hired by Auburn in 1996 as a bookkeeper and eventually promoted to IT server database administrator.

Chaloupka came to see me on March 23, 2017. She had already filed her own race discrimination complaint with the Equal Employment Opportunity Commission (EEOC) in 2016. She was the only black employee under her manager's supervision. She reported being "publicly belittled," "yelled at," and denied the respect and dignity her white co-workers enjoyed. She was also denied valuable training accorded her white co-workers.

Informal negotiations accomplished nothing, so we filed suit. Auburn agreed to mediate through EEOC mediator Jonathan Jones. Long story short, this was successfully resolved with confidential terms. My client was happy, and so was my firm.

REGINA HUTCHINSON & CAMERON BOOZER

Soon afterwards two African American employees of Auburn's "Campus Safety and Security Office" came to see me. Although they knew each other, neither knew the other was consulting me. First was Regina Hutchinson, on June 29, 2017, followed by Cameron Boozer, on October 16, 2017.

The complaint they both shared was that acting head of the Safety and Security Office, Chance Corbett, a Caucasian male, had become interim executive director in May 2016 and was creating bad waves. Hutchinson insisted that, almost immediately upon Corbett's securing his leadership post, he subjected her to a racially cold and hostile working environment and treated her disrespectfully, especially when compared to her Caucasian counterparts. She set forth ample particulars, but defense motions challenging Hutchinson argued she was not specific enough. She complained about disparate discipline (a white co-worker caught sleeping on the job was protected by Corbett, while Hutchinson was docked pay and scrutinized over much less). Hutchinson also questioned Corbett's constant belittling and badgering.

Hutchinson also filed an unlawful retaliation charge under EEOC law, saying the hostile treatment she received at Auburn increased after it was served with her original EEOC charge. Originally we drew Charles Coody, a fair magistrate judge, but when his daughter Emily Marks was appointed to the court, Coody was off the case. Soon Emily was on, but I was dismayed that our new young magistrate judge is Gray Borden, whom I have discovered is ultra-conservative, pro-employer, and can be difficult on discovery issues.

Citing circumstantial evidence, or pattern and practice evidence, Hutchinson also pointed out the unfair treatment experienced by Cameron Boozer.

Boozer also came to see me, on his own initiative, about a case of his own. A 6'11" star forward-center on Auburn's 1990–93 basketball team, the soft-spoken Boozer had ample law enforcement experience in Georgia before being recruited to Auburn's Campus Safety and Security Office. By 2016, Boozer supervised twenty-six employees, the largest number of any division of the Safety and Security department. Yet the politically connected Corbett (son of the late State Senator Danny Corbett) had become interim director of the department. Corbett was stepping on toes, primarily black toes. After coming on board, Corbett received a substantial raise, as did other white administrators, but not Boozer or Hutchinson.

A new associate director position of Campus Security opened up in 2017. Corbett completely bypassed Boozer in the selection process, in favor of three white applicants, despite Boozer's far better credentials. Adding insult to injury, Corbett picked Tony Dean, a white male out of Faulkner University of Montgomery, with minimal credentials and no experience in Auburn's Security Services. Boozer was even required to train Dean, even though Boozer was not a finalist for the job. With my help, Boozer filed his EEOC charge on October 30, 2017, citing, among other things, that Dean received the job without first being cleared by Auburn's EEO office, normally a formal requirement.

Boozer confirmed Hutchinson's observation that Chance Corbett significantly favored white employees, surrounding himself with them, especially in higher-level positions. While conceding that Corbett was too smart to openly use racial epithets, both clients believed Corbett's discriminatory moves were racially based, obvious, and painful.

Both Hutchinson and Boozer received right-to-sue letters in 2018, and we filed lawsuits against Auburn University on May 15, 2018, and July 6, 2018, respectively. Entering 2019, both cases were still tied up on motions claiming lack of specificity. Not until January 7 did one of the assigned magistrate judges, Wallace Capel, issue any rulings, and then it was to dismiss Boozer's "cold and hostile working environment" claim. His primary race discrimination claim remained intact.

As of May 28, 2019, both Hutchinson's and Boozer's cases were still tied up in court on pending motions to dismiss.

MICHAEL STERN AND JOSEPH MAJDALANI (NOT MY CLIENTS)

While compiling this chapter, I was interested to read a September 23, 2018, article by reporter Melissa Brown in the *Montgomery Advertiser* reflecting that I am not the only attorney pursuing discrimination claims against Auburn University. Michael Stern, a professor and former chair in Auburn's economics department, filed a wrongful retaliation and whistle-blowing suit against Auburn on First Amendment grounds. He alleges years of internal administrative battles related to a scandal involving Auburn's public administration major and star athletes. The case drew upon a *Wall Street Journal* exposé in 2015.

Shortly thereafter, also in 2018, I read in the *Birmingham News* that another former client of mine, Auburn University engineering professor Joseph Majdalani, with the assistance of a different attorney, had filed suit in the U.S. District Court for the Middle District of Alabama. He said several Caucasian co-workers refused to accept him as chair of Auburn's Aerospace Engineering department, opposed his efforts, disrespected his authority, called him slurs, excluded him from gatherings, etc.

While Magdalani had come to me first, I am glad to see other Alabama attorneys besides my firm taking on Auburn. McPhillips Shinbaum gets the bulk of this work, but we cannot handle it all.

WANDA JURRIAANS, MARGARET ODOM, SALLY HOOKER, WANDA CARPENTER, AND MELANIE ALLEN

In 2016, seventy-three-year-old Wanda Jurriaans of Oxford (near Anniston) was the first of several older, discontented female clients who came into my office. She was joined in late 2017 by Margaret Odom of Chatom in Washington County, sixty miles north of Mobile. A highly intelligent woman, Margaret is married to an astute attorney, Harold Odom, whose roots go back seven generations to the settlers of St. Stephens, the early territorial capital of Alabama (in 1817–19, when Washington was Alabama's biggest county).

As a land grant institution, Auburn University has a long and ongoing relationship with the Alabama Cooperative Extension Services (ACES), whose "county agents" and "home extension agents" provided farming and living advice to rural Alabamians. In pursuing both age and gender discrimination claims against ACES and Auburn, Odom was soon joined by Sally Hooker of Selma, in Dallas County; Wanda Carpenter of Dothan in Houston County, and Melanie Allen of Florence, in Lauderdale County. The four ACES staffers' jurisdictions each extended out over many other counties spread across the width and breadth of Alabama.

In similar EEOC charges issued in March and April 2018, Odom, Hooker, Carpenter, and Allen agreed in paragraphs three and four of their affidavits that:

ACES is, and has long been, very top-heavy with senior white men in its leadership positions. That includes Dr. Gary Lemme, 65, Director of ACES; Dr. Paul Brown, 58, Associate Director of ACES; and Stanley Windham, 60, Assistant Director of County Office Operations. ACES has recently (since August 2015) included Dr. Kyle Kostelecky, approximately 58 years old, Assistant Director of Family & Consumer Sciences. In addition to becoming a "good ole' boys network," I believe there is no coincidence that Dr. Lemme, Dr. Brown, and Dr. Kostelecky have ties to Iowa State University and the Midwest. It is interesting that Dr. Stephen Leath, recently installed as President of Auburn University is also from Iowa State. This has made it difficult at times for female employees like me to break through what has been a macho or male-dominated mindset which has been challenging for me as well as for other female ACES employees to penetrate.

This male-dominated mindset of ACES's organizational leadership has caused certain jobs at ACES to be unofficially considered "female jobs," and condescending attitudes make it difficult for different views of women to be taken seriously.

Receiving her right-to-sue first, Odom was the first to file suit. Just before Christmas, Hooker, Carpenter, and Allen also filed a suit jointly together against the Alabama Cooperative Extension Service, a part of Auburn University, and sought to consolidate their cases with Ms. Odom's suit, given the great commonality of facts and parties defendant.

Meanwhile, Wanda Jurriaans's case was tied up on a summary judgment motion battle, with Dorman Walker filing a fifty-five-page brief in favor of it, and us a 56-page brief in opposition. Dorman also sought to strike our supporting affidavits, to which we vigorously responded by brief filed on January 18.

In January 2019, the erstwhile Dorman also filed a motion opposing the four ladies consolidations, and Chase Estes filed an excellent response to keep Odom, Hooker, Carpenter, and Allen together. In March, the court granted the consolidation.

KRISTINA DATILLO

I also have a case filed against Auburn University by Kristina Datillo for a violation of the federal Rehabilitation Act because Datillo missed time from work with a health problem recognized as a disability. It was only filed in October 2018, and thus was still in the early stages when this book went to press.

Nonetheless, a deposition taken in May 2019 was very helpful to Datillo. We are proceeding under the Rehabilitation Act because Auburn University receives federal money. A misguided federal court ruling years ago made Auburn and other state entities no longer subject to the Americans with Disabilities Act (ADA) on employment cases. Fortunately, the Rehabilitation Act provides the same relief as the ADA.

19

Alfa the Bully

Power Corrupts

My history with Alfa Corporation goes back to 1976, when as a young assistant attorney general I took on its predecessor Alabama Farm Bureau Insurance Companies and its chief executive Ed Lowder. Battling on behalf of Attorney General Bill Baxley against four major Montgomery law firms defending the Farm Bureau-Lowder powerhouse, we won. As I discussed at greater length in *The People's Lawyer*, it was the talk of Montgomery's legal community at the time. Ed Lowder was so impressed, he later offered a big bucks contribution to my 1978 campaign for Alabama attorney general, which I turned down.

In the mid-1980s the Alabama Farm Bureau empire reinvented itself amidst a battle with the national Farm Bureau organization. The Alabama group dropped the Farm Bureau name in 1981 and dubbed itself Alfa Corporation. By 2016, the Alfa empire had swollen into one of the largest and most powerful insurance companies in Alabama, with millions of policies in its Property & Casualty division and $27 billion in force in its life insurance business.

According to political columnist Steve Flowers, Alfa is the "Big Dog" that "still walks the halls of the State House and . . . controls the legislature" (*Montgomery Independent,* August 9, 2018). Flowers added that Alfa "ran most of the races for their candidates, contributing up to $100,000 in a Senate race and $50,000 in a House race for candidates it supported. They

(Alfa) are the 'kings of Goat Hill,' the same way they were in 1901 when the State Constitution was written." Moreover, Alfa's lobbyist army keeps Alabama's property taxes low, thus depriving public education and other essential state services of badly needed tax dollars. Meanwhile, Alfa's profits soar every year.

Alfa also puts tons of money into federal campaigns that elect U.S. senators, who have the most say-so as to who gets nominated and approved as Alabama's federal judges. President Obama would not even nominate federal judges without the approval of Senators Shelby and Sessions, not to mention what President Trump wants in a federal judge.

Alfa has more than 2,300 employees, including more than 900 in its Montgomery headquarters. It operates 390 service centers in its central market states of Mississippi, Alabama, and Georgia. It promotes itself with the motto of "Alfa Cares." This public relations effort is a "year-round, company-wide initiative to recognize and encourage benevolence and service," to quote the company's website.

But how much does Alfa really care, and for whom does Alfa care, other than itself? The answer is in the famous quote by J. William Fulbright: "Power corrupts, and absolute power corrupts absolutely." And this applies to Alfa's outreach on both the state and federal levels.

FAITHFUL, TALENTED EMPLOYEE AXED FOR
EXCESSIVE HEALTH CARE COSTS

Enter Jennifer Akridge, a faithful Alfa employee for twenty-seven years, who had never worked for anyone else until Alfa unceremoniously dumped her at age forty-seven. Her annual appraisals reflected nothing but excellent performances, from beginning to the end. This included being "Alfa Employee of the Year" in 1995, and in her last year, she helped save Alfa $2 million in strategic underwriting costs. Nonetheless, a shocked Akridge was terminated by an ungrateful Alfa, without notice, on December 2, 2016, and ordered to immediately leave its building. She was physically escorted off the premises. Happening three weeks before Christmas, the ugly events left the single-parent mother—supporting her daughter in college—stunned in disbelief.

And why did this happen?

Akridge became disabled by multiple sclerosis in 1993, causing Alfa's self-insured healthcare costs on her behalf to soar to $11,000 monthly, including migraine headache coverage. When $133,000 annually was added to her $90,000 salary, the $223,000 total was not chicken feed. Notwithstanding her medical condition, Akridge always performed well the necessary duties and functions of her job.

Indeed, in terminating her, Alfa admitted Akridge's consistently excellent job performance but claimed her job elimination was due to "cutting costs company-wide." Yet no other Alfa employee was reorganized out of a job or fired at this time. Other comparable employees were transferred into new jobs. Despite her diverse experience over the years within Alfa, and jobs readily available in other departments in 2016, Akridge was offered no alternative work. At his deposition, supervisor Bob Plaster said Akridge "was just a number," and he confirmed that Alfa made no effort to find her a job elsewhere within the company.

JUST A NUMBER?

You guessed it. Akridge, a tall, slim Caucasian female then in her late forties, came to see me in December 2016, shortly after her termination. We filed a charge of disability discrimination with the Equal Employment Opportunity Commission (EEOC) in Birmingham. Unfortunately, one cannot obtain a right-to-sue letter until more than six months have passed. This gives the EEOC's cadre of overwhelmed investigators time to investigate, which usually means a woefully inadequate review.

Nonetheless, Akridge received her right-to-sue from the EEOC in July 2017, and we filed suit shortly thereafter under the Americans with Disabilities Act. In this regard I was greatly assisted by a recent member of the Alabama Bar, attorney Tanika Finney, who became of counsel to our firm in 2017.

Once we filed suit, I encountered the worst foot-dragging, evasiveness, stalling, and obstruction I have ever encountered from an opposition lawyer. Alfa had one of the best defense lawyers in Alabama in Tom Davis of Birmingham, who said he "had his marching orders." In September 2017 my first interrogatories and requests for production of documents were sent to the defense, which stalled and delayed, and then stalled and delayed some more, for the next nine months. This is a clever game some lawyers play.

BORDEN NO HELP

The stalling necessitated my filing two motions to compel production, which were both most unsatisfactorily handled by a young U.S. magistrate judge, Gray Borden. He did absolutely nothing to help, despite the obvious foot-dragging and Alfa's lame excuses for not answering. Judge Borden reflected the corporate defense lawyer background from which he came, namely the ultra big-business law firm of Lightfoot Franklin of Birmingham.

Notwithstanding his big-firm corporate background, Borden is the son of David Borden, who had helped me forty years ago when I ran for attorney general and is still a respected friend. Moreover, at a judge-lawyer luncheon at the courthouse before the case began, young Borden mentioned knowing one of my daughters from high school. Thus I had no reason to think he would be anything but fair when I agreed to let him serve as head judge on the case, rather than just as a magistrate, due to the shortage of available judges in the Middle District at the time.

I tried very hard to take the deposition of top Alfa human resources official Scott Forrest, since Alfa was claiming "automation" leading to "reorganization" as the reason for Akridge's termination. These topics are overwhelmingly human resources issues, thus key adverse witness Scott Forrest was especially relevant to our discovery, indeed our most important witness. Not surprisingly, Alfa attorney Tom Davis objected, but, most troublingly, Magistrate Borden kept agreeing with every reason Davis threw out as to why Forrest knew nothing and was thus irrelevant as a witness. It blew me away when over my strong objection, Judge Borden blocked me from taking Forrest's deposition. I was dumbfounded; it looked like Borden was solidly in Alfa's camp from day one.

We did not give up. Akridge had earlier issued an affidavit saying that Scott Forrest had asked her out for a date three years earlier, but she declined, and that afterwards he gave her the cold-shoulder treatment, deliberately shunning her every time they passed by one another, which was fairly frequent. No wonder Forrest didn't want his deposition taken. Especially by me; he might have been afraid I'd turn him every way but loose. If that was his concern, he was right.

Given the three-years since the attractive Akridge had turned down Forrest's date offer, pursuing a pure sexual harassment case would have been difficult, made even trickier since Forrest didn't sexually provoke or harass her by words or hand contact. All he did was ask her out for a date, which was not illegal or actionable on the surface. When Akridge refused, she gave no thought to complaining to the next highest Alfa official, namely its president, with its potential boomerang effect. Then several years had passed with nothing more negative than the shunning by Forrest. However, Alfa's contemplated termination of Akridge finally gave Forrest his chance for retaliation. Thus Alfa drummed up a perfect excuse, saying it had decided to "cut back its costs," as if this was the first time it had ever done so.

Notwithstanding, even as several new good reasons emerged for taking Forrest's deposition, Judge Borden kept blocking it. He kept accepting Davis's objection, based on Forrest's affidavit that he "didn't know anything about why Ms. Akridge was fired." In our opinion, this was a bald-faced lie that we could easily prove, but Magistrate Borden wouldn't let us take the deposition essential to our case. At the very least, Forrest knew more about Alfa's human resources procedures than anyone else. That was his job at Alfa. Indeed, Forrest's knowledge in this realm, and his inactions and actions, were central to our case from the beginning.

Even for a huge corporation like Alfa, saving $223,000 annually (Akridge's $90,000 salary, plus her six figure health insurance costs) was significant.

So why did Gray Borden appear so determined to take sides in our case? One can only speculate. Fortunately, there are First Amendment freedom of speech guaranties that protect me in raising this out-of-court question. I was always, and will remain so, respectful in court, including certainly to Judge Borden. He was always polite. It is risky for me to speak out as I am doing, even in the genre of this book. At such a young age, Borden will likely be around for a while longer, and even at age seventy-two, I hope to have some good years left, and our firm may have other cases with him. Thus I should not speculate, and won't, leaving others to draw conclusions about why Akridge's case was treated so harshly by young Borden.

Federal judges, even lower-level magistrate judges, have more power than most public officials, but they are not above the law. Just look at Mark Fuller, a few years ago a U.S. district court judge in the Middle District of Alabama. Fuller twice beat up on his wives, ran an outside business with a U.S. courthouse address, and was forced off the court in disgrace. But before that, with a mean, retaliatory spirit for a certain outcome, Fuller sabotaged Don Siegelman's criminal trial every way he could and gleefully sentenced the former governor to seven years in federal prison for something that was not really a crime (see Chapter 24). I'm not comparing Borden to Fuller, but judges should not be above fair comment, and this chapter falls in that realm.

Back to the Akridge case. We took depositions of four other Alfa officials on June 11–13, 2018. Three were Jennifer's supervisory managers: Tommy Coshatt, Beth Chancey, and Bob Plaster. The fourth was Alfa corporate representative Susie White, who was a former employee of Judge Borden's father's accounting firm; we tried to get Judge Borden to recuse himself for that reason, but he refused. In any case, I peppered the Alfa team with many human resources questions none could fully answer. Only Scott Forrest had the answers, but again he was barred by Magistrate Borden from having to submit to my deposition request.

I still managed to squeeze out some helpful answers from Coshatt, Chancey, Plaster, and White. They admitted that despite automation most of Akridge's job responsibilities continued to exist and had to be handled by other people. These higher managers also confirmed that other workers in the same underwriting department, whose job duties were also "supposedly automated and eliminated," nonetheless ended up with alternative work, either in the same department or another department. The difference was that none of these other employees had expensive disabilities, requiring self-insured Alfa to pay so much money every month for their health costs.

Even more amazing is that during the year preceding her termination, Akridge was the strategic underwriting coordinator who helped save Alfa as much as $2 million. Yes, she really did. Talk about Alfa's lack of gratitude! Her seven-figure productivity was confirmed by Akridge's immediate supervisor, Bob Plaster. In his June 2018 sworn deposition, Plaster blurted, "I'm sure it did" help save Alfa that money.

Revealing how closely related Akridge's termination was to her medical problems of multiple sclerosis and migraines is that for one and a half years after her termination in December 2016, Alfa was responsible under COBRA law for paying all Akridge's medical costs, well into the tens of thousands of dollars per month. Although Alfa was self-insured, under its contract with Blue Cross as plan administrator, Alfa could approve or disapprove Akridge's continued treatment. Thus, Alfa revealed its significant motivation for getting rid of her. If Alfa wanted to "cut costs," especially long-term, this was one big way to do it. Yet if saving Akridge's health care costs was Alfa's motive, it smack dab violated the Americans with Disabilities Act and ERISA protections. When asked at his deposition about Alfa's reaction to Akridge's high cost of health insurance, Plaster said, "I'm sure they (Alfa) were concerned about the numbers."

After Alfa's COBRA obligation to Akridge expired in June 2018, she was no longer covered by any health insurance, neither for her multiple sclerosis nor her migraines. She has been painfully hurting ever since, scurrying to local pharmacies for cheaper and inadequate "over the counter" medicines. Since 1993, Jennifer had tried over "250 medications from doctors to treat her migraines," but none worked as well as the costly medications she could get while she was insured.

The smoking gun proving Akridge health care costs were the real reason for her termination was Alfa's decision in August 2017 (in the middle of her COBRA extension) to discontinue the expensive MS medicines she previously had taken.

RENEWED MOTIONS TO TAKE FORREST DEPOSITION DENIED

On July 16, 2018, I filed a renewed motion for the court to order Alfa to produce Scott Forrest as a deponent, quoting supervisor Bob Plaster that the decision to eliminate Akridge's job "came from Alfa president Jimmy Parnell on down." That "on down" group certainly included executive vice-president Scott Forrest, given his human resources speciality and his next-in-rank proximity to Parnell. On July 23, 2018, Judge Borden again denied the motion. Why?

With clients Jennifer Akridge (far right) and Robert Doll (far left) and Andy Bell (center), chairman of the Alabama-Mississippi Chapter of the National Multiple Sclerosis Society, August 2018.

On August 9, 2018, aided by newly associated attorney David Sawyer, I filed a "Petition for a Writ of Mandamus" in the Eleventh Circuit Court of Appeals in Atlanta. We asked the appeals court to order Judge Borden to allow us to take Forrest's deposition. About a month later, the Eleventh Circuit denied the petition, based on its misunderstanding of Borden's magistrate status. The Eleventh Circuit mistakenly believed a "higher than Borden" district judge in Montgomery could review Borden's ruling and overturn it. Unfortunately, this could not be done, due to the earlier-mentioned agreement between Alfa's attorney and me in January 2017, allowing Borden to preside as head judge for the entire case.

Akridge's situation and story was significant beyond herself. It extended to countless other multiple sclerosis patients across America (including one of my nephews). Not only was the Americans with Disabilities Act designed to prevent such maltreatment, but so were other federal laws, under ERISA, which we tried to amend in, but once again Judge Borden rejected our motion.

Given the public health issues involved and with at least three clients with MS issues, we finally deemed it appropriate to take this to the court of public opinion. So David and I held a news conference on August 13, 2018, in my office with several key officials present, including Andrew Bell, executive director of the Alabama-Mississippi chapter of the National Multiple Sclerosis Society. Also present were Montgomery County Commissioner Dan Harris and Montgomery City Councilman Tracy Larkin. They spoke briefly, as did Robert Doll, another multiple sclerosis sufferer whom I represent on a disability discrimination case against Weyerhaeuser Corporation. Even Akridge answered a few questions.

Also present were many press representatives, including NBC, ABC and CBS News, *Montgomery Advertiser* reporter Melissa Brown and AL. com journalist Michael Cason. I said: "It is a vast understatement to say that Jennifer is a 'David,' fighting against the Goliath of Alfa. . . . It is a joke for Alfa to claim it cares; Alfa truly cares only about its own pocketbook."

Finally, on August 22, 2018, we received the anticipated motion for summary judgment by Alfa. David and I filed a motion under Federal Rule 56 (d)(2) to conduct additional discovery on the health insurance costs of Alfa for Akridge and other employees. A necessary component was to take Forrest's deposition. Uncompromisingly, Alfa attorney Tom Davis still strongly opposed it. Magistrate Borden set the motion down for a hearing in his Montgomery courtroom on October 23. For the first time in two years, our pending motions made it to an open courtroom and a face-to-face meeting with Borden.

At this open court hearing with others present, Judge Borden, for the first time, showed some semblance of even-handedness, granting us the right to take a further deposition of a yet-to-be disclosed "corporate representative of Alfa." Although Borden was always polite on the surface, he kept denying us the right to depose key witness Scott Forrest.

Alfa counsel Tom Davis finally agreed to December 5 for the corporate representative deposition, but continued his fourteen-month refusal to produce important documentary information. Accordingly, on November 20, we filed a motion to obtain those documents, but Judge Borden quickly snuffed it out. We even filed a motion to reconsider, asking that, if he denied it again, would he please certify the question to the Eleventh Circuit in Atlanta. Yet six days later he ruled against us again and would not certify the question. What an uneven playing field my co-counsel Tanika Finney, David Sawyer, and I were on.

Finally, the deposition date arrived. Yet Alfa sprang yet another trick on us. Its corporate representative turned out to be none other than, Susie White, whose deposition we had taken six months earlier. White was a veteran corporate representative, groomed by Alfa counsel to give rubber-stamp denials to Alfa's employment suits. This former Aldridge Borden employee, now a lead Alfa representative, knew well how to pirouette, to act like she knew nothing, and how not to testify on what senior Alfa management had told her. Worse, Alfa's attorneys continuously interrupted with objections, drowning me out with their instructions to White not to answer my questions.

The excuse of Alfa's attorneys was that they were always present when White talked to the executives. Thus the attorney-client privilege extended as the Alfa attorneys continuously objected to my questions. What a charade! Whatever happened to federal discovery rules? The high-powered and well-paid Birmingham lawyer Davis had previously told me he had his "marching orders." His hide-and-seek tactic rendered the attempted additional deposition a complete waste of time and money.

We even produced ERISA documents to Judge Borden clearly stating that Scott Forrest was the "final decision-maker" in what happened to Akridge. Once again the Court refused to consider this as a new important ground for taking Forrest's deposition. Two big questions had emerged: why did Forrest want to hide, and why was Judge Borden going to such great lengths to protect him?

After much hard work, on January 18, 2019, David, Tanika, and I filed our brief in opposition to summary judgment. It was forty-three pages, chock full of case authorities and factual citations supporting Akridge's position, based on depositions, affidavits, and legal research. We naively hoped that despite Judge Borden's one-sided treatment he would have to deny summary judgment. The facts were overwhelmingly in our favor.

Summary Judgment Standard

I knew that, under the standards for granting or denying summary judgment, this one should never have been even a close question. If anything, summary judgment should have been in our favor. At the very least, there were ample questions remaining for a jury to decide.

Here's what the law on summary judgment says. Rule 56(a) of the Federal Rules of Civil Procedure (FRCP) allows summary judgment *only* "if the movant [in this case, Alfa] shows that no genuine dispute exists as to any material fact and the movant is entitled to judgment as a matter of law." Case law precedent, which a judge must follow, provides precise standards as follows:

The court must draw all reasonable inferences in favor of the nonmoving party [that would be Akridge]. *Standard v. A.B.E.L. Servs., Inc.,* 161 F.3d 1318, 1326 (11th Cir. 1998). The trial court's function at this juncture is not "to weigh the evidence and determine the truth of the matter but to determine whether there is a genuine issue for trial." *Anderson v. Liberty Lobby, Inc.,* 477 U.S. 242, 249-50, 106 S. Ct. 2505, 91 L. Ed. 2d 202 (1986). Unfortunately, Borden "weighed the evidence." Further, the Eleventh Circuit in Atlanta has stated:

> A dispute about a material fact is genuine if the evidence is such that a reasonable fact-finder could return a verdict for the nonmoving party. Id. At 248; [A jury could easily have done this for Akridge] see also *Barfield v. Brierton,* 883 F.2d 923, 933 (11th Cir. 1989).

The guiding standard of the Eleventh Circuit, the highest appellate Court short of the U.S. Supreme Court, is:

> In reviewing whether the nonmoving party has met its burden, the court must stop short of weighing the evidence and making credibility determinations of the truth of the matter. Instead, the evidence of the non-movant is to be believed, and all justifiable inferences are to be drawn in his favor. *Tipton v. Bergrohr GMBH-Siegen,* 965 F.2d 994, 999 (11th Cir. 1992)

In *Offshore Aviation v. Transcon Lines, Inc.*, 831 F.2d 1013, 1016, the Eleventh Circuit Court proclaimed the rule of law:

> [C]redibility determinations, the weighing of evidence, and the drawing of inferences from the facts are the function of the jury. . . . *Graham v. State Farm Mut. Ins. Co.*, 193 F.3d 1274 (11th Cir. 1999). If the record presents factual issues, the court must not decide them; it must deny the motion and proceed to trial. *Herzog v. Castle Rock Entm't*, 193 F.3d 1241, 1246 (11th Cir. 1999). Summary judgment is not appropriate where the record, taken as a whole, could lead a rational trier of fact to find for the nonmoving party. *Miller v. Kenworth of Dothan, Inc.*, 277 F.3d 1269, 1275 (11th Cir. 2002).

Our brief stated that, by all the legal precedents cited above, summary judgment against Jennifer Akridge would be denied. We also cited the Eleventh Circuit case of *Beard v. Annis*, 730 F.2d 741, 743 (1984), holding that, in employment cases, involving as they do nebulous questions of motivation and intent, summary judgment is inappropriate for resolving claims.

It was not as if Alfa didn't know about Akridge's disability and its related costs. The record was replete with evidence reflecting that all Alfa managers over Akridge knew she had a multiple sclerosis disability. The record was also clear that Alfa terminated her due to this disability. There was really no other plausible, reasonable, or logical explanation. And that was thus a clear-cut violation of the Americans with Disabilities Act.

Alfa was openly sensitive about saving medical costs, given its self-insurance and another piece of smoking-gun evidence, namely that Alfa had "warned its employees to be careful about such costs." This was proven by Alfa's action during Akridge's COBRA extension, when in August 2017, eight months after termination, Alfa canceled Akridge's prescribed medication, even though she was still on the policy.

More favorable evidence for Akridge was that a "comparator" person existed in Akridge's underwriting department, Hillary McCaleb, who was affected by the same automation as was Akridge. Yet McCaleb was moved to another job, along with several other underwriting department employees. None, however, cost Alfa as much money for disability treatment. All these other employees quickly obtained alternate jobs with Alfa. Moreover, Akridge's immediate superiors acknowledged at their depositions that many of her responsibilities were not eliminated by automation. So why was she removed?

Alfa's "stated reason" for eliminating Akridge's job was to "reduce costs and reorganize the Underwriting Department." That was a tricky subterfuge of wordage that legally is called "pretext." Indeed, Akridge's job elimination did save Alfa money, but by eliminating her high medical costs that were much more than her salary—not from any Alfa automation, which had been ongoing almost daily for two to three decades.

In sum, there was a boatload of evidence, direct and indirect, that Akridge's disability was the primary reason for her involuntary termination. It was at least a significant and motivating factor, more than enough to defeat summary judgment.

Shocked but Not Surprised

How naive we were! On February 20, Judge Borden issued a twenty-two-page memorandum opinion and accompanying order, granting summary judgment for Alfa against Akridge, snatching our case away from a jury, and taking it from us. Yes, we were shocked and dumbfounded, but not surprised. As David Sawyer observed, Judge Borden totally ignored our facts, evidence, and arguments, and simply parroted everything Alfa chirped. It felt like highway robbery.

Despite the prior bad experiences with Judge Borden, I had felt deep in my gut that our summary judgment brief was the best I had filed in my forty-eight years as an attorney. David, Tanika, and I pored over every page, checking and cross-checking the facts and laws.

Magistrate Borden effectively made himself the one and only juror and took the case away from the six jurors who could decide. If he believes he did no wrong, then he must live with his conscience, especially if his ruling leads to a premature demise for Akridge.

As for Alfa? . . . it appears to have no conscience.

How many more Jennifer Akridges, though excellent, superb employees, must suffer through such disabilities as multiple sclerosis without medical insurance? Yes, the world is not fair, but the federal court is supposed to be. Here it allowed the powerful Alfa to make a mockery of the Americans with Disabilities Act, enacted by the U.S. Congress.

FILING ELEVENTH CIRCUIT BRIEF

David and I filed a fifty-two-page appeal brief with the Eleventh Circuit on May 6, 2019. After discussing the discovery issues, the circumstantial facts favoring Akridge were summarized:

Akridge consistently received excellent evaluations, yet did not receive any annual evaluation in November 2016. Alfa's executives and supervisors well knew about her disability. Alfa knew the costs of Akridge's prescribed medications. Alfa had been involved in automation since 1986, while Akridge worked individually with Alfa's agents and district managers to reduce losses and costs, taught Alfa workshops, provided monthly reports to Alfa's agents, and educated agents by people-to-people contact. These circumstantial facts scream!

Alfa produced no evaluation or other document indicating that Akridge's services were no longer needed. Alfa immediately terminated Akridge without notice. Alfa's termination documents were addressed to Scott Forrest, Alfa's HR Director, who had access to all employees' medical costs. Ms. Susie White spoke with Scott Forrest about Akridge's termination, which had previously been discussed for some time before it was implemented. These circumstantial facts also scream.

Alfa's entire "senior leadership" including Scott Forrest, decided to eliminate jobs and expenses. Yet, Alfa singled out, with a mark on its employees with higher medical costs, suggesting they were being targeted. (Doc. 126-1 Pg 17); (Doc. 126-2, Pgs 77-84).While Alfa's policy is to check for other opportunities within its organization, Alfa never considered transferring Akridge to another job, nor provided her the opportunity to apply for another job. Susie White stated that Akridge, after 27 years of diverse experience at Alfa, would not "be a fit" for another job. These additional circumstantial facts help make Ms. Akridge's case.

Ms. White knew of no other jobs eliminated in December, 2016; and for the four-year period prior to Akridge's termination, Alfa eliminated only two other underwriting jobs, and eliminated not a single marketing job. Alfa's number of employees increased during the period from 2013 through 2017. Following Ms. Akridge's termination, Alfa continued to post jobs and hire new employees, but never contacted Ms. Akridge to ask if she were interested. Again, these circumstantial facts bellow out, as do the following:

Ms. Chancey never asked Ms. Akridge about other type work or job responsibilities she could perform at Alfa; and Al Dees, Vice President of Alfa's Marketing Department, advised Akridge, upon her termination, that he had already created two positions for 2 other people coming from the Underwriting Department (Kayla Dill and Emily Davenport), and could not create another one.

Other employees in Alfa's Underwriting Department affected by the Guidewire automation retained their jobs and their salaries remained unchanged. Alfa gave Ms. Akridge's duties to others in her department. Alfa allowed Ms. Hillary McCaleb, the comparator with a similar position on the "property/ home" side of underwriting, to keep her job. Finally, while Ms. Akridge was on COBRA following her termination, Alfa cancelled her previously covered medication for treating her disability.

Let you, the reader, be a juror! Please decide if this was fair.

HANDICAPPING THE HANDICAPPED

By handicapping our case with such an uneven playing field, and by continually blocking us from taking the deposition of key witness Scott Forrest, Judge Borden caused my handicapped client to suffer much pain and legal wrong, after Alfa first did the same to her.

Our filing an appeal to the Eleventh Circuit was no problem for Alfa. With all its financial might, it can easily weather the appeal. Not so easily, Akridge. She is hurting from the lack of appropriate medication, with barely the resources for a much cheaper and less effective brand. Her migraine headaches have flared again, especially with all the tension and unfairness. On Easter weekend of 2019, Akridge said the first two days, Friday and Saturday, were "very very painful," but she felt better by Easter Sunday.

It has been tough for Jennifer to pay litigation expenses, while paying her attorneys nothing for the many hundreds of hours of work between David Sawyer, Tanika Finney, and me. Of course, we knew when we took her case on a contingency basis that it was risky and we would be paid nothing unless we recovered more than the $47,000 severance base Alfa offered her in December 2016. But we assumed we'd be on an even playing field.

We also knew the risk of standing up to the financial gargantuan that is Alfa, but we didn't realize how unfairly things would go with a magistrate judge, sitting as a full district court judge. This, of course, is our opinion, and it is daring to express it. I still retain the greatest respect for all the other federal judges in Montgomery, who are paragons of integrity. They have always treated me fairly, even when ruling against my client.

LIFE GOES ON

After filing our appeal to the Eleventh Circuit, wouldn't you just know that on that same day, March 5, 2019, Alfa filed a "Defendant's Motion for Attorney Fees and Sanctions" against plaintiff Akridge and her counsel, that is, David, Tanika and me, "pursuant to 42 United States Code and this Court's Own Inherent Power." This was adding insult to injury. Alfa also filed a "Bill of Costs," seeking reimbursement for its deposition expenses of almost $2,000, a more normal filing.

The sanctions motion was obviously an attempt by Alfa to scare us off from pursuing an appeal. Alfa's strategy and hope, not unique, is that we might trade away the appeal to avoid potential sanctions and fees against our client and us. Amazingly, the motion for sanctions was based primarily on our repeated efforts to take Scott Forrest's deposition. This again reflects what an out and out bully Alfa is.

It is our humble opinion that unless the Eleventh Circuit reverses this case, Alfa and Judge Borden will have succeeded in completely gutting the Americans with Disabilities Act, at least in the Middle District of Alabama.

Life goes on, but this story is not yet finished. We pray that God will help Akridge and us ultimately reach a better resolution against this injustice. In this regard, we are comforted by the Epistle of James 1:2 and will never forget Luke 6:37.

20

Tuskegee University Struggling

The Tuskegee Institute of Booker T. Washington and George Washington Carver was a great citadel of learning well before the civil rights movement of the 1950s and 1960s further energized its meaning and purpose.

Tuskegee (now University) has been a proud part of the HBCU (historically black colleges and universities) movement, respected as one of the best such schools in all America. Students from across the South and beyond have attended Tuskegee. Its professional schools, from veterinary medicine to architecture to engineering are first rate. Its liberal arts college is sound. Its football and basketball teams have won national championships. Its faculty and students have excelled on the world stage in science, art, music, literature, politics, and education.

Yet I've had to wonder what was going on when I kept getting contacted by professors, deans, coaches, and students claiming harassment, wrongful discrimination, and other misdeeds by the Tuskegee administration.

Several years ago, with the assistance of attorney Scott Golden (a former mayor of nearby Wetumpka, Alabama), I took on Tuskegee University on behalf of Leslie Porter, a former senior vice president of administration. After much persistence we achieved a great confidential settlement for him; Porter returned to his home base in Florida.

And then there was Coach Belinda Roby, an ultra-successful basketball coach wrongfully let go. She had led Tuskegee to a women's national basketball championship. She was beloved by students and faculty. Who knows what she did to deserve termination. The answer was nothing really. After sending Tuskegee a draft of the lawsuit we intended to file, the university caved in. Roby was all smiles, though the usual confidential settlement agreement language prevents me from saying more.

And then there was Dean of Liberal Arts Dr. Lisa Hill. Exceedingly astute academically and with an enthusiastic personality, how did this brilliant mind run afoul of the "powers that be." Somehow she did. She moved quickly to another exciting opportunity in northern Virginia. It was Tuskegee's great loss, but our firm's legal efforts made her departure much more comfortable than it otherwise would have been.

Likewise, Tuskegee's loss of Daya Taylor, former dean and department head in Tuskegee's Robert R. Taylor School of Architecture and Construction Science, should never have happened. She, too, sought my help. Law partner Joe Guillot shared the privilege of representing Taylor in attempting to right the wrongs she suffered. After depositions were taken, the case was resolved. Taylor had just given birth to her third child, had a prominent architectural job in Florida, and was ready to move on with her life.

While Taylor's case was pending, I was even retained to represent a member of Tuskegee's board of trustees, whose name will remain undisclosed. He said he was wrongfully defamed by another trustee and then subjected to a threatened termination. I agree that he was badly wronged. This mid-1970s trustee, African American like most other board members, was a former high public official from another state. The trustee was wrongfully challenged on issues the board failed to disclose to him, despite our repeated requests for information. Talk about lack of transparency. Understandably this trustee didn't take it lightly. Our client was fuming.

I tussled with a Washington, D.C., attorney representing the board of trustees. I even consulted my long-time friend Charles Price, knowing he was a former Tuskegee trustee and a now-retired Montgomery County circuit judge. My trustee client and I had a lawsuit ready to file if a Friday, July 13, 2018, vote went against him. At the last moment, the trustee, compelled by loyalty to Tuskegee University and not wanting to embarrass it, chose to voluntarily resign. I appreciated getting to know this good gentleman of conscience and conviction. Yet this brief representation gave me close, genuine insight into how disorganized is the state of Tuskegee trustee matters.

I now focus on an outstanding client who personifies it all, Vinaida Robnett, a senior African American faculty member. While she historically was very loyal to TU, unfortunately the university didn't reciprocate that loyalty.

Robnett first came to see me on March 19, 2015. Employed on Tuskegee's veterinary faculty since 1983, she had a distinguished academic record, a very likable personality, and looked much younger than her seventy years. For her modest annual salary of $57,847, the College of Veterinary Medicine received an extraordinarily good return. Robnett was an excellent teacher, beloved by students. She was also a scientific visualization specialist, a co-ordinator of projects, and an associate director of the Center for Computational Epidemiology Bioinformatics and Risk Analysis (CCEBRA). She led the team that redesigned and renovated a student study area, winning first place in an institutional design competition.

When Robnett first came to see me, she still had a job. I wrote Tuskegee President Brian Johnson. We articulated the mistreatment she was receiving from Dr. Patricia Patterson, financial manager of Tuskegee's veterinary teaching hospital.

My letter eased Robnett's problems for the next sixteen months or so. In the summer of 2016, she was even honored with appointment by the director of CCEBRA as the "person of contact for dignitaries." Unfortunately, Ms. Robnett's elation was short-lived. On August 31, 2016, she received a RIF (Reduction in Force) notice, costing her job. Tuskegee made no suggestion that her work performance was inadequate, and truly it could not, given her many accomplishments and deep popularity with students.

I carefully analyzed her plight. Certain facts stared me in the face. This was a "reverse national origin discrimination" case, if ever I saw one. Although we are in America, it was Robnett's American national origin that disadvantaged her in her own department. Amazing, but consider the numbers.

First, of the nine to ten people left in Tuskegee's BIMS/CCEBRA unit, Robnett was virtually the only native-born American. The non-natives included: Drs. Tsegaye Habtemariam and Berhanu Tameru and Mr. Addegid Bogale, all of Ethiopia; Dr. David Nganwa of Uganda; Dr. Ehsan Abdulla of Sudan; and Sunday Adalumo and Monday Offem, both of Nigeria. Two other women in the unit, one from Pakistan and the other from Nigeria, had recently transferred to other teaching areas of the College of Veterinary Medicine.

Robnett noticed that not only were the other employees mostly of African nationalities, they were also much younger than she. In an EEOC charge, we claimed wrongful discrimination, based on national origin and age.

Robnett also noted in her charge "that [reductions in force for budget reasons] had disproportionately hit female employees of Tuskegee University, including most recently Dr. Lisa Hill, dean of the College of Liberal Arts, Sarah Stringer, director of Career Development and Placement Services, and Belinda Roby, the very successful head coach of the female basketball team, as well as many others." Robnett thus alleged that she experienced a painful sex discrimination at Tuskegee. She specifically set forth in paragraph 11 of her EEOC charge:

> I am aware that President Brian Johnson, who sent me my letter of termination, is the subject of vast disapproval by the overwhelming majority of faculty staff, students and alumni at Tuskegee University. I attach hereto a petition of signatures of 349 supporters calling for the removal of President Brian Johnson. This petition was recently delivered to the Board of Trustees of Tuskegee University, as was a similar letter sent to the Board of Trustees calling for Dr. Johnson's removal. I have heard that Dr. Johnson's tenure at Tuskegee University may be short-lived.

The EEOC in Birmingham received Robnett's charge on September 30, 2016, and issued a right-to-sue letter on May 8, 2017. Attempts to negotiate proved unsuccessful. Hence we filed suit in the U.S. District Court for the Middle District of Alabama.

Long story short, before depositions were taken, a mediation was agreed to and occurred in March 2018. A confidential resolution was reached. Although not fully satisfied, my client received a measure of justice. However, Robnett's EEOC charge had proved prophetic with regard to TU President Brian Johnson—his successor took office in July 2018.

On November 5, 2018, I was called upon by long-time Tuskegee University professor Dr. Marshall Burns, a Caucasian seventy-three years old.

What a brilliant man! He had obtained his PhD in theoretical solid state physics from Kent State University in 1972. After teaching at Kent State and in New Jersey, Burns accepted an offer in 1976 from Tuskegee University to join its faculty as an assistant professor. He was promoted to associate professor in 1978, and to full professor by 1980. Burns was voted "Teacher of the year" by Tuskegee students and later named most outstanding professor by a panel consisting of the Tuskegee president and a committee of faculty. Textbooks that Burns wrote have been used by other colleges and universities throughout America. While lobbying for more funding, Tuskegee's administration displayed one of his books to the Alabama legislature as a sample of its astute scholarship.

Yet in 2018, after forty-two years of professorship, Burns was making only $60,500 annually. Meanwhile, much younger full professors, virtually all of a different race, color, or national origin, were being paid from $70,000 to $80,000.

Dr. Burns was an academic and a scholar, not a politician or legal advocate. He had nonetheless taken the underpayment issue to Tuskegee provosts and its president at least twelve times from the year 2000 to the present. The replies Burns received from the administration, while feigning sympathy, always cited reasons why funding was inadequate to pay him more.

Tuskegee, like Auburn University and many other colleges and universities, needs to be more concerned about the low salaries paid their faculty. The university receives ample funding and grants from the federal and state government, despite its status as a non-governmental entity. It also gets significant funding from private sources. Indeed, on November 7, 2018, I read in the *Birmingham News* that Birmingham-based Encompass Health had contributed $250,000 to fund scholarships for nursing and occupational therapy students at Tuskegee University. This is typical. Yet despite these state and federal grants, and healthy tuition amounts charged their students, Tuskegee doesn't pay its faculty nearly enough, as Dr. Marshall Burns's case reflects.

Has the great Tuskegee University been in decline? I hope not, though others contend to the contrary. Whatever, the university has been struggling. The powers-that-be at TU need to regroup and take a long hard look about what they can do to restore this storied school. As often as the university keeps changing presidents, hopefully the trustees have finally found the better leadership this historic institution needs in its new president, Dr. Lily McNair. I recently learned that she and I are fellow alumni of Princeton University, classes of 1979 and 1968, respectively. I wrote a nice letter to congratulate her and offered to help.

21

Merrill Todd

One excessive force case with strong racial overtones took exactly eight years, from August 2010 to August 2018, to be resolved in east Alabama. All the facts set forth in this chapter can be found in federal courthouse records, accessible to the public, mostly in an opinion written by senior U.S. District Judge Myron Thompson.

It began on a late summer day with the enforcement wing of the Alabama Alcoholic Beverage Board sweeping into the town of LaFayette, combining with the Chambers County sheriff's department and the La-Fayette police in a so-called "Joint Task Force." Typically, it did far more harm than good.

The worst victim of this police overkill was thirty-five-year-old Merrill Todd, a modest African American man guilty of "walking while black." He was not engaged in any crime and was never charged with one. His bevy of cousins had organized an extended family outing at the Club Blaze in LaFayette. Todd arrived early to help set up for the party. Food and alcoholic beverages would be served. It was simply a celebration, and good old family fun. One of Todd's cousins naively advertised the event on her Facebook page.

That was bait for the overwhelmingly white police entourage that showed up and came close to killing Todd.

Todd was in the parking lot in front of the building when he saw a string of law enforcement vehicles arriving. With only two days left on parole, he decided to slip away and avoid controversy or risk of being arrested. Accordingly Todd and cousin Brandon Story quietly withdrew to the back of the building, Todd just ahead of his relative.

As Todd rounded the corner, he saw the headlights of a truck bearing down on him from the opposite side of the building. Todd made a dash for the nearby adjacent woods. He never made it.

The next thing Todd remembers was waking up in the Lanier hospital in the nearby Langdale, Alabama, badly injured after being struck by a suddenly accelerating truck. He had also been beaten up by the cops, tasered, and chewed on by a police dog. Todd had two facial fractures, one to the bone surrounding his left eye that was splintered or crushed into numerous pieces. The other was to the side of his face near his ear. He endured multiple surgeries, with holes drilled in his skull. This resulted in long-term facial numbness and severe headaches, with sharp pains and blurred vision in his left eye.

This also damaged Merrill's memory. At deposition, he could remember much before the incident, and very little afterwards. Adding to his evidentiary woes was that none of his witnesses personally observed the assault, beating, and chewing. Yet there was a mountain of circumstantial evidence.

I didn't get involved until 2015. Todd reminded me that he first sought my help in 2010, but that I declined, for whatever reason. Later in 2015 I represented Mark Overall, the attorney who originally took Todd's case in 2010. I had helped Mark with disciplinary proceedings in 2014–15, but in late 2015 Mark decided to move to Maryland and urged me to take over Todd's case. I relented, first assigning the case to associate attorney Chris Worshek. But when Chris left our firm in mid-2016, the whole voluminous file bounced back into my lap.

Summary judgment motions filed in 2012 by the defense had been outstanding were still unruled upon three years later. Little did I realize the amount of work I had stepped into. There were three sets of diligent opposition attorneys fighting for the City of LaFayette, the Chambers County Sheriff's office, and the alleged individual wrongdoers. The governmental entities were subsequently dismissed, but thank God for U.S. District Court Judge Myron Thompson, a long-time hero.

In December 2017, five years after suit was filed, Thompson ordered all attorneys in the case to answer key questions related to liability. We submitted additional briefs.

Finally, on April 6, 2018, almost six years after the initial defense motions were filed, Thompson released a 107-page opinion, a magnum opus if ever I saw one. Written and footnoted like a book, Thompson laid out the case against the defendants. The opinion in *Merrill Todd v. Jerome Bailey* (3:12 CV-589-MHT (2018)) should be required reading for police cadets in training. Although Thompson dismissed co-defendants Jerome Bailey and Larry Clark, he wrote a strong opinion explaining why defendants Terry Wood and Steve Smith must stand trial before a jury. The circumstantial evidence was strong.

The defense attorneys artfully appealed Thompson's ruling to the Eleventh Circuit Court of Appeals in Atlanta. They raised the complicated "qualified immunity" doctrine as a defense. The opposing counsel also filed a $5,700 bill for deposition expenses leading up to the trial court's dismissal of the governmental entities and Clark and Bailey. I viewed both moves as strategic leverage, usable by the defense in future negotiations.

Not long after the appeals were filed, a telephone mediation occurred on July 30, 2018, with Atlanta mediator Clifford Alterkruise, defense at-torneys Robbie A. Hyde of Auburn and Jamie Kidd of Montgomery, and me at my Montgomery office. I was ably assisted by paralegal-office manager Amy Strickland.

While much legal work was behind me, I knew that if we didn't settle, we faced several big hurdles. First, the Eleventh Circuit could easily reverse and render the case against us in Atlanta, particularly on the qualified im-munity issue, notwithstanding Judge Thompson's brilliant opinion. The second was that, even if we won in Atlanta, we would still be going to trial, with several significant risks. One bad juror can do you in, or a large verdict at trial can be appealed again to the Eleventh Circuit where it could be chopped down or reversed.

Sometimes one's toughest challenge at a mediation is not the opposing counsel. Instead, it is one's own client. This was one of those times. At the end of Monday, July 30th, we were getting closer, but still not there. I had to leave Montgomery late the next day to pick up my granddaughter Laurel at Camp McDowell in North Alabama. The rest of the week Leslie and I would be in Huntsville with family.

Thanks to my Iron Lady of an office manager and paralegal, Amy

Strickland, with her tough charm in batting down medical providers' subrogation claims and helping to temper the expectations of Todd and his fiancé Candace, a settlement was finally reached on Thursday, August 2, 2018, by continued telephone mediation. The usual confidentiality clause limits us to saying that the case "was resolved." Nonetheless, Todd was smiling, and we, his legal team, were relieved.

22

Dee Parks, No Shrinking Violet

Inspired by Rosa Parks, her legendary cousin, Dee Parks is no shrinking violet.

I first met her about 2008 when she was running a restaurant, Mammanems, which specialized in Southern home-style foods and catering. Located on Carmichael Road, her restaurant's food was delicious. I also helped her resolve a few legal issues that had popped up. She was full of energy, with an engaging personality and relentless drive.

Thus I was not surprised to learn in October 2016 that she had built up a successful pharmacy business. Parks Pharmacy had two stores in Montgomery, one in Gadsden, and a convenience store operation in Hayneville.

Parks opened Parks Pharmacy in 2008 to fill a need in Alabama. As a small pharmacy, in contrast to the Walgreens, CVSs, and Rite-Aids of the world, she reached out to remote communities, especially those poor, black, and elderly, where the other pharmacies didn't care to go. She provided free courier service to clients who were immobile or mentally or physically challenged. Many came from low-income African American homes. Parks also engaged community members to research what they needed. She learned there was a need for novelty items, including beauty products. Accordingly, Parks opened a novelty store in Hayneville, the county seat of Lowndes County, one of the poorest parts of Alabama, southwest of Montgomery.

Parks's boundless energy encountered a major obstacle in 2015, when she ordered Alabama Board of Pharmacy investigator Glenn Wells to get out of her Gadsden store. That was after he had shown up, unannounced, without a warrant, and had started rifling through her records. Parks, in a bold, commanding voice, ordered Wells out and said the police were being called if he did not leave. This state investigator, from a different ethnic background and full of his own importance, didn't appear to take kindly to being so commanded by a black female, and soon the fight was on. Wells wasted no time in bringing the full force of the board down upon Ms. Parks.

Parks's impatience with investigator Wells's tactics accusing her of misdeeds at her variety store in Hayneville soon led to her being confronted by the power of the State of Alabama.

On a warpath that Parks considered racist, the Alabama Board of Pharmacy on February 5, 2016, issued a thirty-five-count "Statement of Charges and Notice of Hearing" against Parks and her pharmacies. A month later, the board, led by its long-time attorney Jim Ward, piled on eleven more charges. Following an August 2016 hearing, the board spewed out a final order on October 6, 2016, finding Parks and her pharmacies guilty on all counts.

The unprecedented punishment meted out by the Board of Pharmacy was way in excess of what the board normally did with anyone else:

Parks's owner's license to practice pharmacy and controlled substance permit was suspended for five years; the permits of her two Montgomery pharmacies and her Gadsden pharmacy were placed on probation for five years; and Parks individually was ordered to pay a fine of $27,000 and her three pharmacies $47,000 more. That totaled $74,000, a hefty fine for a scrappy businesswoman of modest resources.

On top of that, the board's investigator inspired a local client of Parks, Sara Tate, to file a class action malpractice and HIPAA violation suit against Parks and her pharmacies. The worst insult was the televised report on Montgomery's Channel 12, the local NBC affiliate, which is the most widely viewed news program in Alabama. It made Parks look negligent and stupid. I remember watching it myself and being astonished. This wasn't the Dee Parks I had known. Especially harmful was that the report was picked up by the national data board and became the basis for certain drug suppliers, like Cardinal and Leadernet, cutting off Parks and her pharmacies from badly needed supplies.

With all that weighing down on Parks, she came to see me in late October 2016. She unloaded her legal problems and her heart. What to do? Where to go? How to battle this plague of injustice?

Conferring in my office in Montgomery with, from right, client Dee Parks, attorney Tanika Finney, and Parks's associate, Necey Glover.

I listened to Parks. I looked at her paperwork and tried to decipher what was going on. I asked her why she didn't come to me first, since I knew attorney Jim Ward of the Alabama Board of Pharmacy, and maybe we could have headed some of this off. Dee replied that she did try to see me, but at the time I wasn't available. She saw another partner, and decided to go elsewhere.

I determined that we had two major pieces of legal work. The first was defending the class action suit. The even bigger battle was with the State Pharmacy Board. I involved law clerk Adam Andrews. His energy level, tenacity, and sensitivity to the racial aspects of the situation made him a good assistant, although he sometimes got into boisterous arguments with Parks.

I filed a Notice of Appeal on November 4, 2016, and followed it up with a petition for judicial review on November 22. By December 1, the

Circuit Court of Montgomery granted a stay of Parks's suspension, with agreement from the Board of Pharmacy.

My knowledge of the board's attorney, Jim Ward, came from forty years earlier when we had both worked under celebrated Alabama Attorney General Bill Baxley. Jim came from Minnesota originally. He is both quite smart and quite liberal, but headstrong. Although he was supposed to be only the board's attorney, and not a board member or executive director, everyone knew Jim was the "real power" at the pharmacy board. Talking to him by phone gave me an earful of how insulted Jim personally felt by Parks. Compromise was not on his radar screen.

At the same time, I started vigorously defending the class action suit. That included taking a revealing deposition of Sara Tate. Not surprisingly, she knew nothing about her case. Shortly thereafter the whole case was dismissed upon my motion for summary judgment, granted by Montgomery County Circuit Judge J. R. Gaines.

Undaunted, Parks was not satisfied with just having the suspension stayed. She wanted critical language about her on the State's Pharmacy Board website and the national data site NPBD removed. Meanwhile an ill Jim Ward missed two hearings on motions I filed in December. By early January 2017 Judge Gaines gave us the additional language on the "stay order" we wanted.

When attorney Ward recovered, that language sent him into orbit, causing him to file a petition for a writ of mandamus with the Alabama Court of Civil Appeals. After extended briefing over several months, the higher court on June 9, 2017, granted the board's petition on the procedural ground that the board had not been adequately heard in the lower court (*Ex parte Alabama State Bd. Of Pharm.*, 240 So. 3d 594 (2017)).

That really didn't hurt us that much, since Judge Gaines quickly ruled again in our favor. This sent Jim Ward screaming foul again. He petitioned again for writ of mandamus, claiming we were trampling upon federal pre-exemption rules in requiring the National Board to remove harmful language about Parks and her pharmacies. While the Court of Civil Appeals again ruled with Ward, it gave Parks the "gift" of ruling that the stay of Parks's suspension did not "endanger the public." Moreover, the court said the board itself never asserted that a denial of the stay was necessary to "protect the public" (*Ex parte Alabama State Bd. of Pharmacy*, 253 So. 3d 972 (2017)).

During this time, months were passing on, and Dee Parks kept working hard with her top assistant Necey Glover, augmented by occasional bursts of activity between Parks and my assistant Adam Andrews. However, by May 2017, Adam left to take the bar exam again. Taking his place and employing her bar licenses from Alabama and Georgia was a bright, young female attorney of African American descent, Tanika Finney, whose help was invaluable. I have called her "Manna from Heaven."

Meanwhile Parks pushed us into additional litigation on two fronts. The first was a lawsuit against Medicaid for not giving back her share of the costs she incurred in receiving Medicaid. Judge Roman Shaul dismissed the suit, despite an anguished opinion saying he would have ruled otherwise, had it not been for a recent change in a relevant statute.

We also had a collateral suit against the former major supplier of drug materials, Cardinal and its subsidiary Leadernet. After a year of duking it out in federal court on our claim of tortious interference with Parks's contracts and business relations, Cardinal agreed to a mediation with us in Atlanta. The mediator was the distinguished Judge Leah Sears, formerly the first and only black female chief justice of any state supreme court in America, when she held that office in Georgia. On June 19, 2018, Finney, Parks, Necey, and I piled in for an early morning car ride to Atlanta. The mediation went extremely well for us, and we dismissed the lawsuit. A confidentiality clause prevents us from saying more about the settlement.

Finally, on July 24, we were back in front of Judge Gaines to finalize our opposing positions on the still-pending issues before the court. Jim Ward showed up with the entire membership of his Alabama Board of Pharmacy, as if that would impress the court. I had Parks, Necey, and Finney with me. The judge gave both sides a month to file draft memorandum opinions and orders.

On November 7, coming back to my office from another case, I fielded a call from Parks. She had received Judge Gaines's opinion before I did, as Tanika Finney had earlier forwarded it to her while I was out. Parks blurted out, "I can live with this."

Indeed it was a great victory. Although Judge Gaines found there was a basis for the board's action against Parks and her pharmacies, he also found that the severe sanctions imposed against her were "arbitrary, capricious, and unreasonable, and were due to be modified under the authority of §41-22-20(k) of the Code of Alabama, 1975."

Hence, the suspension of Parks to practice pharmacy and her controlled pharmacy permit was reduced from the board's original five years down to three months. The five-year probations of her two Montgomery pharmacies and her Gadsden pharmacy were reduced from five years to one year. Finally, the fines levied by the Board of Pharmacy against her three pharmacies, originally totaling $74,000, were reduced to $1,000 each, for a total of $3,000.

Parks breathed a huge sigh of relief, and I did as well. It was great to help relieve a client of such an unnecessary and unjust burden.

I wrote Jim Ward, attempting to persuade him not to appeal Judge Gaines's ruling to the Alabama Court of Civil Appeals or eventually to the Alabama Supreme Court. I said "let's bury the hatchet," and I apologized for any of Parks's or my excesses (I had once referred to the board's action as a "legalized lynching," which had sent Ward into orbit again). It didn't work. The intransigent Ward appealed anyway, and in May 2019 Tanika and I were working hard on our reply brief.

Having defended against the Board of Nursing and other administrative agency appeals, I know we have a tough challenge. Prior Alabama appellate case law serves as precedent and guides newer high court decisions. Those decisions are replete that a "presumption of correctness" is due to an agency's "recognized expertise in a specific area," and that decisions cannot be reversed unless shown to be "clearly unreasonable or arbitrary" (*Hamrick vs. Alabama Alcoholic Beverage Control Board*, 628 So. 2d. 632 (1993)).

Unfortunately, on May 17, 2019, the Alabama Court of Civil Appeals continued its favored relationship with the Alabama Board of Pharmacy by ruling for it once again. Its opinion said the lower court did not adequately justify its ruling for Parker and reversed for a third time.

As this book went to press, Tanika and I were filing a motion with Judge J. R. Gaines to provide more information to the Court of Civil Appeals. Alternatively, we lawyers and client Parks were pursuing an appeal to the Alabama Supreme Court.

23

The Confederate Memorial Park

I have been a civil rights attorney most of my professional life, at least during the forty-four years since returning to Alabama in April 1975. Yet I am descended from at least four Confederate soldiers by the names of McPhillips, McGowin, Poole, and Dixon. Notwithstanding my heritage, I never had a moment's hesitation in enthusiastically representing two employees of the Confederate Memorial Park (CMP) in mounting a race discrimination case against the park. The mother body of the park is the Alabama Historical Commission (AHC), a state agency headquartered just two buildings north of my law office on South Perry Street in Montgomery. I respect the good work of the AHC.

The Confederate Memorial Park is in southeastern Chilton County, just north of the Elmore County line, about thirty north of Montgomery. It was founded in 1901 and has long been funded by an annual $1 million tax initially pledged to support a home for disabled and indigent Confederate veteran soldiers that operated on the same site until the 1930s.

The two employees were Anthony Toby, an African American man born in 1982, and Robert McDonald, a Caucasian man born in 1964. The pair got along remarkably well, even when the CMP kept putting pressure on both, or perhaps because the CMP put pressure on Toby because Toby was black, and then on McDonald for standing up for Toby.

I was first visited by the twosome in 2012. I helped them prepare charges of race discrimination and wrongful retaliation against CMP Executive Director Bill Rambo, who looked and acted like Nathan Bedford Forrest, a notorious Confederate general, former slave trader, and KKK leader during Reconstruction. The "N word" was occasionally used, and making fun of blacks also existed at the CMP. One egregious incident involved Rambo laughing out loud in the presence of others about a two-sided Christmas card he received. One side displayed a "White Man's Christmas" with a white family enjoying a large mansion and plenty of food. The other side displayed a "Darkie's Christmas" with a black man in dirty clothes carrying a possum on a stick to feed his family (this is in the public record in the federal courthouse).

The pair sought my assistance in combating a racist atmosphere. Ultimately, after meeting with the administrators at the AHC in 2013, the tension subsided temporarily. Rambo kept his job, as things cooled off a bit during 2014–16. But by 2017, the CMP atmosphere had heated back up, as both former clients came back to see me, describing their work at the CMP as a "living hell." They said Rambo screamed at them frequently.

Accordingly, in 2017, I filed a new charge of race discrimination for Toby and a race and retaliation charge for McDonald. Specific incidents were set forth, including harassment and negative treatment of Toby, compared to his white co-workers. McDonald said he was also denied a promotion that should have gone to him.

Both plaintiffs received rights-to-sue in late 2017, and accordingly suits were filed on March 14, 2018. Depositions were taken in November 2018. At deposition, Rambo testified that people think he looks like Nathan Bedford Forrest, that Forrest was a symbol to African Americans of a racist figure, and that Forrest had something to do with the Ku Klux Klan. Rambo also confirmed he didn't like McDonald sticking up for Toby and that he had stated in writing that both were "jerks."

As groundwork was being laid for trial, defense counsel Todd Hughes and I agreed to mediation before U.S. Magistrate Judge Wallace Capel Jr. Hence, we all gathered together in federal court on February 6, 2019, and hours later agreed to state that "this matter has been resolved to the mutual satisfaction of the parties." Accordingly, I make no further comment about this resolution, but one is free to draw his or her own conclusion.

I want to add that the Alabama Historical Commission is overall a very good state agency, one charged with necessary work across Alabama in preserving structures and places of historic value. My friends, both black and white, liberal, conservative, or independent, generally agree that this is important work.

24

Opening Up the Floodgates

In two news conferences in October 2018, attorney Melissa Isaak and I urged, "Return the $735,000 in illegal PAC to PAC transfer money," publicly calling upon Alabama's attorney general to do so.

The Alabama legislature passed a law in 2013 banning such transfers between political action committees in Alabama because they are a device to conceal the identities of the original donors. The intent of the law was to stop opioid manufacturers, toxic environmental polluters, criminals, and others from disguising their huge donations to politicians, and later seeking to pull strings.

If anyone knew well that this law banned such illegal transfers, it should have been Alabama Attorney General Steve Marshall. Indeed he made that same argument before the U.S. Supreme Court in early 2017 in a case against the Alabama Democratic Conference, a black arm of the Alabama Democratic Party.

Yet, in the height of hypocrisy which stinks to the heavens, Marshall, the top law enforcement officer of Alabama, disavowed his earlier position. In his 2018 state campaign for election to attorney general, Marshall suddenly decided it was okay to take such "hidden identity" PAC contributions. He simply needed the money.

In this 180-degree turnabout, Marshall disgraced the office to which he was first appointed in 2017 by the subsequently ousted and convicted governor Robert Bentley after Bentley had appointed then Alabama Attorney General Luther Strange to fill the U.S. Senate seat vacancy created when Alabama's junior senator, Jeff Sessions, was appointed U.S. attorney general by Donald Trump. Dizzying, isn't it? It seems that one disgrace begets another.

As I mentioned earlier, working with Baxley from April 1975 to June 1977 as an assistant attorney general inspired me to run for the office myself in 1978 (Bill was running for governor). A lot of people were surprised when I finished second out of nine in the unofficial results in the Democratic primary. Then I was the one surprised when my run-off berth was shockingly stolen. Although I did not win, all was not lost, as the prodigious effort of the campaign catapulted me into a very successful law practice.

By 1983, the Associated Press had dubbed me as "the public watchdog," and the *Montgomery Advertiser* called me "the private attorney general." Pursuing public-interest cases without holding public office became my trademark. The 1980s saw a meteoric rise in precedent-setting and landmark cases I was bringing. The '90s, '00s, and teens were similar, except for my 2001–02 run for the U.S. Senate and an illness in 2006, both taking some time away.

For many years, every four years after 1978, the press and public speculated I would be running for attorney general again. Yet I was having so much fun raising our children Rachel, Grace, and David and traveling with them and Leslie, while making many times financially what the state attorney general did.

I well recall in 1986 that Don Siegelman, a Democrat, honored me by first asking if I was going to run for attorney general. He said he would not if I were going to. We were friends, and I appreciated the courtesy. I told him no, I wasn't. He did and won.

I also got along well with Jimmy Evans, a Democrat elected in 1990. But the red tide had begun to turn, beginning in 1986 with the Baxley-Graddick fiasco in the governor's race, which led to the fluke of Republican Guy Hunt being elected. In 1994 Jeff Sessions became Alabama's first Republican attorney general since the Reconstruction era. From Sessions onward, the office has remained solidly in GOP hands, while I've continued to enjoy private life. That is far better than what happened to my friend Siegelman, the last Democrat elected governor of Alabama in 1998.

As history knows, Don was subsequently subjected to the most corrupt political prosecution ever in Alabama, which he suffered in 2006 at the hands of the Riley-Canary machine. The Republican prosecutor Leura

Canary was the wife of Republican operative Bill Canary, who was a top aide to Republican governor Bob Riley. They all desperately wanted to stave off a tough challenge from Siegelman, the strongest Democrat in the state. It was an assassination of a different kind, in some ways worse. The Republican federal judge, Mark Fuller, contributed by ruling against Don at every twist and turn in a trial on a trumped-up bribery charge. Fuller joyfully sentenced Don to seven years in federal prison. Only a few years later, Fuller was forced off the bench for beating up on his wives too many times.

What was so outrageous is that Don never received any money personally, nor did his gubernatorial campaign. Instead money was steered by health care magnate Richard Scrushy toward promoting a lottery which, had it succeeded, would have put badly needed dollars into public education. It was almost inconceivable that Scrushy and Siegelman could be railroaded to prison as a result, but it happened. I go into more detail about this in my previous book, *Civil Rights in My Bones*.

My friendship with Don grew as I periodically sent modest financial help (which he never asked for) to him at the prison in Louisiana (unbelievably, one $250 check was embezzled by prison officials). I also helped Don's son, Joseph Siegelman, pursue legal initiatives to help his dad after Don's conviction.

Thus my answer was a quick yes in 2018 when Don and Joseph asked me to help Joseph in his attorney general campaign that year. Joseph announced at the last moment, just before the qualifying deadline. With good name identification and his father calling on old friends to help, Joseph beat a very decent opponent, Chris Christie, in the statewide Democratic primary. I liked Chris but was already committed, and devoted, to Joseph.

Joseph then faced Republican Steve Marshall in the November general election. Accordingly, twice in October 2018 Melissa Isaak and I publicly called upon Montgomery County District Attorney Daryl Bailey to do something about the illegal PAC-to-PAC transfers received by Marshall in his campaign. No action was taken by Bailey.

Joseph lost on November 8, 2018, by roughly the same 40 to 60 margin as other statewide Democratic candidates in the Republican sweep of our now thoroughly red state.

Marshall was also before the Alabama Ethics Commission, which in a very political vote in early December 2018, but on a different issue, ruled 3–2 in his favor. Ethics Commission member Judge Charles Price was one of two votes saying Marshall had violated the State Ethics laws.

I later spoke with DA Bailey about the issue again. He is a highly ethical prosecutor, but he was concerned that his pursuit of Republican Marshall might appear too partisan, or too political, since Daryl is a Democrat. He also pointed out that his office and Marshall's office had to work together on several cases, which presented a conflict. Therefore, I was satisfied on January 30, 2019, when I received a call from Daryl informing me he had turned the matter over to Governor Kay Ivey with a recommendation that she appoint an independent special prosecutor to investigate the case.

Again, this issue was a very different question from the one the Ethics Commission voted on, as opposed to whether Marshall violated the state's ban on PAC to PAC transfers. Instead the Code of Alabama at §17–5-15(b) makes what Marshall did unlawful. Moreover, the Code, § 17–5-7.1 requires that any such PAC to PAC money received by a candidate must be returned within ten days or its receipt. A person who violates this statute, § 17–5-19(c), is guilty of a class B felony and can be sentenced to up to two years in prison, per violation. There were five such violations by Marshall.

Thus Marshall's actions, in a bad example for our chief law enforcement officer, opened up the floodgates for illegal campaign contributions from sources so obscure and sinister that Alabama voters will never know who's controlling the state officeholders. Some not so benign powers must be licking their chops.

Once again, only in Alabama! Hold your nose!

I have nothing against Steve Marshall personally. On the surface, he appears to be a fairly nice guy. Further I deeply sympathize with his tragic loss in his wife's suicide death during the campaign. I lost a brother that way forty-three years ago, and it still hurts. It matters not to me that Marshall is a Republican. He was once a Democrat and is probably overall a moderate. Although still a Democrat, I've become increasingly independent in recent years on many issues, local, state, national, or international.

But unless Daryl Bailey or someone else appointed by Governor Ivey pursues the case (within a two-year statute of limitations), our current attorney general, by his deed and example, will have voided a very important protection in Alabama for maintaining integrity in the election process. By late February 2019, I learned that Kay Ivey had decided not to assign a special prosecutor to investigate or pursue the wrongdoing. How blatantly political, how unsurprising, how dangerous to the political integrity of Alabama. Columnist Josh Moon, writing for the *Montgomery Independent,* railed on again for the umpteenth time, as did Kyle Whitmire of AL.com and the *Birmingham News,* but to no avail. Ugly power politics!

As stated in Chapter 17, "Selma in Turmoil," the current Alabama attorney general's office under Steve Marshall has also wrongfully indicted three Selma policemen, with no specifics of wrongdoing set forth. Moreover, rather than provide documents disclosing the wrongdoing, the AG's office inundated assistant co-counsel David Sawyer and me with a USB drive containing thirty thousand unindexed documents, something that would take us months to plow through. Talk about hiding a needle in a haystack.

It's gotten so bad for Attorney General Marshall that survivors of E. J. Bradford Jr., an African American man wrongfully killed by police in a shopping mall in Hoover, Alabama, on Thanksgiving night 2018, have publicly called upon the attorney general's office to step aside, and let the local Jefferson County district attorney handle the case. On February 4, 2019, Marshall added insult to injury to the Bradford family by announcing that the police officer who fired the fatal shots had done no wrong. What does that say about the competence of the current Alabama Attorney General?

I do commend Marshall for his January 25, 2019, rehearing request to the Alabama Supreme Court, after that court earlier granted a defense motion to change venue from Montgomery in another highly controversial case. This involves the trial of Montgomery police officer Aaron Smith, charged with murdering an unarmed African American civilian, Greg Gunn, who was shot in the back by Smith. I have full confidence in Montgomery Circuit Judge Greg Griffin's fairness. Moreover, a local jury needs to consider the case. Unfortunately, in March 2019, the Alabama Supreme Court ruled that Griffin could not be judge over the case, and that it must be tried outside the Montgomery area.

I am certain the AG's office under Marshall has done other good things. Nonetheless it pains me to see how this once great office of the Alabama attorney general, despite many bright, competent assistant attorneys general still working in it, has lost much respect. We can and must do better.

25

Scott, Zelda & Helen

Only in Alabama is there a museum for the great F. Scott Fitzgerald and his renowned Montgomery-born and -bred wife, Zelda Sayre Fitzgerald.

Only in Alabama, just two doors west on the same north side of Felder Avenue in Montgomery, is the home of the only full-blooded sibling of Helen Keller, world-famous champion of the deaf and the blind. Keller frequently visited her dear sister Mildred at this home from the 1920s to the 1950s. A 1955 picture of the two of them seated in white rocking chairs on what is now Leslie's and my front porch adorns the wall behind where those chairs were sitting.

Legend, lore, hearsay, and speculation abound that from 1931–32, when the Fitzgeralds and their daughter, Scottie, were staying in their Old Cloverdale home, they ambled down the sidewalk and met their famous sometimes neighbor while she was visiting at what was then the home of Mildred Keller Tyson and her husband, Warren. One can only imagine the conversation that must have sparkled in that meeting. Those three international icons have positively impacted the lives of my better half Leslie and me and countless millions of other human inhabitants of planet Earth.

The Keller connection started for Leslie and me when we signed the contract in 1981 for our home at 831 Felder Avenue in Montgomery. The Tysons had occupied the home beginning in 1923. Captivated by the architectural rave of the 1920s, they converted the original white clapboard exterior to a Tudor style. This still provides eye-pleasing diversity to the early 1900s homes in the neighborhood.

Meanwhile, during this same era, Scott and Zelda were kicking up their heels internationally, attracting attention not only in Scott's novels and short stories but also in Zelda's convention-defying behavior and three-pronged artistry. Three prongs, you say? How so? Influenced by Picasso in Paris and on the Rivera, the elongated limbs in Zelda's impressionistic paintings echoed her surroundings and her mind. Her one novel, *Save Me the Waltz*, was favorably reviewed by the *New York Times*. Her short stories were always colorful, and her famous quote "plagiarism begins at home" alluded to her literary influence on her famous husband's work. Her ability as a dancer got her featured as a flapper on a 1921 cover of *Hearst's International* magazine, a progenitor of the modern *Cosmopolitan*.

What makes Zelda especially heroic is that she did all this while defying recurrent episodes of schizophrenia and bi-polar disorder before modern-day medications. She also defied the conservative mores of her day, making her an inspiration to early feminists.

Scott, meanwhile, was inspiring the Jazz Age through his now-classic novels, though he largely financed his and Zelda's lavish lifestyle by publishing hundreds of short stories in such magazines as *Esquire*, the *Saturday Evening Post*, and the *New Yorker*. This was well before radio and television governed so much of the public's recreational time.

BEFORE 1986, WHEN REALTOR Martha Cassels came running to Leslie and me, beseeching us to buy the Fitzgerald home to keep developers from tearing it down, I had gradually soaked in the Fitzgerald legacy. The first source was while I was a cadet at Sewanee Military Academy in the early 1960s, where influential English teacher-wrestling coach Bill Goldfinch had me read several of F. Scott Fitzgerald's novels. My four years at Princeton, which Fitzgerald attended, caused me to hear much about the university's greatest literary light. Finally, in my post-Columbia Law School days as a young Wall Street lawyer, I made summer forays to Long Island beaches. My contemporaries would talk about East Egg and West Egg, the Gatsby locale, and Fitzgerald's mystique, as if it were just yesterday.

Then, in about 1973, I met Scottie Fitzgerald Smith at my parents' Lake Logan Martin home, east of Birmingham. Scottie, the Fitzgeralds' only child, had driven up from Montgomery with her friend Mary Lee Stapp.

After Leslie and I moved from New York to Montgomery in 1975, Scottie soon invited us to several parties at her Garden District home on Gilmer Avenue. During the summer of 1978, when I ran for attorney general of Alabama, Scottie generously allowed my brother Frank, managing my campaign, and his wife Louise, to stay in her home while she was summering up East. Following the initial newspaper story in December 1986 about the possibility of the museum, some of Scottie's friends tried to shoot down the idea, saying "Scottie wouldn't have approved." (She had died that summer.) The celebrated Virginia Durr, an early board member, said, "Oh, they're just jealous and want to be keepers of the flame."

I created a nonprofit corporation for the museum in January 1987, and after thirteen years of private ownership, Leslie and I conveyed the museum house and its acre and a half lot, worth perhaps half a million dollars, to the Scott and Zelda Fitzgerald Museum Association.

The Fitzgerald Museum soon took on a life of its own. Mirroring the *Field of Dreams* notion, "If you build it they will come," Fitzgerald scholar Matt Broccoli's appraisal in 1988 was that we needed "more bait." Leslie and I traveled to the Princeton University Library's rare book section that year to make copies of precious letters, and Zelda's great-niece Sayre Godwin generously donated items from her collection of artifacts and memorabilia. By May 1989, we had enough bait to have a public opening of the museum with a big party. We also filed and won a suit against the city Board of Adjustment after it voted 3–2 to deny us a zoning variance following our grand opening.

Carroll Dale Short's 2000 biography of me, *The People's Lawyer*, described the museum's creation in more detail, as did my autobiography fifteen years later, *Civil Rights in My Bones,* adding further description about the museum's rapid growth over the next decade.

The stars of the later chapter, Willie Thompson and Shawn Sudea Skehan, made great contributions, but were replaced in 2017–2019 by a hard-working executive director, Sara Powell, and more recently by our current director, Dr. Kendra Doten, our former curator. Also, president Dr. Kirk Curnutt and publicist and vice-president Daron Harris made great contributions in 2018–19. Curnutt, head of Troy University's English Department, as

Leslie and me having a fine time at the Fitzgerald Museum's 30th Anniversary Gala fundraising party on May 4, 2019.

vice president of the International Fitzgerald Society, has deftly organized biannual meetings of that group in Europe and America.

Curnutt's connections and energy helped the museum in hosting an International Fitzgerald Conference in November 2013, attracting participants from all continents but Antarctica. Both Fitzgerald granddaughters, Bobbie Lanahan and Cecelia Ross, were present.

Our collection of artifacts and memorabilia has increased, more Fitzgerald scholars are researching or speaking at the museum, and more publications online and in print are treating the museum as the precious international resource that it is. Our leadership (including me as board chairman, and resuming the presidency in February 2019) sees the museum not as just a shrine for Scott and Zelda but as promoting literary awareness, education, and revival. The Southern Literary Trail organization in Mississippi, Alabama, and Georgia has had board meetings at the Fitzgerald Museum, and the *New York Times* finally began giving the museum recognition it has long deserved. Montgomery's ascension on the literary map appears secure, and hopefully the museum will continue in full force long after Leslie and I are no longer around.

We also instituted in 2016 the annual Fitzgerald Museum Literary Prize for Excellence in Writing. The first winner was Birmingham's Kim Cross for her book, *What Stands in a Storm*, a gripping literary nonfiction account of the 2011 deadly tornadoes across Alabama. The 2017 winner, Katherine Clark, also of Birmingham, was honored for her four novels satirizing Mountain Brook, Alabama. The 2018 winner was the highly respected Wayne Flynt, Auburn University emeritus history professor, for his lifetime body of work and especially his recent book relating his friendship with the late writer Harper Lee. The 2019 winner, Frye Gaillard of Mobile, was recognized for his outstanding historical memoir about the decade of the 1960s, *A Hard Rain*, as well as other works.

I am especially proud of younger Fitzgerald board member Foster Dickson, a high school creative writing teacher and mentor. While on the board, he was inspired to write *Closed Ranks*, a nonfiction account of the infamous 1975 police murder of Bernard Whitehurst Jr., and the subsequent cover-up. Special gratitude goes always to long-time museum advisory board member Randall Williams, whose (with partner Suzanne La Rosa) NewSouth Books has published many hundreds of books in the last twenty years, including all of mine and Gaillard's and Dickson's volumes mentioned above.

Our Fitzgerald board has recently been strengthened by other new members, including artists M. J. Kirkland and Bill Ford, journalist Andrew Yawn, portrait artist-musician Joel Kelly, and two Beasley Allen lawyers who combine literary flair with the ability to raise money, Leslie Pescia and John Tomlinson. Pescia and another Beasley attorney, Rachel Boyd, successfully ran this year's thirtieth anniversary gala. Cloverdale community president Brian Daniel Mann has also strengthened our board, helping especially with neighborhood relations.

One of the most promising recent developments has been the transformation of the two second-floor apartments of the Fitzgerald House into Airbnb locations. Give Sara Powell, Kendra Doten, and new museum employee Kimberly Newman much credit for this. The double benefit has been much-needed funding for the museum and intrinsic online advertising for travelers who might not otherwise hear about the museum. Meanwhile, the grounds and gardens continue to improve, with Mobile's Bellingrath Gardens as an inspirational model.

I am especially grateful to State Senator David Burkett, the Montgomery County Commission (most notably Dan Harris), and certain city councilmen (Bollinger, Larkin, Lee, and Bell), and Mayor Todd Strange for their financial assistance. The Fitzgerald Museum is also very appreciative of the leadership help from state tourism director Lee Sentell in getting financial assistance to replace ancient air-conditioning and heating systems.

A sad footnote was the loss in August 2018 of landscape architect and long-time enthusiastic board member Janie Wall, who died of cancer at the too-young age of sixty-one. For many years, Janie was a spirit and driving force behind the museum's annual fundraising gala. Living just across the street, she also helped look after the Museum's grounds. She is missed.

THE HELEN KELLER CONNECTION deserves more comment. In the 1950s, my mother put me up to reading three different Helen Keller biographies, each written for different stages of a child's development. But until Leslie and I bought our house in 1981, I never realized that Keller lived all the way to 1968, and the age of eighty-eight. In my mind, she ranked with the long-ago heroes like George Washington, Abraham Lincoln, George Washington Carver, and Booker T. Washington, whose biographies I also read in the 1950s. Instead, Keller was very much alive, vibrant, and influencing the world until she finally graduated into the heavenly realm. They must have thrown a big party up there when she arrived, seeing and hearing perfectly.

What blows me away is that Helen Keller was not only a "champion of the deaf and blind" but also traveled the world, from Europe to Japan to South America, promoting the cause. Just as amazingly, without being able to see or hear, and with diction tough to follow, Helen Keller spoke out for the rights of workers and for women to vote. What further amazes me is that during the 1930s, during the height of racist America, Helen spoke out against the travesty and injustice of Jim Crow laws. No one dared retaliate.

The woman was a saint! She, Mother Theresa, and Mother Mary are in rare company. Add in Rosa Parks, Eleanor Roosevelt, and for me more personally my own mother and wife, and you can see why I frequently say my greatest heroes are women.

To think that Helen Keller frequently visited my home in Montgomery and sat on our front porch visiting with her sister—holy ground it is.

We have well preserved the room where, according to her sister's grand-children, "Aunt Helen" frequently slept. It became my actress daughter Grace's bedroom. Standing eight feet tall in the room is a five-hundred-pound chiffonier (or colloquially mispronounced "chifforobe") dating from the Alabama pioneer days of the late 1700s to early 1800s. The panels are secured by wooden pegs, not nails. Having seen an identical piece of furniture at the Keller family home, "Ivy Green" in Tuscumbia in northwest Alabama, our beautiful chiffonier obviously came from Helen's childhood home. We frequently take friends and strangers upstairs to see this room. One guest sighed and no doubt spoke for many when she earnestly remarked that she "could feel Ms. Keller's presence."

Helen Keller has inspired me as much as anyone on planet Earth. She has encouraged me in all my civil rights work, especially for people with disabilities, for blacks, women, immigrants, and any other group or person wrongfully discriminated against or unjustly treated.

Keller's spirit lives on, and continues to influence many people worldwide! And I can simply sit out on my front porch, lean back in the rocking chair where she once sat, close my eyes, and reflect upon her. Wow!

26

The Grand Finale

"Man does not live by bread alone."

Those famous words explain what distinguishes humanity from the rest of creation . . . which mostly searches for food, shelter, safety, or mates. Meaning and purpose in life are the magnets of our existence, whether we realize it or not. Yes, the needs of the animal kingdom also exist for humans, but much more is needed.

Mankind is the unique, highest form of God's creation, unique as a combination of body, mind, soul and spirit. We are more than the five senses of seeing, hearing, smelling, touching, and tasting. There is a sixth sense, in the realm of the Spirit, in which we hunger and thirst for the Divine.

As we get older, and at seventy-two I'm getting there, our priorities begin to shift . . . at least that has been my experience. Yes, the cornerstone needs of good health, peace, economic well-being, and fellowship with family and friends are of utmost importance. Yet there is a great desire for knowing something more, whether we realize it or not, an attraction for the Light and Truth of God.

Why are we on planet Earth in the first place? Where are we going when this life ends, and what will we be doing once there? Where did we come from? When I was a teen, I frequently questioned, if not pestered, both my parents about many of these ultimate questions of human existence.

My grandfather Julian McPhillips and uncles David Dixon and Warren McPhillips all added to my wonderful father, the Reverend Julian L. McPhillips Sr., in providing excellent role models. My mother, Eleanor Dixon McPhillips, couldn't have been a better influence. (I put an excellent profile of both parents in the 2005 edition of *The People's Lawyer*.) Yet neither parent could answer these ultimate questions, as much as they may have wanted to, because neither had yet entered heaven, of course. I expect to see them again on that holy ground and can hardly wait for them to help answer these questions.

By word, deed, and example, both parents did share, however, their faith in Jesus Christ as Lord, Redeemer, and Saviour. Dad's famous words in 1959, in leaving a prosperous family business to attend seminary in Sewanee, Tennessee, and then become a priest, have rung in my heart, mind, and spirit ever since. He said, "Son, I have decided to bet my life that everything Jesus said in the Gospels about himself and about life in general is true . . . and I'm convinced that I will live my life far better if I do." He called it the "leap of faith."

What a foundation! It became my foundation, too. It helped that I respected Dad and Mom enormously and knew I was a wonderful recipient of their love, reflecting God's love.

Obviously, not everyone is so fortunate, which I knew early. And that explains the next part of the godly wisdom my parents passed on. Coming from Mom's moral Presbyterian background, she gently admonished, "To those to whom much has been given, much is required" (by God). Mom articulated this frequently, as she repeated our Lord's message from the Gospel of Luke 12:48.

I kicked around in the pews of Sacred Heart Catholic Church in Cullman the first four years of my life. Mom and Dad decided to split the difference in 1950 between his Catholic and her Presbyterian backgrounds and become Episcopalians, a reasonable compromise. I watched Grace Episcopal Church in Cullman grow from ground zero the next nine years of my life until 1959, when we moved to Sewanee, Tennessee. There Dad began three years of seminary, and I had five years at Sewanee Military Academy with a strong religious orientation. This enthusiastic experience of the 1950s to early 1960s was punctuated by my—and my brother David's—favorite hymn, "I Sing a Song of the Saints of God." We sang it with gusto at Grace Church and believed in its words. Family prayer together at night, including all five of us children, was routine in both Cullman and Sewanee. While in high school, I fully expected to follow in Dad's footsteps into the priesthood.

The years at Princeton, 1964–68, and at Columbia Law School, 1968–71, prepared me for my life's work. The lawyering I first did on Wall Street from 1971–75 was educational but I saw what I *didn't* want to do the rest of my life. Helping the little guy and the underdog became my true calling. It flowed naturally from the Gospel message.

Both my parents emphasized the "Sermon on the Mount," including Jesus's oft-quoted challenge: "Inasmuch as you do it unto the least of these my brethren, you have done it unto me." Jesus did not say except for this group of people, nor that type of person, nor that color of skin. Neither did he say except for children still in the womb.

Those precepts have motivated my law practice at McPhillips Shinbaum and my ministry at Christ the Redeemer.

Like Cornel West, quoted earlier, I admit I am "a broken vessel," still a "work in progress," and will be so until I kick the bucket. I have my faults, and I believe we're all sinners in need of the mercy, forgiveness, and grace of God. I'm in need of more humility and patience and of being less sanctimonious. I also recognize that the Christian Gospel, and Jesus's words, compel us to love not just our neighbors but our enemies (unique for Christianity among the world's faiths). And Jesus told us to forgive others seventy times seven times, especially if we want to be forgiven by God (Luke 6:27–38). I also take seriously the Ten Commandments, including its warning against idolatry in the first two commandments. God should always be our "first love." It is a challenge to keep other things from becoming more important, whether it is one's work, sports, or relationships.

While enormously blessed, I've had enough hard knocks to know what they are, from losing a dear brother to suicide, to experiencing my wife's three miscarriages, to having one state political campaign stolen from me and another sabotaged, to experiencing depression, to breaking my leg twice in one wrestling season.

I am no longer politically ambitious; my running days are over. I still plan to be active advocating for issues that concern me and helping good candidates in other races. Increasing gun violence is a huge concern that needs to be stopped. Justice, the environment, education, infrastructure, and civil rights issues concern me, as well as the need for heightened conscience about unborn life in the womb and adoption as a great alternative to abortion.

As far as meaning and purpose go, I commend and encourage those with less exciting jobs, more daunting health problems, or economic struggles. There are many such folk out there, and we, as children of God, are called to be loving to these, our brothers and sisters. The joy and peace that flow from helping others are worth more than silver and gold.

Also great joy comes from the cornerstones of the Christian walk: praise and worship; prayers; spirit-inspired scripture reading; and fellowship. Those four should motivate one to the fifth, service to mankind, either in outreach to the community, mission-related, or through inreach to others in a church.

None of us know how many years we have left. I consider life an enormous gift from God, and see getting into Heaven as depending far more on God's grace, mercy, and love than anything we can do. The Gospels also quote Jesus as saying there is accountability. Yet I expect he'll be there, hand extended, as we graduate from earth to heaven. He will welcome us into the greatest healing of them all. While I respect and love people of all faiths or no faith, I deeply believe Jesus is the Way, the Truth, and the Life (John 14:6). He is also the Light who brightens the darkness.

Evangelism I agree with, as well as its goal of spreading the good news of Jesus, because it is so helpful to people. Yet proselytism is counterproductive, and thus I avoid it. It is important to be sensitive and to show respect to people of all faiths, and of no faith. In so doing, one encourages a reciprocal respect more receptive to the Christian view. I'm not advocating lukewarm Christianity (see Revelations 3:16 for advice against that) but believe a bold faith is important and necessary, along with compassion, for an effective healing ministry. (See chapter 38 of *Civil Rights in My Bones*, and chapter 25 of *The People's Lawyer*.) And Leslie and I have seen many such healings.

Unselfish love, also called *agape* by the ancient Greeks, is very important. Best described by Saint Paul in First Corinthians 13 (the love chapter) and perfectly embodied in Christ, this type of love has world-changing, transformative potential. This is the usual love of a mother for child—daughter Rachel gave me Ed Bacon's *The 8 Habits of Love*, which is an excellent guide for this type of love; even Archbishop Desmond Tutu said this book left him "tingling with excitement." But given human nature's often selfish and backsliding ways, this super love must be spurred by the Holy Spirit to be maintained long-term.

Flowing from this kind of love are forgiveness and reconciliation, which are the heart of Christ's message and important to both the Jewish and Christian faiths. Christ's message to love your enemies can be a daunting challenge. In any case, given all the animosities, chaos, egos and unforgiveness, such love is much needed on planet Earth.

Most writers, from the epistle writers Peter and Paul to twentieth-century fiction writers Fitzgerald and Hemingway, to more modern-day *écrivains*, draw from their own experiences. I am no exception. Hence the preceding chapters recounting my work on legal cases have been drawn from a reservoir of faith, shared in this chapter.

I tell folks with a chuckle, and sometimes tap on wood for humorous effect, with hands genuinely cupped in prayer, that I am aiming for age 105. The chances are great I will fall short, possibly far short. But I add that "maybe I'll get further down the pike, because I aimed high." This makes good sense, because the goal encourages better habits, including daily exercise, a decent diet, twice daily prayers with Leslie and a happy marriage, and generates a more positive attitude. The best habit is a close personal relationship with God through Jesus. Our Savior brings healing in both this world and the next. He did it in ancient times and still does it in modern times. Thanks be to God the Father, Son and Holy Spirit, and thanks to you, the reader, for making it this far, to the end of my epistles. May God bless you.

Appendix

A. Our Fortieth Anniversary as a Firm (1978–2018)

How well I remember September 1978! Running for attorney general of Alabama at age thirty-one, surprising everyone by finishing second out of nine candidates in the unofficial tallies compiled by the AP and UPI, then campaigning hard in the run-off . . . only to wake up a week later and discover that my run-off spot had been stolen . . .

The floodtide of emotions, from top to bottom, ran the gamut. I challenged the theft for one week, only to discover that it was going to cost me $200,000 to post a bond, when I was down to my bottom dollar. Moreover, the final election was only a week later . . . the practical realities caused me to abandon the challenge.

In the midst of that mist, my good friend and fellow attorney Tommy Gallion called me. In his deep, resonant voice he said: "Julian, I know how you feel; my family knows what it's like to lose an attorney general's race we should have won. Why don't you come over to my building, and practice with me. I'll give you free rent for three months to help you get started."

I decided his offer was a good idea, thanked him, and took off with Leslie for a week's recovery vacation in Cancun, Mexico. There the two of us did far more sleeping than anything else.

We returned in late September 1978, and entered the Perry-High Building, 516 S. Perry Street in Montgomery, and have remained there continuously for forty-plus years. My dear wife Leslie was my first secretary that September–October of 1978; toddler Rachel, barely one, was crawling around in the reception area. Leftover stationery from my campaign was initially used, and the telephone was transferred from my campaign office a few blocks away. Overhead was close to zero. $5,000 in attorney fees came in October, $10,000 in November, and we were off to a good start. I bought the building (ten thousand square feet) from Tommy's in-laws in 1982. Thanks be to God.

Much of the ensuing four decades of work and life has been summarized in the two books I have been referring to throughout this one, *The People's Lawyer* (2000; 2005) and *Civil Rights in My Bones* (2016), both published by NewSouth Books, still my publisher. Highlights from the next three years, 2016–19, are in this book.

In looking back, I must insist that top credit and honor for all my professional successes, and for life in general, goes first to God the Father, Son, and Holy Spirit. I owe everything to my Creator, Redeemer, and Sustainer. In the human realm, top credit definitely goes to my awesome wife Leslie. Her assistance and encouragement during the first month of the law firm's existence helped me then, and she continued to help the firm in many ways in the forty years since, as backup receptionist, my driver on long journeys, and by her friendships with others in the firm and her moral support to me. She has also been very supportive of all of my books (this one makes five; see page ii for the full list).

B. Celebration of the Law Firm

On September 27, 2018, the firm partners, that is Kenneth Shinbaum, Aaron Luck, Joe Guillot, and me, but minus Jim Bodin, together with other firm attorneys Chase Estes and Tanika Finney but minus David Sawyer (away on a family trip), assembled in downtown Montgomery for a big celebration organized by office manager Amy Strickland. We were joined by long-time process server/firm chaplain Kaylon Jenkins; paralegals Tori Bozeman, Jennifer Lee, Page McKee, Lillian Neace, and Patricia Williams; and by receptionist Carrie Sheets Jones. We had fun together at SaZa's Restaurant. I passed out a single page entitled "40th Anniversary Statement of Appreciation and Memorial," which read as follows:

I thank Kenneth for 32 years of loyal partnership and invaluably helping

The Firm, September 2018: front row, from left, Joe Guillot, Kenneth Shinbaum, Julian McPhillips, Aaron Luck, and Jim Bodin; back row, from left, Jennifer Lee, Page McKee, Patricia Williams, Carrie Sheets Jones, Chase Estes, Tanika Finney, David Sawyer, Karen Willis, Amy Strickland, and Lillian Neace.

In 2019 with several members of our outstanding law firm team/ family: Right, seated, paralegal Lill Neace; standing, office manager Amy Strickland and receptionist Carrie Jones. Below, left, process server and firm chaplain, Kaylon Jenkins, and right, my newest paralegal, Bridget Strength.

me and other firm attorneys see the obstacles and possibilities in cases.

I thank Aaron for his hitting the long ball, his common sense, his communication skills, and consensus-reaching in partnership meetings.

I thank Jim for his level-headedness, his ability to bring in fruit at unexpected times, and his trying a case with me on September 10–11, 2001.

I thank Joe for years of friendship, both before and after coming to the firm, great legal skills, especially in criminal cases and at the appellate level, and his enormously helpful book-keeping skills.

I thank Amy for her friendship and incredible range of talents, including serving as office manager, book-keeper, paralegal, advertising and public relations manager, computer guru, and Fitzgerald Museum treasurer.

I thank Chase for his great electronic skills, rapidly-developing knowledge in employment law, his sense of humor, and heart for the little guy.

I thank Kaylon for over 20 years of excellent professional services as a process server, runner, and firm chaplain.

I thank Tori for coming here in June 2017, working for a year, and, after taking off much of the summer, returning. The quality of her professional service is first-rate, and I do much better when she is here.

I thank Patricia, Page and Jennifer for many devoted years of service (over 20 for Page and Patricia). All three have other primary partners they work for, but all three have loyally helped the entire firm in so many ways.

I thank Lill for not only helping to keep Kenneth straight, as her primary attorney, but also for typing the chapters on my next book, *Only in Alabama*.

I thank Carrie for holding the fort down at the Reception desk, helping me with copying and mailouts, greeting clients well, reminding me of waiting clients, and improving her skills.

I thank Tanika for, like manna from Heaven, showing up almost 2 years ago, just after Chris left, providing much needed attorney assistance on employment cases.

I thank the entire firm for working together as a team, realizing that we're all on the same boat together, and will rise or fall together.

40 years as a firm is no small achievement. It is indeed a Biblical number, and with God's continued help, and giving Him all the honor and credit He deserves for our many blessings, I foresee many more good years for the firm.

The point is that I never could have done the legal work of the past forty years without great backup support from everyone listed above. That includes several other attorneys, including my long-time friend and fellow attorney Bobby Segall (only three weeks my junior), just down Perry Street at the Copeland Franco law firm. I still consider Bobby the best attorney in Alabama, and at times he's been a guardian angel, helping me a few times when the ox was in the ditch. Recently I have added attorney David Sawyer, whom I recruited to go to Princeton and who graduated there in 1987. (David was an All-State football center and straight-A student at Montgomery's Jefferson Davis High School. At Princeton he dated his classmate Brooke Shields, the famous movie star.) David showed up at the firm for legal advice in June 2018. At that time, I had two pressing employment cases headed towards the Eleventh U.S. Circuit Court of Appeals and needed help. With good appellate writing skills, David was drafted by me. Returning the favor, he artfully drafted the briefs for me. David came on board with the firm in July 2018 as an "of counsel" attorney, the same status as Tanika Finney.

I would be remiss not to mention several former partners over the years who helped build the firm into what it became. That included Jim DeBardelaben (1981–90); Frank Hawthorne Jr. (1985–93); William Gill (1988–2004); Allen Stoner (1991–96); Mary Goldthwaite (1992–2006); Kay Dickey (1996–2004); and Karen Rodgers (1997–2006). I also include of counsel attorneys Bill Honey and Gary Atchison for their help in the 1990s. Several star paralegals included Regina Lee Barron, (1978–87) (who became an attorney for the firm in 1990), Carroll Puckett (1978–2006), Carlton Avery (2014–15), Lynelle Howard (1987–96; 2007–13), Denise Bertaut (2013–14), Vicki Morrison (2007; 2011; 2018), Tori Bozeman (2017–19); and, just before this book went to press, a new talented paralegal with a pleasant disposition, Bridget Strength.

C. Community Outreach Helps the Book

My outreach into other parts of the Alabama community has also broadened my writing, contributing to this book. I refer especially to Christ the Redeemer Episcopal Church, of which Leslie and I were among the co-founders in 1981, and the Scott & Zelda Fitzgerald Museum, which Leslie and I founded in 1987. Founding and enhancing high school wrestling programs in Alabama and engaging in Democratic politics have continued my "work in progress." Traveling with Leslie and enjoying our adult children and grandkids are also primary passions. I wrote about all these topics at length in *Civil Rights in My Bones*.

D. Additional Good Influences in Writing, Especially My Parents

The two individuals to whom I owe the most in shaping my writing are my awesome parents, Julian (1920–2001) and Eleanor (1920–2002) McPhillips. They were the first to instill faith, character, broad-mindedness, an expanded world view, and good health. In addition, they both enjoyed writing, inspiring me by their own four-volume autobiography, *The Drummer's Beat*. Their acorn—me—didn't fall far from the tree.

My mother was probably the greater influence, because she encouraged me in reading books early. She also motivated me to ride my bicycle to the Cullman library in the 1950s to check out biographies, mysteries, and later classic novels. Through good letter exchanges, Mom also taught me how to write, as if by osmosis. She could write with color and flair. Dad's sermons were also well-written and well-delivered. He practiced them in front of Mom, who gave him constructive feedback. As I have mentioned before, both Mom and Dad encouraged my first published writing, which was a letter to the editor of the *Alabama Journal* expressing anguish over the assassination of President John F. Kennedy.

My grandparents Julian and Lillybelle McPhillips, grandmother Stuart Sanderson Dixon, and uncles Dave Dixon and Warren McPhillips also sparked me with their knowledge, keen insight, and winsome personalities, inspiring my writings. On top of that, I enjoyed two paternal great-grandmothers: Petronilla "Mare" McPhillips, of Spanish descent, lived until I was twelve. The other, Lulabelle Graham McGowin, lived until I was nineteen—"Mamoo," we called her; born in 1870, she shared many stories with me about returning Civil War veterans. No wonder I love history, and enjoy writing about it. I'm steeped in it and living in Montgomery and Alabama only deepens the appreciation.

Also inspiring my writing is continued avid reading—thanks, Mother.

As the manuscript for this book was being completed, I had just completed Bob Zellner's *The Wrong Side of Murder Creek*. I was also reading Steven Gish's *Amy Biehl's Last Home*, Richard Gergel's *Unexampled Courage*, and L. D. Reddick's *Crusader Without Violence*, the first biography of Martin Luther King Jr. I previously mentioned my reading of Frye Gaillard's outstanding memoir of the 1960s, *A Hard Rain*. The common denominator of all these books is civil rights, which is still in my bones. I also read theology daily, beginning mornings with Sara Young's *Jesus Calling* devotional and related scriptural citations. My favorite magazines are *Charisma, Christianity Today, Time, Sports Illustrated*, and the *Princeton Alumni Weekly*.

Enormous credit, and I mean enormous, goes to Lill Neace of our law firm. Although primarily a paralegal to partner Kenneth Shinbaum, Lill devoted great professional talent to typing all the chapters of this book, with good cheer and encouragement. In addition, Lill retyped the chapters of my April 1968 senior thesis, published by NewSouth Books exactly fifty years later on April 17, 2018. The original title remained: *From Vacillation to Resolve: The Role of the French Communist Party in the Resistance Against the Nazis, 1939–45*.

I also thank office manager Amy Strickland and paralegals Tori Bozeman and Bridget Strength for their help in typing and/or reviewing parts of this book, and especially for their general assistance around the office. My new nickname for Amy is "Powerhouse." A former one was "Superwoman," because she wears so many hats in the office, managing the law firm. Amy is my right arm and Bridget is my left arm, and I couldn't do my legal work without them.

I must also thank Randall Williams and Suzanne La Rosa, who together comprise NewSouth Books, the publisher of my books. Both have great integrity and have encouraged me enormously in my writing. They have polished my writing and helped shape me as a writer. They are also dear, influential friends. We have much in common philosophically, politically, and personally. I also thank Daron Harris, Bobby Segall, Bill Baxley, Joe Guillot, and Don Siegelman for reviewing and commenting constructively on this book.

E. Assistance in Life Generally

While my parents Julian and Eleanor McPhillips and devoted wife Leslie have done the most, my writing has also been encouraged directly or indirectly by my siblings Sandy, David, Betsy, and Frank, and by my adult children, Rachel, Grace, and David. I also appreciate my daughters' fine husbands, Jay Plucker and Corbett Lunsford, my sister-in-law Louise Jones McPhillips, my nephews and nieces, and some Dixon, Sanderson, McPhillips, and McGowin relatives with whom I stay in touch.

A little more about the Big Four of my life, who are "my heart." There is no way I can adequately express my gratitude to Leslie, a font of common-sense wisdom and unselfish love. These qualities flow from our three grown children: Rachel, the wise mother of three and a leader in school; Grace, equally devoted mother of two and an actress; and my only son, David, conscientiously beginning his career. They all sparkle with creativity and kindness but humbly recognize that in our weakness God's strength is made perfect.

A person's life is like a river that twists and turns. It encounters boulders and forks, smooth water and rough currents. My life has been divided into four stages: Cullman, 1946–59; Sewanee, Tennessee, 1959–64; Princeton-Columbia-Wall Street (1964–75); and Montgomery, 1975 to the present. Along the way there have been several especially influential people at each stage. Their friendship and support have influenced me for the better, inspiring my writing and undergirding this book. My thanking them in these subsequent pages is therefore appropriate, and will help a reader better understand the reservoirs from which I draw, and why I write as I do.

1946–1959

In the Cullman years, outside of good family influences, I mention three childhood friends, each born in the same year, 1946, as I was. The first, Courtney McKoy, I came to know as a fellow toddler in the late 1940s; our friendship grew through the '50s and remains strong. The second, my next-door neighbor, Don Weaver, was a great athlete and very independent-minded and influenced me in both regards. The third was John Shaw, my battery-mate, as catcher, to my pitching for the Cullman County Little League All-Stars. We all stay in touch to this day.

1959–1964

The most positive influences in my Sewanee days were wrestling coach and English teacher Bill Goldfinch, now deceased, and Dad's seminary professor, the Right Reverend C. Fitzsimmons Allison, still sharp spiritually, intellectually, and physically, at past ninety. Fellow cadet Tommy McBee, two years my senior, like me a football player and wrestler, and one who attended a near-Ivy school, Franklin & Marshall, deserves mention, as we've stayed in touch over the years. Ditto for John Alexander, one year older, also a fellow cadet at SMA and a year ahead of me at Princeton, and a Rhodes Scholar. We were both members of Ivy Club and remain in touch.

1964–1975

The most positive influences from the Princeton-Columbia-Wall Street years, together with their wives, have been Tim and Ilia Smith, Princeton '66 of San Francisco; Walter and Mimes Bliss, '66 of Princeton; and Cliff and Judy Fenton, '65 of Chicago. All are full of personality and purpose and joined me at Columbia University Law School (or I joined them), except for Cliff, who attended Columbia Business School. Since 2007 Leslie and I have joined them for annual reunions in Chicago, San Francisco, Princeton, or Alabama. In all honesty, I'd have to add Bill Bradley of Princeton's class of 1965 as a great motivator and good influence by example, not only in my Princeton undergraduate years '64–'68 but also for many years afterward, including in 2000 when I ran his presidential campaign in Alabama and in 2002, when he helped me in my U.S. Senate campaign.

Also influential, and remaining so to this day, are Princeton classmates Fred Billings, '68 of Baton Rouge; Bill Potter, '68 of Princeton; and Steve Pajcic, '68 of Jacksonville, Florida. A mini-reunion of Princeton '68-ers was held in Montgomery on April 4–7, 2019, which has helped classmate Bob Faron, '68, whom I didn't know before our fiftieth reunion in June 2018, also become a good friend. I also add classmate Tom Johnson '68 as becoming a much better friend. That is the beauty of reunions, the making of new friendships in our seventies. I also include some of the most outstanding recruits of the approximately one hundred teenagers I recruited to Princeton from 1977–91, namely Barbara McElroy '81, Steve

Among the students I have recruited to Princeton over the years were two who also clerked for me in the summer of 1983: future Congresswoman Terri Sewell and Farris Curry.

Williams '81, Farris Curry '83, Steve Stearns '84, Terri Sewell '86, David Sawyer '87, Shannon Holliday '89, and Rick McBride Jr. '92. My more recent recruiting also included several younger Princeton graduates from Montgomery, namely Jud Matthews, Will Davis, and William Haynes Jr., all Montgomery Academy graduates and sons of attorneys, and all now contributing significantly to the world.

1975–

My longest span has been in Montgomery to date. On the professional end, I credit most former Alabama Attorney General Bill Baxley, Montgomery attorneys Tommy Gallion and Bobby Segall, and my law office partners Kenneth Shinbaum, Aaron Luck, Jim Bodin, and Joe Guillot. They have also been good friends personally. Associate attorney Chase Estes, forty-two years my junior, has been fun to work with. More recently I also credit the two newest lawyers at our firm, Tanika Finney and David Sawyer. Their help was badly needed and came largely unsolicited. They just showed up and were put to work. Distinguished Montgomery attorneys and former U.S. Magistrates Vanzetta Penn McPherson and Delores Boyd have motivated me by their high standards, intelligence, and good will. I am also inspired by the recent elevation of three new bright, younger female judges, Emily Marks, to U.S. District judge, Brooke Emfinger Reid to Montgomery County Circuit Court judge, and Tiffany McCord to Montgomery County District judge. All are well qualified in joining other very competent judges at their levels. This bodes well for the future of justice in Montgomery. The same is true for the storied Jere Beasley and Joe Espy and their firms, which have helped many people. Thank you Lord.

I also include Daron Harris, a young Princetonian, '96, a professional publicist whom I only met in April 2018 shortly after he moved to Montgomery. We have fast become the best friends. Daron helped publicize my *From Vacillation to Resolve*, mentioned earlier. Daron helped arrange speaking engagements on the book for me in Mobile, Birmingham, Selma, and Montgomery. Daron has also helped energize the Fitzgerald Museum as its new vice president, and he attends Christ the Redeemer Episcopal Church, Resurrected, the reborn version of our dear church, which resumed on April 28, 2013, following a six-year dormancy.

As far as a pure personal friend, I have had none better over the past forty years than the late Reverend John Alford, a long-time Baptist minister, civil rights leader, and the most valuable player in my 2002 U.S. Senate campaign. Only my wife Leslie ranked higher as a friend. John encouraged me, assured me, and vice-versa. A month shy of seventy-eight, John graduated to greater life beyond the grave on November 20, 2018. I wrote a long column about him in the *Montgomery Advertiser* (December 13, 2018) recounting his church-leading and civil rights activities in Alabama over the decades. I also gave a eulogy for him at his funeral at the historic Beulah Baptist Church (Leslie and I were two of only three Caucasians present among the several hundred mourners). John was an extraordinary human being with a heart of gold. I miss him tremendously.

Also still influential friends from my 2002 U.S. Senate campaign are Sundra Escott of Birmingham, Sim Pettway of Mobile, and Janet May of Montgomery. All have great spirits, senses of humor, and dedication to making the world

Program from my friend John Alford's funeral service.

a better place. I cherish their friendships. Just before this book went to press, Sundra brought her esteemed sister, Deborah Lumpkin, to seek my assistance with legal issues in Montgomery. Sim calls me every few weeks from Mobile to let me in on his latest insights. Former Montgomery councilwoman May and her son, Alan May, are longtime friends and clients. Bravo to them all!

Likewise, former Tuskegee mayors Johnny Ford and Ron Williams remain influential friends. Clayton Thomason (a.k.a. "Wildcat" or "Tamedog") of Montgomery is a friend, client, and roofing contractor on my office building and the Fitzgerald Museum. I am influenced by his indomitable spirit and enthusiasm.

Several other African American reverends, two of them bishops, deserve mention for their good influence, namely the Right Reverend Frank Bozeman and his minister wife, Hurtis, of the Global Evangelical Christian denomination, and Bishop A. L. Dowdell of Auburn of the Potter's House New Testament Full Gospel Church. I also add Carol and Mike Jones of the United Community Church in Montgomery. For many years Carol and I teamed up on a TV show called "Conversations with Carol and Julian," with a predominantly religious message, reaching a large cable audience. I have certain rhetorical flourishes that are honed from preaching, or being preached to, in black churches. Listening to black preachers probably has also impacted my literary style, at least in terms of cases that are the subject matter of my books.

Several Caucasian bishops have also foundationally influenced me. Charles C. J. Carpenter of the Episcopal Diocese of Alabama, Princeton '22, and his son, Bishop Doug Carpenter, '55 were among the reasons I went to Princeton, and Doug at eighty-six remains close today. Also Anglican bishop William Wilson, eighty-one, close friend of both my parents and present with our family at their deaths, helped the dormant Christ the Redeemer Episcopal Church become resurrected in 2013. I also credit and thank Bishop McKee Sloan of Alabama, eight years younger than me, for his allowing Christ the Redeemer's resurrection, and the previously mentioned Bishop Fitz Allison of South Carolina, eighteen years older than me. We've had great letter exchanges on salvation theology.

Although I didn't know him personally, I still remember the controversial but colorful Bishop James Pike of California, whose famous words at Princeton in 1966 were that "If I make it into Heaven by hook or crook, and, once there, discover that other poor sinners are down in hell suffering, the only thing I'd know to do, consistent with my Christian faith, would be to lead a demonstration in front of the throne of God, to petition him to bring up those poor sinners to Heaven." I realize that this statement is in tension with certain words in the Gospels and Epistles, but it is consistent with other portions. By contrast, I believe both Bishops William Spong and Eugene Robinson, whatever their intentions, have done much harm not only to the Episcopal and Anglican worlds, but to Christianity in general. Of course, being a bishop or priest gives one no claim to sainthood. They are made of human clay like everyone else.

The public officials in Alabama most positively influencing my writings have been former Attorney General Bill Baxley (thanks also for the "Foreword," Bill), U.S. Congressman Terri Sewell (a great talent helping the entire U.S.) and former governor Don Siegelman, for his incredible perseverance under unjust persecution. Thank you all. I also thank Don's son, Joseph

Christ the Redeemer congregation, 2018.

Siegelman, for helping his father so much and raising badly needed public justice issues in the 2018 Alabama attorney general's race.

In the institutional realm, the most foundational influences in these Montgomery years have been Christ the Redeemer Church and the Scott and Zelda Fitzgerald Museum, both founded by Leslie and me. The church and museum are covered well in the two previous books, *The People's Lawyer* and *Civil Rights in My Bones*. As to the church I especially thank the Reverends Mark Tusken (1986–94), Coleman Tyler (1995–99), and David Peeples (2015–2019) as our best priests. My wife Leslie has been a great partner, growing in faith at CTR over the years, 1980–2019, and is now my co-minister there. I also thank our musicians Curke Dudley, Frank Grey, Unita Newsome, Isaiah Thomas, and Charise Dudley for spirit-filled music at the church, and Peggy Gelpi, Michael Kerr, Mary Tuell, Daron Harris, Jenny Hwang, and Kendra Doten for their encouragement and attendance at our small church body.

As to the museum, I thank especially long-time leader Kirk Curnutt, my wife and co-founder, Leslie McPhillips, long-time treasurer Amy Strickland, co-founder Martha Cassels, and the late Janie Wall. Valuable new leadership came in 2017–19 from former executive director Sara Powell, new vice president Daron Harris, and curator Dr. Kendra Doten, now also our new executive director. Kendra attended Montgomery Academy before earning two bachelor's degrees in Japanese and design from the University of Florida, a masters' from Ochandmizu University in Japan, and a PhD in art history at the University of Melbourne, Australia. Bravo!

Fitzgerald Museum 2019 leadership includes, from left, Kendra Doten, executive director; myself and Leslie, co-founders; Daron Harris, vice president; and Jenny Hwang, international liaison.

We also have had some exciting new museum board members, including two from the Beasley Allen law firm, John Tomlinson and Leslie Pescia, Old Cloverdale president Brian Daniel Mann, and artist Bill Ford. They join energetic existing board members Brian Jones, Foster Dickson, Joel Kelly, M. J. Kirkland, Andrew Yawn, Meg Lewis, and our new museum secretary, Bridget Strength. Another Beasley Allen attorney, Rachel Boyd, has become our legal counsel.

Speaking of Beasley Allen, that juggernaut of a plaintiff's law firm, its founder Jere Beasley and lead partners Greg Allen, Tom Methvin, Cole Portis, Mike Crow, Dee Miles, Graham Esdale, and Gibson Vance, have impacted our whole country for the better. Their work ethic and organizational skills are a great example to me and others. The Southern Poverty Law Center, its founder Morris Dees and president Richard Cohen have done much good work over the years, though I have not agreed with some of their initiatives. Just before this book went to the publisher, the SPLC abruptly terminated its founder Dees, and Cohen resigned shortly thereafter.

The Equal Justice Initiative (EJI) and its founder Bryan Stevenson I admire immensely and unequivocally. Thanks be to God, they have helped spring from prison numerous wrongfully convicted people. The National Memorial for Peace and Justice, honoring four thousand-plus victims of lynching and the Legacy Museum are attracting national and international attention. This influences my law practice and writings. All three of these legal powerhouses, the SPLC, EJI, and Beasley Allen have contributed much to the "only in Alabama" theme of this book.

I add the Appleseed Society and Alabama Arise, both based in Montgomery, which have done much, especially on the legislative front, to help poor and needy people. I am especially proud of my brother, Frank McPhillips of Birmingham, for his presidential leadership of the Appleseed Society.

In the civil rights realm, so many people have inspired me that I simply refer to my book, *Civil Rights in My Bones*, especially its first two chapters. Special appreciation goes to my co-counsel in several tough cases, Eric Hutchins of Alexander City, to national SCLC president Charles Steele, to NAACP president Benard Simelton, and to civil rights icon and Rosa Parks/MLK attorney Fred D. Gray Sr. I also give great credit to Joe Reed, John Knight, and Alvin Holmes for years of opening up public service opportunities for African Americans in Alabama.

Three other sets of civil rights icons have deeply influenced my life. They are Virginia and Clifford Durr, Bob and Jeannie Graetz, and the Reverend Fred Shuttlesworth. I first met Virginia in 1965 in Princeton at the home of her daughter Lucy and son-in-law Sheldon Hackney's house. Sheldon taught me three history courses at Princeton. Virginia raved about my letter to the *Alabama Journal* in November 1963 on JFK's assassination. The Durrs insisted that Leslie and I stay at their Wetumpka (Pea Level) home in April 1975 upon our return to Alabama. Virginia introduced me to such civil rights leaders as Rosa Parks, E. D. Nixon, Johnnie Carr, and many others. Virginia also sent me many of my best civil rights cases, several of which became landmarks. My devotion to the Durrs and their high ideals continues with my annual leadership participation in April of the Clifford and Virginia Durr Lecture Series.

The Graetzes in the 1950s endured two KKK bombings and a third attempted bombing of their Lutheran Church and home in west Montgomery. They are now our adjacent neighbors on Dunbar Street, across from the Fitzgerald Museum. At ages ninety and eighty-eight respectively, Bob and Jeannie exemplify better than anyone I know the "beloved community" that MLK espoused.

Fred Shuttlesworth was an enormous personal hero, on several levels. He personally encouraged me to stand up to police brutality in the 1980s and 1990s, campaigned hard for me in my 2002 U.S. Senate campaign, and twice paid me pastoral visits in Montgomery in 2006, to pray with me during a four-month depression that was induced by overly strong medication. His famous words: "It's okay, Julian to be depressed; just don't let it become despair."

I'd be remiss not to throw in the Montgomery Lions Club for its influence on me over the past forty-three years since I joined in 1976. The frivolity and relaxation on Friday afternoons, (listening to some of Alva Lambert's imitations) together with meaningful charity work, are a positive influence, influencing the more light-hearted side of my writing. I especially enjoy seeing there my ninety-one-year-old second cousin, once removed, David Sanderson, who shares my November 13 birthday that we've celebrated together.

A few other random individual friends deserving mention include Ken Mullinax. At age nineteen, Ken drove me up and down Alabama while I campaigned for attorney general in 1977–78. Originally from Anniston, Ken has long lived in Montgomery and has been the public relations director for Alabama State University for many years, doing a great job while surviving five different presidencies. Devoted friend Doug Ghee of Anniston, his wife Brenda, and incredible family (see chapter 13) have also influenced me.

Taylor and Martha Jane Dawson were inspirational early friends at the Church of the Ascension in Montgomery in the 1960s–'70s and are still friends today and models for longevity. Taylor turned ninety on April 2, 2019, and looks as healthy as ever, as does Martha Jane, only a few years younger. They were kind to my family when we first arrived in Montgomery, 1962–64, and to Leslie and me in the years since returning in 1975, including recently. I see Taylor when I attend the Thursday morning men's breakfast group at the Ascension.

I also include the humble Art and Ellen Sanborn, the uncle and aunt of our son-in-law Corbett Lunsford, and a great encouragement for both Leslie and me. They have been missionaries in Thailand and Burma but regularly return to their home base in Tampa, Florida. Their keen devotion to Jesus as Lord, and their radiating warmth and kindness are contagious, gladden many hearts, and uplift spirits, including mine and Leslie's. Both effectively prayed for me when I was ill in 2006. The prayers of the righteous avail much, says the Bible, and theirs did for me. Their prayers in Tampa a year ago for a former secretary's mother, to whom I referred the Sanborns, resulted in the Holy Spirit lifting the seventy-year-old lady from near death to an extended period of joy and better health.

An author's location nourishes his work. Consider Henry David Thoreau and Walden Pond. Similarly, the McP Retreat at Lake Martin, just forty-five minutes north of our Cloverdale home, has been fertile ground for me. It is our home away from home many weekends. The rustic mix of water and woods, together with exercise and rest, soothes my soul and stimulates creative writing.

The wonderful peace and quiet are occasionally joyfully disrupted when five grandchildren ages one to eleven burst in with their doting mothers, Rachel and Grace, their husbands, and our son David. The biggest weekends are Memorial Day and the Fourth of July, patriotically enhanced at the Chapel in the Pines near Children's Harbor. There on those dates the legendary brother-ministers George Mathison and John Ed Mathison regale the masses with uplifting messages.

Leslie and I both support, and are greatly inspired by, including in my writing, LaDonna Brendle, founder of Reality and Truth Ministries. She aids the homeless in the Montgomery area and in Israel. LaDonna takes an annual retreat at our Lake Martin place.

Perhaps the most inspirational of all spiitually over the years have been Mahesh and Bonnie Chavda, now of the Charlotte, North Carolina, area. Their healing ministry is legendary and worldwide. They spearheaded successful healing conferences at Christ the Redeemer Episcopal Church in 1994, 1996, 1999, and 2003. Their good influence on Leslie, me, David, Grace, and Rachel has been enormous, and continues, influencing me also as a writer.

Leslie and I have many good friends in Alabama and beyond, and many good neighbors, clients, and acquaintances. We apologize to anyone left out who should have been mentioned, but this book was never intended to be a Who's Who about anybody or anything.

Montgomery has been a great city and Alabama a great state to live in, despite their many imperfections. We're all a "work in progress" and "broken vessels" and I close this book by thanking again the Great God who created us, redeemed us, and continues to sustain us.

Left: Our three children: Grace, David, and Rachel

Below: Our five grandchildren, from left, Sage, Jude, Nanette, and the oldest, Laurel, holding the youngest, a sleepy Emmanuelle.

Index